BEHIND THE
BLACK ROBES

Volume 160 Sage Library of Social Research

RECENT VOLUMES IN . . .
SAGE LIBRARY OF SOCIAL RESEARCH

BEHIND THE BLACK ROBES
Juvenile Court Judges and the Court

H. TED RUBIN

Volume 160
SAGE LIBRARY OF
SOCIAL RESEARCH

SAGE PUBLICATIONS
Beverly Hills   London   New Delhi

For information address:

SAGE Publications, Inc.
275 South Beverly Drive
Beverly Hills, California 90212

SAGE Publications India Pvt. Ltd.
M-32 Market
Greater Kailash I
New Delhi 110 048 India

SAGE Publications Ltd
28 Banner Street
London EC1Y 8QE
England

Printed in the United States of America

Library of Congress Cataloging in Publication Data

Rubin, H. Ted, 1926–
  Behind the black robes.

  (Sage library of social research ; v. 160)
  1. Juvenile courts—United States. 2. Juvenile
justice, Administration of—United States. 3. Judicial
process—United States. I. Title. II. Series.
KF9794.R83   1985   345.73'081   85-11923
ISBN 0-8039-2500-X   347.30581
ISBN 0-8039-2501-8 (pbk.)

FIRST PRINTING

CONTENTS

To Bunny, who has loved me with and without robes,
and to Marjorie, Steve, and Jefferson.

The drawings of the judges and of the author are by the author's wife,
Bunny Rosenthal Rubin.

PREFACE

I would like to invite you to journey through an important American institution, the juvenile court, and to meet five of its better judges. This road map is easier to read than many, so don't be deceived that the picturization is lacking in far-reaching considerations or academic substance. It is an insider's view. Your guide was a juvenile court judge in Denver, Colorado, from 1965–71. Since then, I have spent most of my professional hours researching juvenile courts, training juvenile justice professionals and future professionals, and writing articles and other books about juvenile justice developments.

This work is more than a treatise on five people who act so fatefully on so many, though this is a major focus. It is also an examination of the very critical issues and conflicts that need to be confronted daily in this forum. In a nutshell, the court must blend concerns for public protection with an interest in the rehabilitation of juveniles and the protection of children, all within a legal regimen. This is not easily done or done well. The presentation considers any number of pressing concerns. Many allow for very individualistic interpretation and clearly different application. The background experiences that five judges bring to their positions helps in understanding how these jurists view these matters and apply their beliefs on the firing line. This, then, is a book about a place, a socio-legal process, and about how and why five juvenile court judges administer their particular brands of justice.

The book begins by illustrating six cases, similar to those heard in juvenile courts across the country. These cases, as is the rule, range from the less serious to the more serious. They portray the three major types of juvenile court stock-in-trade: juvenile delinquency, for which this court is best known and most criticized; status offenses, or conduct-illegal-only-for-children, such as school truancy, runaway, and incorrigibility, matters now less frequently heard in this setting; and child neglect and abuse, increasingly a target of this court's and this nation's attention.

The opening chapter depicts the interchanges that might occur between judge, child, parents, lawyers, probation officials, and social workers during a juvenile court day. Following each instance of dialogue, I have entered comments and analyses, not just as to what is happening in this hearing, but also as to juvenile court history, current trends, competing principles, pertinent United

States Supreme Court decisions and other legal guidelines, workloads, decisional influences, rehabilitation aims and methods, and research findings. The disputes and problems that face this institution are reviewed through this mechanism, are further assessed by the judges in their chapters, and are considered in the final chapter where the judges, actual strangers to each other, come together in a mythical meeting. In this interaction they discuss and question each other about juvenile court directions and policy matters, their own legal and social philosophies, what has shaped their values and viewpoints, their concerns regarding youngsters and the treatment of youngsters, the satisfactions and frustrations they experience, the uncertain future of the juvenile court. The words are those of the individual judges or were constructed in character with their beliefs and personal singularities.

The purpose of this work is to bring readers inside this essentially private sanctum in order to become familiar with five high-caliber people who are largely known only in their home communities or their states, and to ponder the juvenile court's dilemmas. The judges have their critics and their deficiencies, as do we all. But their accomplishments are striking.

Their robes make it more difficult for people to learn what judges are like; the book eases this pathway. Their robes also make it more difficult for judges to relax and be like other people. What they shared with me in more relaxed moments is also shared here.

Many, but far from all juvenile court judges, since this court was born in Chicago in 1899, have felt and implemented a special mission. They are child advocates and child guardians, in a unique position to do good. They are also the expression of the public's conscience, censors of those who do not do well.

The juvenile court is being reshaped, and it is necessary that informed persons join in the debates that need resolution in this highly controversial setting. Indeed, some readers may want to enlist as volunteers, assisting juvenile court youths, or enroll in a career design to work in this forum and, perhaps, even become a judge. Others, hopefully, will activate their communities to ensure strongly qualified judges for these courts.

Any number of today's juvenile court judges sit just part-time on this bench, otherwise handling criminal or civil cases, since the juvenile workload does not require their full energies. In other courts, judges may rotate to full-time status on the juvenile bench for a year or two and then go on to a specialized criminal or civil division of the court. The judges profiled here are among those who specialize as juvenile court judges, either because their court is structured as a separate court or because, as in one case, a judge who is a member of a general court has chosen and receives approval to preside here continuously for an extensive period. These five judges have maintained these positions for from seven to twenty-four years. My design was to capture for the reader the long-tenured, specialist juvenile court judge who has had a widespread opportunity to place his or her imprint on a court and a community, and who has distilled an approach and a perspective that have matured over time. I wanted variances in regions of the country, structures of court, community cultures, religious, and ethnic backgrounds of the judges. I also sought courts several serving varying sizes of population, but particularly those processing rather large numbers of juveniles.

The five judges are above average, if not outstanding, yet other holders of this office demonstrate keen skills and expansive achievements. There are also many others who care little about this opportunity, have never mastered a mature use of self, prefer directive to reflection, or do a reasonably good job for a year and then move to another court division. Still, there is no pretension that the five are typical jurists.

I knew two judges well before I embarked on this adventure. A third I had met and talked with briefly while conducting a study. I had read an interesting legal opinion by a fourth, called him, and he opened his doors. The fifth came highly recommended when I sought out a judge from a particular part of the country. He also welcomed this examination. I think you will agree these are intriguing people.

I spent an initial week with each judge, returning some months later for another week of extensive court watching and interviewing. In addition to running the judges through hundreds of questions, I interviewed their judicial colleagues and any number of local juvenile justice system officials, citizens who were involved with these courts, media personnel who had covered court matters, critics of the judges. I suggested dinner invitations to their homes so I could observe the judges in a more informal setting and also talk with their more intimate support group: wife or husband, children, and even two judges' mothers. I also went with the judges to their meetings with community organizations, listened as one lectured to a university class, and accompanied one to a wedding reception. In several courts I asked detained juveniles about how they saw their judge; as expected, they had words both kind and unkind. As desired, no two judges were alike in personality, standards or hearing style. As anticipated, the procedures in each court differed, heavily influenced by particular state laws, and the nature and extent of juveniles' law and legal-norm violations were disparate. But clearly, there were many common threads sewn onto these five black robes.

Much has been written from divergent perspectives, in both popular and academic literature, about juvenile justice and juvenile injustice, the abbreviation of legal safeguards in this forum, the effectiveness or ineffectiveness of intervention efforts, the need for less coddling, the need for more cuddling, the necessity for more resources to do more, the uncertainty whether more resources will do more, individualization versus equalization, the failure of the promise. These issues are recast here, but in a different format. Polarity from the author is absent; the hyperbole is that of good judges in their real worlds. The centerpiece is the nature of judges and judging rather than more abstract theory, or complex research, or rigorous system analysis, or journalistic exposé.

Come and look at this rich process, at what is happening in what was once termed a noble invention, at what is behind five black robes.

CHAPTER 1

A DAY IN A JUVENILE COURT

The judge takes the bench and scans the docket . . .
Across the country, in courtrooms and in judicial chambers, juvenile court judges face up daily to the problems of children and young people. The court's clients are faceless to the public, since protective juvenile codes have prohibited, with exceptions, picture identification of these youngsters in the media and their names and addresses.

Ten delinquency cases between now and noon . . .
Juvenile law violations are the basic stock in trade of juvenile courts. Law breaking, as everyone knows, is not confined to adults. Deliquency charges range in seriousness, from the petty to the very serious. Some are victimless crimes, like drug use, though the youth himself may suffer injury. Most often they are property crimes, like shoplifting and home burglary. Least often they are crimes against persons, like assault or rape.

The judge calls the first case, a burglary, and looks across at the thirteen-year-old boy he has not seen before . . .
The juvenile courtroom is often less austere than other courtroom structures. The judge's bench, frequently, is just one-step-up, a deliberate design to reduce formality and facilitate communication between the judge, the child, and other participants. Judicial communication with youngsters can be an art form, counted by many judges as an important skill, indeed, a necessity. Others, less artful, use the law and procedural formalities as their canvas.

You are James Bellamy — do people call you Jim? . . .
This is the communicative judge beginning his work. He has quickly sensed that the child's age, offense, and first offense status do not mandate strict formalities. The judge can begin to balance his awesome powers with a first attempt to show interest.

Uh-huh...
Some judges prefer a "yes, your honor" response, but this will bother another judge who thinks the polite response has been rehearsed. Many judges are pleased to obtain even a minimal verbal answer, one that does not require the judge to point out that the hearing is being recorded and the record does not pick up nods of the head.

And you are Jim's mother?...
A parent is required to attend juvenile court hearings. Several reasons support this requirement. The child is a minor and, despite a law violation charge, is a legal non-person. Accordingly, a parent's consent to how the child exercises his legal rights in a court proceeding is a necessity. The second reason is the public policy position that parents should be involved when their child is involved with the court. Much of what the court might hope to do to assist the child requires parental support. To conduct hearings without a parent jeopardizes this support.

Yes, your honor...
Parents tend to dress up for court and put their best foot forward. But the fact that one's child is accused of delinquency is a threat to parents, an acknowledgment that their parenting has been imperfect and their ability to handle their own adjustment problems may be deficient. Parents may seek to avert a focus that they, too, are on trial and may line up with the judge in criticizing their child's misconduct. "Your honor", they may say, "I work very hard to provide for my children, but James has gotten headstrong and just won't listen to me anymore." Perceptive judges understand this diversion strategy, indicate that neither child nor parents are perfect, and suggest that the probation officer will be pleased to assist them in becoming more effective parents. But perceptive judges may also be more straightforward and state sharply that both the child and the parents have to do a better job.

Oh, yes, good morning Probation Officer Neilson...
Probation officers are at the center of a juvenile court's control/rehabilitation venture. Their employment in Massachusetts antedated the 1899 enactment of the nation's first juvenile court act

in Illinois. That act's authorization of these officials, together with numerous other provisions, served as the model for similar enactments across the country in the following years. The use of probation officers gave a juvenile court a vehicle to provide direct counseling assistance, to explain and enforce its regulations, and to refer or channel youths to other service agencies and institutions that might assist or control them. Probation officers, most commonly, are employees of the court, appointed by the judges to assist their purposes and functions; elsewhere, they are employees of an executive-branch agency directed, by law, to assist court purposes and functions. In different jurisdictions they may be titled probation officer, court services officer, or court caseworker. Within the generic probation officer role there are three primary specialties: intake officers, investigation officers, and field supervision officers.

First, I must advise Jim of his legal rights . . .
A radical reshaping of juvenile court proceedings was touched off by the 1967 United States Supreme Court decision, *In re Gault.* Except for juvenile code modernizations enacted several years earlier in a few states, juvenile court proceedings were characterized by informality, a non-adversarial quality, an absence of legal rules, regimen, and attorneys, and a focus on what the court should do for or to the child. In short, these courts acted as authoritarian social agencies using proceedings bereft of ceremony. Since juvenile court matters may result in the deprivation of a child's liberty, the *Gault* case held that children are entitled to due process protections. Because youngsters were accorded constitutional safeguards in this forum, judges now had a duty to advise one of his legal rights.

the right to a lawyer and a free lawyer if your parents cannot afford one . . .
There are sharp differences in the frequency of lawyer representation in different juvenile courts. Some courts now operate in a more adversarial atmosphere and all formal hearings are accompanied by defense counsel representation. This is more characteristic of large, urban juvenile courts. These judges do not wish to proceed without a lawyer for the child. The dominant urban defense lawyer is a public defender, not a private attorney. Other judges carefully advise youngsters of this right, frequently accept

waivers of this right, but may well insist that an attorney be secured where there is a reasonable likelihood of institutionalization. When the family can afford counsel, their access is restricted to private attorneys, although in some courts public defenders will represent the child in this situation and the parents will be ordered to pay for the defender's service. Some judges prefer to proceed without attorneys, and, in ways both subtle and not so subtle, may encourage waiver of this right. The *Gault* case did not require counsel, but required only notification of the right to counsel. The *Gault* decision did not require notification of this right in all cases, only where institutionalization was a possibility. Most juvenile codes go beyond this holding and require notification of the right to counsel more generally. At least two states, Iowa and New York, mandate that this right cannot be waived.

the right to a trial if you deny the charges, . . .
Trials occur in juvenile courts, though they are not frequent. Fewer than five percent of juvenile court cases result in trials. This ratio in adult criminal courts rarely exceeds ten per cent. The 1971 United States Supreme Court decision, *McKeiver*, held that the United States Constitution did not mandate that states provide jury trials in delinquency cases. Nonetheless, states may authorize jury trials and approximately fourteen states permit this, though the frequency of jury trials is very modest in those jurisdictions. Ordinarily, the general public is prohibited from attending juvenile court proceedings. A small number of states, reacting to concerns regarding juvenile offenses, now permit the public to attend these proceedings. Whether the media is a member of the general public which is barred from observation or whether it can attend under a First Amendment right to report on public proceedings is not totally clear. In any event, newspaper reporters do not sit in juvenile courts day after day, reporting on hearings. They do interview judges and probation personnel regarding delinquency developments, may report on a spectacular case, or probe into judicial sentencing patterns or allegations of abuse in juvenile facilities.

the right to remain silent; the right to cross-examine witnesses testifying against you, . . .
As with criminal proceedings, it is the obligation of the state to

present sufficient evidence to convict a juvenile defendant. If a trial occurs, a juvenile need not testify. Further, the United States Supreme Court, in the *Winship* holding of 1970, ruled that the Constitution required the same beyond-reasonable-doubt proof standard in juvenile as in criminal proceedings. Historically, juvenile court proceedings have been civil in nature, owing to the express rehabilitation purpose. The *Gault* decision had penetrated this "civil label-of-convenience" in pointing out the similarity between juvenile institutions and prisons and the comparable restraints on freedom. Another aspect of the *Gault* decision was to ban the use of hearsay testimony at a juvenile trial; witnesses against a child must testify under oath in court and are subject to cross-examination.

Judge, I want to go ahead and admit to what I did . . .
Most juveniles admit to their offenses whether or not they have had the benefit of legal counsel. Prior to their formal appearance in court, most juveniles have been questioned by law enforcement officials, typically admitting their offense; commonly, also, they have been interviewed by probation intake officers and have admitted their participation in the offense. This is the usual, though not universal response. Some juveniles deny their guilt at one or more stages. Occasionally, a youth admits his guilt to police or intake officers, but reverses himself and requests a trial. Admissions made in the pre-court stages, often done with limited understanding by juveniles of their rights or whether a valid defense may exist, tend to pave the way for the child's formal admission before the judge.

Do you agree, Mrs Bellamy? . . .
Parental acquiescence to a child's waiver of rights is obtained due to the minor's lack of legal capacity. Incongruously, few states require a parent to join in a child's relinquishment of his right to counsel or to silence in agreeing to discuss the offense with police officers. While law enforcement officials are required to provide advisements of rights to the child before interrogation, one research study has indicated that youngsters invoke the right of silence in only 9 percent of occasions. An adult study found that 42 percent of criminal suspects refused to talk with police officials.

My name is now Mrs Hudson, but, as James' mother, I agree to his telling you what he did . . .

A substantial number of delinquent youths come from home settings that do not have both the natural father and mother. The "broken home" theory, which related the absence of a parent as an important cause of delinquency, was prominent earlier in the century. It has lost some favor, but has not been totally discarded. Other explanations of delinquent conduct have been suggested, stretching from psychological causation to social and economic reasons. That delinquent offenses are often committed by small groups of youths provides some support for a peer group phenomenon theory. Labeling theorists complain that the way society reacts to delinquent behavior through the responses of the juvenile justice system may further delinquent misconduct. Opportunity theorists believe that the absence of legitimate means for low-income youngsters to achieve parity with middle-class juveniles explains at least certain delinquencies by economically deprived youths. Delinquency is sometimes seen as a relatively normal reaction to growing up in a complex, disparate-value society. There are other theories as well. Judges, on the firing line, tend to be more concerned with the control of delinquency, though they often explore with a juvenile what factors led to the commission of the offense.

Let the record reflect . . . tell me what you did, Jim . . .

Since the *Gault* decision, most juvenile courts make verbatim records of formal proceedings. Usually this is done by court reporters using stenotype machines or by tape recording devices. No record of the hearings was made with the Gerald Gault case in Globe, Arizona, in June, 1964. In the first appeal of this matter in the Arizona courts, there was the unseemly spectacle of the juvenile court judge, other court officials, and Mrs Gault attempting to recount what had occurred at this hearing. The absence of a court record was one of the grounds certified to the United States Supreme Court for review. The Court did not rule on this question, having overturned Gerald's conviction for other reasons. One justice, who wrote a separate opinion of this case, stated that trial courts should be required to maintain written records in order to permit effective review on appeal. The aftermath of the *Gault* decision was a far more widespread acceptance that the juvenile court was now a court of law and that a record should be a requirement. The growth of appellate court decisions since then, reviewing juvenile court proceedings, has been noteworthy.

I saw this house door was open and I went in. I quickly stole the radio from a table, but the police caught me with it five minutes later over on Oak Street . . .

The judge has asked for these explanations for several reasons. It gets the youth to accept, openly, culpability for his actions. He has now admitted that he has committed the offense before his parents and the judge. This is an additional communication strategy. Although adults will largely dominate juvenile court proceedings, the juvenile's explanation here provides further opportunity for the youngster to join in these proceedings. Further, judges believe it is important to compare a youth's explanation with the allegations of the petition. Now and then, these do not square. The boy may acknowledge that he struck another youngster, but that he was defending against the other youngster's assault. The theft may be acknowledged, but it is learned that it had substantially less value than what had been alleged. A youth may state that what he had done was coerced by an adult. These statements, though they may not always be totally accurate, are listened to carefully.

Probation Officer Neilson, what do you have to say that supplements the social history report I am now reviewing? . . .

The social history report is also known as the social study or predisposition report. With consent, the gathering of this information often begins following the child's informal admission of the offense to the probation intake officer. It is therefore in readiness following the entry of a plea so that the judge can move immediately into a disposition hearing. More adversarial juvenile courts delay the preparation of the report until after the plea has been entered or the trial completed. In such courts the disposition hearing will then take place four weeks or so following the plea hearing or trial. Defense lawyers prefer this latter approach since some youngsters will be found innocent at trial and because the negotiations between prosecution and defense may result in a prosecutor's dismissal of a case due to evidentiary shortcomings. Further, a judge may dismiss the matter at the time a plea is entered for the reason that the case is not serious and that it is unnecessary to proceed further with this matter. Defense lawyers contend that information provided during this study constitutes an invasion of privacy unless, first, there is a formal admission or a finding of guilt, or unless the attorney has consented to gathering this information.

Just to emphasize further that Jim is a good probation risk. Intake did not adjust the case due to concern about the seriousness of a house burglary and because Jim's mother has had trouble controlling him lately. I also recommend that he perform twenty-four hours of community service work . . .

The earlier intake decision is influenced both by the legal facts, for example, the seriousness of the offense, and by social facts, in this case the mother's difficulties with her son. Virtually all juvenile codes authorize intake officers or, in some states, prosecutors to resolve cases without a formal petition to the court. Some communities view house burglaries more seriously than others. Media attention to burglary waves triggers more formal rather than informal dispositions. Since Jim was just thirteen years of age at the time of the offense, many juvenile courts would have decided to handle this case informally. The use of social facts in decision making is an irritant to some attorneys and theorists who are pessimistic about the court's rehabilitation achievements. They believe that a child whose parents are less able to mobilize private resources to help are discriminated against and handled formally more often than youngsters who come from more wealthy or more "together" families. Throughout its development, the juvenile court has been hinged far more on an individual justice approach than an equal justice construct. The individual justice model weighs the needs of the individual, the overall quality of his adjustment, his family's capability in assisting and controlling him, together with offense information and prior record in reaching decisions. An equal justice philosophy would seek to mete out equal punishment or handling to youngsters with like offense severity and prior record. Restitution, in the form of repayment to a victim for losses suffered, or to the community as symbolic repayment for violating society's laws, is a growing requirement of juvenile courts. Probation departments or youth restitution programs arrange supervised work placements at public parks, libraries, nursing homes, United Way agencies, and other governmental and non-profit organizations.

But, Jim, I don't really understand — why did you go into someone's house and why did you take the radio? . . .
The judge wants to understand more. This is a typical quest for the causation of delinquency in a particular case. Jim's explanation may well be included in the social history report. The judge may not have arrived at that part of the report by now or he may have reviewed it and be asking Jim to state this as part of his ongoing effort to obtain a dialogue with the youth. If Jim were to say that he wanted a radio at home but didn't have one, the judge could then tell him this was not the way to go about this; rather, he should get a job and earn the money so he could feel good knowing that he had bought his own radio. If Jim were to say that an older boy had promised him $25 if he obtained a radio for him, the judge's admonishment would be to learn to say no to such a temptation.

I don't know . . .
This is a very common juvenile response. It may be painful for him to explain reasons. Or he may be untruthful in his explanation. Or whatever he says may be unacceptable. He may think that it is safer to leave it as it is. His mother has already asked him why, as has the intake officer.

He had had an argument with his mother and either wanted to punish her or himself . . .
Probation officers sometimes jump in here. It may be because they recognize that it is no easy thing for most youngsters to talk in the courtroom. Or, they may want to enhance their status with the judge. If they volunteer this information, the judge may note that the probation officer is informed and has individualized this youngster. Experienced probation officers are extremely sensitive to their judges' styles. If they know that a judge normally probes further into such reasons, then they will hold off volunteering an explanation since they know the judge wants to put some pressure on the youngster to talk further about his offense. Also, whether an argument with the mother factored substantially in the offense may be more a statement of rationale by the boy rather than the fact occasioning the delinquency. A stated reason may not be the real reason. The real reason, like "getting something for nothing", may appear invalid to officials. There are different games that are played

by different juvenile court actors. This may be part of the child's game. Not only the judge has power here. Not only the judge manipulates the scenario. The child may be wiser than his years.

Mrs Hudson, Mr Neilson indicates you have had some trouble with Jim? . . .

The judge is still scanning the social history, but seeks more verbal involvement from the mother. He will comment on her statement, however she replies. The court has noted a rather good relationship between mother and son. She may be more a part of the solution than the problem. Parents are aware that most judges expect them to make some statements in court.

Yes, but it's better. I grounded him when this happened and he's been cooperative. His concern about coming to court has him doing everything right . . .

This may be another play in the juvenile court game. Judicial fears are being allayed. The mother suggests she now has control over Jim. She took disciplinary action and has probably earlier received favorable comment on this from the probation officer. She also appears to be a smart mother. She has let the judge know that her son is cooperating and that he is in some awe of the court's powers. A less positive response might provoke more severe intervention by the court.

Okay, I'll go along with Mr Neilson's recommendation. But Jim, I want you to see Mr Neilson regularly and to obey the conditions of probation I'm signing. Do a good job with your community service work. You've also got to follow your mother's rules and be in school each day . . .

The social history had recommended a stint on probation. Probably, the probation officer had told the youth and his mother what the recommendation would be. The disposition was predictable with a thirteen-year-old first offender, this type of offense, and seeming parental strengths. Nonetheless, Jim undoubtedly experienced substantial anxiety. This is what a court wants; indeed, this is what most parents want. Further, the judge has reinforced the mother's rules and control. There is, in this case, a certain harmony. The judge is also reinforcing the school's authority with the boy. The written conditions of probation require that a probationer not offend any laws, attend school if he is regularly enrolled, meet with the probation officer upon request and not leave the jurisdiction without this official's approval, avoid drug or alcohol use, and comply with parental rules and local curfew requirements. Certain special conditions may be attached that are tailored to the particular case.

Thank you, your honor . . .
The successful ceremony has concluded and everyone feels positive. At this moment, no one expects Jim to be back in court on a second offense. What court officials did not know was whether Jim had committed other offenses for which he had not been apprehended. Self-report delinquency studies, replicated widely, have found juveniles reporting, in anonymous questionnaires, that they have committed vastly more offenses than those for which they have been apprehended. Studies of crime frequency have revealed that the extent of crime committed by both juveniles and adults is substantially more than that reported, and that which is reported is far more frequent than the arrests which follow. Since a judge, in sizing up a youngster's demeanor and socio-economic status, may believe that the youth in front of him has committed additional offenses that did not result in apprehension, or that the admitted offense was plea bargained down from a more serious charge, this belief may well result in a more restrictive disposition than appears merited. But a judge is on firmer legal ground in basing his disposition only on the official offense or offenses before the court.

The next case involves a sixteen-year-old boy charged with drug abuse. The judge has seen this youth before. Good morning, Mr Public Defender, and good morning, Earl and Mr Kyle . . .
Judges do not always address the child's attorney first, but when this is done it indicates that lawyers are talking with lawyers and that the judge and the public defender, both legal professionals, are members of the ongoing array of juvenile court participants. Although a public defender's responsibility is to represent the child's best interests, both in regard to the legal charges and any disposition the court may enter, public defenders, like private attorneys, need to maintain continuing professional relationships with judges. The

judge, in governing his or her forum, administers law and discretionary authority in the best interests of both the community and of the child. The public defender and the judge may be quite interested in the welfare of the child, but they also seek to maintain a professional cordiality and relationship.

Lawyers for children charged with delinquency have special problems in discharging their functions. They are often uncertain as to the degree that they should contest these proceedings or challenge what the court and its probation arm believe is best for the child. They, too, hold to some of the public's reservations that an exploitation of procedural deficiencies which results in a dismissal of a juvenile case will disadvantageously affect the character and development of the child. There are three primary modes of defense representation for juveniles charged with delinquency. If their parents can afford private counsel, the child is represented by private counsel. When a family is indigent and unable to retain counsel, a public defender service may be appointed to represent these juveniles. Elsewhere, private lawyers are appointed by the court and paid from public funds to provide attorney services.

There are advantages and disadvantages to each of these modes of representation. The privately retained attorney has special problems in determining who his client is and what his client wants. The parents will pay his bill. The child is dependent upon the parents for underwriting the attorney's services. Probably, the parents will influence what the attorney will do on behalf of the child. The parents' interest and the child's interest are often, but not always, the same. The parents may prefer that the attorney not challenge a procedural technicality, preferring that the court's authority be accepted though the state might not be able to prove the wrong was done. The technicality, however, may be a constitutional violation in the face of which a lawyer should not remain silent.

Your honor, Earl denies the petition and requests trial . . .

Particularly in large cities, juvenile courts essentially serve poor youngsters. Public defenders are appointed quite routinely, parental indigency being assumed, generally. The defenders assigned to juvenile courts often are relatively inexperienced employees of this office and frequently carry quite heavy caseloads. However, they are in a position to gain familiarity and specialization with juvenile court law and procedures and are in a position to use their knowledge of the juvenile justice system to enhance the fate of the juveniles they represent. There is a special language to the juvenile court process. The terms "guilty" and "not guilty" are not used. Juveniles either admit to a petition or deny a petition. The formal document charging a juvenile, usually, is called a petition. In criminal courts this is termed a complaint, an information, or a grand jury indictment.

The earliest trial I can provide is four weeks from now . . .
Juvenile courts in more populous communities often experience a crunching workload; there, public defenders tend to make these courts more adversarial. Their style is more contentious; they know that their client is the child and not the parents; they tend to be more distrustful of the system and its promises. In less populous jurisdictions, the judge of the juvenile court may carry numerous other judicial responsibilities and may be able to allocate just one day each week for juvenile matters. All juvenile courts are responsible, in addition, for other types of children's cases, such as those relating to dependent, neglected, and abused children. A juvenile court may be a family court, also having jurisdiction over dissolution of marriage (divorce), adoption, child support, and other family-related matters. The court's calendar administration is also impacted by a judge's attendance at judicial education seminars and a variety of workshops related to the juvenile court and to the rehabilitation enterprise, both locally and nationally. These judges sit on numerous planning committees and community agency boards. They are sought-after speakers. They lobby legislatures and also take vacations.

But, Earl's in detention and I'd like to get this resolved quickly . . .
A repeat offender, like Earl, is more often held in pre-trial detention pending the court's disposition. In only a small number of states is a juvenile entitled to a right to bail. Laws that guide when children should be detained vary as to their breadth or overbreadth. Often they recite that a child should be returned to his parents' custody unless it is likely that upon release he will endanger the person or property of others, endanger himself, abscond from the court process, or if there is no adult able to provide suitable supervision for the child. Administering such a broad policy grant, on the spot, means that almost any youngster can be held in detention if the

doorkeeper should so choose. There has been strong criticism that broad provisions, such as these, have encouraged substantially more detention use than is necessary to protect either the community or the child. Some states have tightened these criteria to allow detention only where there is a serious threat of substantial harm to others or when a child has a history of failing to appear in court. There is a conventional wisdom, that, despite the presumption of innocence that surrounds a juvenile suspect, a stay in detention has a deterrent effect upon an errant youth. In effect, detention is used as punishment. If one is detained, one is more likely to be formally petitioned before the court rather than to be dismissed through informal procedures. Many detained youngsters are dismissed without formal court consideration of an offense due to a variety of screening procedures that decide this case is not serious enough or legally sound enough to go forward.

The United States Supreme Court, in the *Schall* decision of 1984, held that pre-trial juvenile detention is not punishment but, rather, is a reasonable assumption by the state of the parental custody role in order to facilitate a crime-reduction objective. The court ruled that juveniles may be preventively detained when there is a serious risk a youth may reoffend prior to the next court hearing so long as there are the safeguards of a judicial determination of probable cause for the detention, counsel for the child, and speedy adjudication proceedings. The New York serious risk provision, under review in this case, was a narrower authorization for detention than those used in most states. This decision has been criticized for its failure to recognize the imperfections in predicting reoffenders and to require clear guidelines and criteria for operationalizing what constitutes a serious risk. Juveniles, in this context, have fewer rights than adults.

Why don't you meet with the prosecutor? . . .

Prosecutors, late entrants into this scenario, had long regarded juvenile courts as "kiddie courts". Making sure that a youth was convicted was no big thing in prosecutor offices where attorney colleagues boasted of convicting adult homicide defendants and armed robbers. For generations, juvenile court judges preferred to dominate their setting without the assistance of either prosecutors or lawyers for children. More recently, the frequency and severity of juvenile offenses has prompted public concern, if not alarm, precipitating far greater prosecutor activity in juvenile courts. While this setting remains more a training ground than a prized assignment for prosecutors, lead juvenile prosecutors in a number of cities have retained this role for two to five years and longer. They enjoy the specialized nature of this job, their working relationships with other professionals, the opportunity they have to obtain improvements in the juvenile justice system, and their function to protect the community's interests in these proceedings. In a growing number of states, prosecutors have moved up front of their trial role to influence, if not control, the intake process where decisions are made as to whether referrals shall or shall not be formally petitioned. Initially, the police dominated this decision. More recently it has been probation intake officials. It is now proceeding toward prosecutor dominance. In suggesting that the defender meet with the prosecutor, the judge is communicating a message that a plea bargain may be struck and the need for a trial may be obviated.

Denial entered and trial set four weeks from today . . .
Earl has been in detention anywhere from several days to a week at the time of this particular hearing. The delay in the resolution of this case for an additional four weeks is a prolonged wait. Yet, trial preparations need to be made, witnesses interviewed, the police investigation examined, the law researched, the judicial calendar accommodated. A growing number of statutes and state supreme court rules now place priority on expediting trials for detained youngsters. They mandate release of a child from detention if the trial fails to occur within two to four weeks, unless a time extension has been requested by the child or his attorney. If the allegations of the petition are proved at trial, these regulations require that a dispositional hearing be held within, for example, an additional fifteen days. This time is needed to prepare the predisposition report following resolution of a contested matter. Releasing Earl from detention pending these proceedings would allow the lengthier time frame permitted for non-detained youngsters to apply. Many jurisdictions, however, have not yet promulgated such time guidelines.

Next up is a transfer hearing. The judge observed to himself that he had experienced more of these during the past year . . .
In most states, the maximum age for initial juvenile court

jurisdiction is seventeen years. On the eighteenth birthday, one becomes an adult, subject to criminal court proceedings. Eight states shut off juvenile court jurisdiction on the seventeenth birthday, four states on the sixteenth birthday. For years, now, any number of legislatures have sought to reduce the maximum age. These efforts have not been successful. However, all but a few states permit the juvenile court to hold a transfer or waiver hearing for more serious or repetitive juvenile offenders and to determine, on the basis of whether it is likely that the juvenile can be rehabilitated by the juvenile justice system services, that the youngster should be transferred to a criminal court proceeding or retained within the juvenile system. The transfer option is the counter argument to dropping the juvenile age. In some states, juveniles are eligible for transfer proceedings at age sixteen, elsewhere at age fourteen or even younger. Generally, the commission of a felony or one of certain specified felonies is the offense requirement for transfer consideration.

The transfer-hearing "escape valve" has not been a sufficient placating force to many legislatures in recent years. A supplementary, harder-line response has gained currency. This is known as direct filing. For youngsters above a specified age who are alleged to have committed a certain felony offense or who have had several prior juvenile court convictions, the prosecutor may file this matter directly in criminal court without proceeding through juvenile court and a transfer hearing. This approach constitutes a threat to the role and identity of the juvenile court as the essential processing center for all juveniles. It suggests, in effect, that the juvenile court and its rehabilitation apparatus should be reserved for less serious and less chronic juvenile offenders. At this writing, however, transfer constitutes the more frequent route for handling juveniles as adults.

Yes, probable cause as to the knife assault is found . . .
The first stage of the transfer hearing requires the submission of evidence as to the alleged offense. The legal proof standard for this stage is not a high one, only that sufficient evidence has been presented to believe that a crime has been committed and committed by the particular individual. If transfer is ordered at the completion of this hearing, full trial on the offense can be held in a criminal court. Prior to the juvenile court legalization trend in the late 1960s,

youngsters could be transferred to criminal courts without prosecutor or defense counsel representation or even the limited probable cause proof requirement.

Fourteen months before the celebrated *Gault* holding, the United States Supreme Court ruled for the first time on juvenile court procedures in the *Kent* case. This case involved a transfer hearing in the District of Columbia juvenile court. The mother of Morris A. Kent, Jr had obtained a lawyer and psychiatric and psychological evaluations. The lawyer filed a motion for a hearing on the question of transfer, though a hearing was provided by statute. The attorney offered to prove that if Kent were provided psychiatric treatment, he would be a suitable subject for juvenile court rehabilitation, and moved for access to juvenile court probation records regarding Morris's probation status prior to the new offenses. The juvenile court judge did not rule on these motions. Without conducting a hearing, he entered an order reciting that after full investigation he was transferring jurisdiction to the criminal court. He made no findings and entered no reasons for the transfer. Subsequently, the Supreme Court held the juvenile court proceedings to be defective. Kent should have been afforded a hearing, counsel should have been granted access to the probation records, the judge should have recorded the statement of reasons for the transfer.

Justice Fortas, for the Court, stated that the juvenile court hearing "must measure up to the essentials of due process and fair treatment". In his now famous words, Fortas continued with a critique of juvenile court proceedings that was to lead to the reform of juvenile courts into more regularized and formal forums: "There is evidence, in fact, that there may be grounds for concern that the child [in juvenile court] receives the worst of both worlds: that he gets neither the protections accorded to adults nor the solicitous care and regenerative treatment postulated for children."

Testimony relating to whether the seventeen-year-old juvenile recidivist, Ellis, could be satisfactorily rehabilitated within the juvenile justice system began with the investigating probation officer. When Ellis was fifteen, he was first placed on probation for breaking windows at his school . . .

Probation is a typical sanction for this type of offense, committed at this particular age. In some courts he would have been handled informally and required to repay the damages. That this type of offense, of limited seriousness, was formally petitioned may indicate that the youth may have been handled informally for an earlier offense and that the window breaking was not the first referral for this boy.

Three months later he threatened his teacher, Mrs English, with an uplifted chair. After a psychological examination, he went into our therapy group . . .

The seriousness of this offense prompted the mental health examination. Larger juvenile courts employ full-time psychologists to evaluate youngsters and recommend different treatment directions based on their examinations. Elsewhere, such evaluations are obtained through community mental health clinics or by contract with private psychologists. The courts also tend to have access to psychiatrists through one of these means. Such evaluations are particularly used with youngsters showing signs of significant emotional disturbance, more chronic offenders, and with such offenses as fire-setting and sexual assault. The treatment group may be led by the court psychologist, a highly trained probation officer, or provided through the mental health center.

At age sixteen, he knocked over an old lady in the process of stealing her purse. We tried to get him into a private treatment center, but they didn't think they could help him. So we placed him on intensive probation and now he has reoffended . . .

Privately-administered residential treatment centers serve some juvenile court youngsters. They also serve neglected children referred by local social service departments and children whose parents arrange placement through their own means. The cost for this service is often substantial. Public funds underwrite the payment for these first two sets of children, though parents are required to pay what they can toward these costs. Family-maintained health insurance policies may provide some of the fee. The probation department's intensive supervision program may be not very intensive. It may mean one counseling visit with the child each week and a collateral phone call to the family or school. Or, it may mean that the child is in a counseling group that meets for an hour three or four times a week. The child remains with his family.

The court psychologist then testified that Ellis has unresolved hostility. He evidences a character disorder. He requires a structured institution with consistent requirements and expectations . . .

This is a frequent observation of many court youngsters. The character disorder reference is parlance for psychopathic or sociopathic behavior. It evidences, in part, a deficiency in the development of conscience. Institutions, then, are seen as providing consistent rules which the psychologist attests are necessary for this boy. The assumption is that the youth will grow better emotionally when permissible behaviors are clearly set forth and some form of institutional punishment constrains impermissible behaviors.

The prosecutor next contended that Ellis's delinquencies have escalated, and that nothing has worked. If the juvenile court sentences him to a state institution, he will be out in six months. Rather, he needs to be confined, incapacitated if you will, in an adult institution. Society has to be protected . . .

There is much to the prosecutor's advocacy. The knife assault is the fourth official offense. The duration of stay in state delinquency institutions often terminates after six or eight months, a period which may seem short to the public but is long in a juvenile's sense of time.

The defense countered: Nothing has worked because nothing has been tried. His first probation officer had only one visit with Ellis before the teacher incident occurred. The therapy group just sat around in a circle while the therapist told the boys their silence meant that they were angry. The treatment center doesn't like ghetto kids because they want to work with easier offenders, or, preferably, mixed up kids who are not offenders. He's never been helped in his own home; he's never been helped outside his home; he'll be chewed up if a criminal court judge sends him to prison. Only you can orchestrate what Ellis needs: weekends in the detention center, tight probation that I would like to have shifted to Mr Wray who knows how to work with kids like Ellis, transfer to the vocational educational school, since auto-mechanics is the one thing he's good at, a part-time job we've lined up for him, and an order that he make restitution of $250 for medical bills, which he has agreed to do . . .

Defense counsel, like prosecution counsel, look for the soft spots in a judge's armor. Judicial preferences and prejudices are well known to attorneys who practice regularly before a particular judge. The judge may have expressed questions about probation department effectiveness, psychologists' opinions, or the suitability of prisons for juveniles in prior hearings. The prosecutor has emphasized that Ellis has been unresponsive to rehabilitation efforts. Defense counsel has tried to shift the ground, and to place on trial the failure of the rehabilitation system to meet the needs of this minority youth. Certain public defender organizations employ their own social work personnel, part of whose role is to help the defender outline a more attractive alternative plan to the judge. That defense counsel has not suggested he will plead Ellis guilty and that the judge should commit the boy to a state delinquency facility may be due to the fact that the prosecutor has already rejected such a suggestion in going ahead with the transfer hearing. Possibly, also, Ellis may have rejected this idea, opting for more freedom and a less restrictive alternative such as a sentence to a series of weekends in the detention center. Although detention facilities are intended to serve youngsters on a pre-trial and pre-dispositional basis, a growing number of states have authorized their use for sentencing purposes as well, though those awaiting hearings are rarely segregated from sentenced youths in the facility. The stage has now been set for the judicial finding.

The judge avoided the defense attorney's eyes, looked toward Ellis, and announced he was granting the transfer. Ellis requires more institutional time than is guaranteed in the juvenile system. He has rejected the court's interest in assisting him. Instead of improving, his offenses have become more serious. But, privately, the judge wondered whether shortcomings in the court's efforts really justified his "getting rid of" Ellis. He wondered whether the criminal court judge would incarcerate Ellis, place him on probation, or use his authority to institutionalize Ellis back in a state delinquency facility? He also wondered whether he was becoming too concerned with protecting his own judgeship from prosecutor and public criticism . . .
The judge was justified in transferring Ellis. Still, he had some nagging doubts. Punishment available to the juvenile court, a training school commitment, might end up as more severe handling than is actually awarded in the criminal court. Something like 50 percent of transferred youngsters are not incarcerated by adult courts; instead they are placed on adult probation, fined, ordered to

make restitution. In juvenile court, the youth is at the "end of his rope"; in the criminal courts, he is at the beginning. The criminal court judge might provide Ellis with a chance to demonstrate that the severity of punishment facing him now as an adult, were he to offend again, will act to conform his behavior. Alternatively, the criminal court judge might consider that juvenile probation caseloads are generally smaller than adult probation caseloads and that the juvenile system has a reputation for being better able to arrange a wider array of services than the adult system. Since this appears to have failed, and Ellis is now in the adult system, and also because of the seriousness of the offense, the judge might indeed sentence Ellis to prison.

Ellis will pick up a new public defender in the criminal court who will probably try to bargain the case down to a misdemeanor and agree to a term of up to one year in the local jail. The lawyer will also request a jury trial. He will try to arrange Ellis's release on bail, encourage Ellis to get a job and stay out of trouble, and delay the criminal court process for six months or longer in order to show that Ellis has remained trouble-free and merits a stint on adult probation. Criminal court commitment of a transferred youth back to a state delinquency institution occurs in some states, though infrequently. This would be unlikely in Ellis's case due to his age, particularly if he was over eighteen at the time of the criminal court sentence.

A detention hearing is next. Her mother joined fourteen-year-old Margaret in waiving the right to counsel for this hearing. The judge needed to explore whether Margaret could be safely returned to her mother today...
Detention hearings have been a reform to impose legal checks on keeping youngsters in pre-trial detention. Frequently, on about 50 percent of such occasions, youngsters are returned to parental custody at this stage. Prior to the hearing, a probation officer has reviewed the police report, checked out previous court records, met with the child, and talked with a parent by telephone or in person. Probation officers generally dominate this hearing since they possess much of the relevant information. Increasingly, prosecutors and defense attorneys attend these hearings as well. The right to a defense counsel applies at this stage since the child presently has been denied liberty. These hearings tend to be brief. Court systems develop norms as to who should be held or released. Youngsters with

more serious offenses or offense patterns and those presently on probation status are more likely to be held.

The relationship has been strained for a long time and Margaret's not controllable by her mother now, said Probation Officer Mascarenas. The mother is very upset because this is Margaret's second shoplifting charge in six months . . .

Shoplifting is one of the most common girls' offenses. Female delinquency occurs far less often and far less seriously than male delinquency. If her mother had made a strong push for her return earlier, Margaret quite possibly would have been returned to her mother's care prior to the detention hearing, despite the second charge.

What about it, Margaret? You are going to be charged with shoplifting, your mother told Miss Mascarenas that you're staying out late, not helping around the house, and that you tried to bring home a new skirt you hadn't paid for . . .

The judge recognizes that the probation officer favors retaining Margaret in detention. The second offense and a weak relationship with the mother factored into the probation officer's opinion. While a second shoplifting offense in six months does not constitute a serious endangerment of the property of others, the inability of the mother to supervise Margaret effectively at this stage would provide the judge with a rationale for retaining Margaret in detention.

I want to go live with my father. My mother doesn't understand me . . .

Judges know that imperfect parenting prompts youngsters to manipulate their parents, as, indeed, they may have been manipulated by their parents. Judges are also aware that youngsters manipulate court systems. The mother and daughter are in conflict, not an uncommon denominator, but the judge needs more information on the father and the father's interest in Margaret.

I'm going to hold her longer. Check out her father. Also, see whether Margaret and her mother cool off after awhile. You can release her to one of her parents, if one of these situations works out. Otherwise, bring everyone back before me in ten days. I will appoint a public defender for her and you should get social services involved in this case . . .

The shoplifting charge will receive formal court attention later. The main problem at this moment is the child-parent relationship. The judge, in suggesting the involvement of the local social services agency, senses that ongoing family counseling is indicated and that Margaret's placement away from her mother might become necessary. She is being handled more as a dependent or status offender than a delinquent child in terms of this preliminary disposition. The judge sees utility in appointing a lawyer for Margaret, wanting someone to be an unambiguous advocate for the child. The idea of a review detention hearing in ten days is used to force rapid interim resolution of this matter. The probation officer has been authorized to release Margaret if that becomes viable. If not, the promotion of quick action by the probation officer and the social services department is aimed at thwarting unnecessary and prolonged detention. If return to a family member does not develop, the judge may well direct, at the next hearing, that Margaret be released from detention and placed in a non-secure shelter care facility, a more normal setting for Margaret to reside in while efforts are undertaken to work out where she will live.

The judge completed hearing the other cases just before noon, recessed the court, and hurried off to a League of Women Voters luncheon. There he would be the featured speaker, addressing proposed legislation that would amend the juvenile code. He would also speak to the need for additional programs, governmental and privately sponsored, to assist children . . .

Appearing before public groups is a particular characteristic of the juvenile court judge role, though some judges shun this function or prefer to be highly selective about how they use their time to seek improvements to the juvenile justice system. Juvenile court judges have their own national organization and, often, statewide councils. They are particularly strong advocates for increased services. They also tend to prefer to have both greater power and greater discretion to exercise, as witnessed by their usual preference to administer probation and often detention services within the judicial branch of government and their opposition to legislative constraints as to what they are authorized to do with certain classes of juvenile offenders.

At the time, judges took quite strong exception to the *Gault* ruling, considering that its radical departure from informality threatened the value of what this court was about. Today these judges accept the *Gault* direction and defend it. They are able to perform their functions effectively within legal mandates. Extremely influential in their communities, their speaking engagements and conference participation enhances their visibility and encourages groups and individuals who wish to assist juvenile justice or alter current approaches to solicit the judge's opinion and support.

Next is Juanita and she has run away again. Juanita, you know you can have a lawyer, but do you want to take care of things right now? . . .

Runaways have been a major workload of juvenile courts until recently. They form part of a classification now known as status offenses. A status offense is noncriminal misbehavior, conduct-illegal-only-for-children. The status of childhood has subjected children to state-imposed controls that has not accompanied adult sanctioning. Truancy, incorrigibility, runaway, under-age alcohol use, and curfew violations are the most prolific status offenses. For years, these matters had been classified within juvenile delinquency and a judge's powers were undifferentiated as between delinquents and status offenders. Runaways could be shipped off to delinquency institutions as readily as armed robbers. Girls, particularly, were confined in pre-trial detention and state institutions for status offenses. Historically, juvenile codes had sought to compel juvenile conformity by proscribing often vaguely defined activities such as associating with immoral persons, growing up in idleness or crime, endangering one's morals or health or that of others, patronizing poolrooms or saloons, and smoking tobacco. Beginning in the early 1960s, legislatures began to repeal the archaic descriptions and reclassify these youngsters separately from delinquent youths who had violated criminal laws, structuring a separate category for status offenders and constraining what courts could do with these youths. They are now known by such names as person in need of supervision (PINS), child in need of supervision (CHINS), youth in need of supervision (YINS), unruly child, and by other terms. Judges tend to be less meticulous in affording these youngsters the same legal rights as delinquent youths.

Okay, but Judge, I really had decided to come back when the policeman stopped me . . .

Police officers are granted authority to take these youngsters into custody under juvenile code provisions. There is some evidence that law enforcement officials are now less inclined to take these youngsters into custody due to the substantial constraints on detaining or institutionalizing them which have been widely enacted, particularly during the 1970s. Most states still permit status offenders to be detained for from twenty-four to seventy-two hours. But the general public policy preference now is to hold these youngsters, if holding is necessary, in non-secure facilities, though further "runs" are not uncommon. Since these youngsters have not committed crimes, as the contemporary supporting rationale goes, their liberty should not be curtailed. Another argument which supports this view is that mixing status offenders with delinquents in pre-trial detention facilities and state institutions will contaminate the former group. But concerns with today's diminished court powers with status offenders remain acute. There is no longer the same authoritarian backup to flagging parental controls and to school truancy violations as there had been. Courts can still order counseling and orchestrate a range of community-based programming. But courts, too, have lost some interest in these youngsters since they can do less with them.

I did run away from my mother's home on September 20 but it's my stepfather's fault. He's jealous of my mother's interest in me. He nags me all the time to clean up the house, wash the dishes, get to bed early. He's no good for Mom and no good for me . . .

Another reason for the diminished juvenile court interest in these youngsters is the recognition that a court may not be a good setting for "hanging out the family wash". Further, though parents may contribute to the child's decision to run away, more typically it is the child who is the focus of the court sanctions. The tangible symptom of the runaway is more prominent than the more distant factors of intrafamily conflict. Judges, however, often encourage or order family counseling with these matters.

But that's not the way to handle it, Juanita. You're already on supervision. You're to talk this over with your probation officer, and not take off . . .

Until recently, a status offender placed on probation supervision who again ran away, was beyond parental control, or was truant could be transferred to delinquency status by a legal contrivance known as the violation of a lawful order of the court. Where status offenders could not be institutionalized for a status offense only, a subsequent status offense converted the child's status to delinquency and enabled institutionalization. This approach is still used in some jurisdictions but is now more generally banned. Still, the practical issue confronts judges daily: How shall I deal with youngsters who may injure themselves or hurt their potential achievements?

The probation officer indicated she was counseling with the mother and stepfather. The stepfather was trying to accept Juanita. Juanita was obstinate. She used her stepfather as a reason for not accepting the rules of the court. Probably, Juanita should be locked up in detention to show her that she cannot get away with refusing to follow supervision rules . . .

The probation officer is not a strong advocate for Juanita. We also do not know whether the counseling session occurred once or more often. Little has been said as to the intricacies of household dynamics. The probation officer is control-oriented. Juanita, also, may enjoy all this attention. She now has a lot of people interested in what she is doing.

But, remember, Mrs Glenn, I can't lock up a kid for runaway anymore. I can put Juanita in a shelter or return her home again. I know this is frustrating . . .

Beginning in 1974, the federal government enunciated policy and funding support for deinstitutionalizing status offenders. The policy strongly favored non-coercive intervention with these youngsters. A variety of community agencies were funded to provide alternatives to court intervention. Still, courts can intervene, but their sanctioning powers have been sharply curbed. Faced with such an obstacle, some judges have begun to fall back on an old authority, the use of contempt of court powers. A reoffending status offender, in such courts, can be placed in secure detention for a contemptuous refusal to follow the court's requirements. Other judges frown on such an approach.

I'll go to the shelter and stay there, Your Honor, Juanita said. I think she will, commented the mother; this is hard for all of us and we need more time to work things out. All right, said the judge, but stay put, Juanita, while everyone works with Mrs Glenn . . .

This has been a useful conference. There appears to be a positive working relationship between Juanita and the judge. The authority of the court, though limited, has been constructively used. The judge feels good about this hearing, but experience has taught him another crisis may well lie down the road.

The last case this afternoon is the day's most eventful matter: Whether to terminate the parental rights of an interested but neglectful and abusive mother . . .

Child dependency, neglect, and abuse are the other major workload of juvenile courts. Public policy, expressed through legislative action, has long interposed these courts in protective roles for children who receive substandard care from their parents or guardians. The parenting deficiencies range from children left alone while their parents are away for hours or even days to child victims of sexual abuse, physical battering, and severe emotional abuse. In its less drastic forms, the determination of neglect is not an easy one. An official's conclusion that neglect exists may differ from another person's perception. More serious cases leave no room for doubt, though there may be questions of proof. A one-year-old suffers broken bones. The child cannot speak for himself or herself. The parent claims the child crawled away and fell off the table during a diaper change while the parent had gone for a safety pin. The hospital physician has a different theory. The state's interest in protecting children comes into conflict with another state value, that of family autonomy. Some question whether the state should intrude into family autonomy short of more severe derelictions. But a failure to intervene may result in further damage or even death. It is the juvenile court role to protect the welfare of children. More and more juvenile court judge time is engaged in overseeing proceedings and social service provisions with these cases. The punishment of parents and others who abuse or mistreat children is the responsibility of a criminal court. Criminal prosecutions have increased substantially as the magnitude and grim quality of these injuries have become more visible.

You will recall, Your Honor, that you found Marlene an abused child a year ago and approved her placement in a foster home, the county attorney began . . .

There was an earlier hearing where proof of the mother's neglect and abuse was established. Generally, the proof standard at that stage is the usual civil case measure, a preponderance, where 50.1 per cent or more of the evidence establishes the allegations. A foster home is the basic placement resource used for young children. Forty and more years ago, institutions were generally utilized with these children. But child research demonstrated that young children need close nurturing relationships which are not obtainable in congregate institutions. Foster homes and parents may be licensed for one or several children. They are often the unsung heroes of child care services, though a number of such homes are far from ideal and more than a few later have been found neglectful, despite their licensure. A prosecutor brings these matters in some courts; elsewhere, as in this example, it is a different attorney, a lawyer who handles civil matters for the local governmental entity. Terminating parental rights to a child, the proceeding being conducted here, requires a higher proof standard, clear and convincing evidence of a parent's unfitness and of the unlikeliness that this condition will change in the foreseeable future. This was the ruling of the United States Supreme Court in *Santosky*.

Further, at a review hearing held six months ago, it was brought out that the mother's adjustment remained in great disarray. The department was concerned about her care of Marlene's five-year-old sister and sought to remove the sister, as well. A petition in the sister's case has just been filed, the county attorney continued . . .

In finding one child in need of the court's protection, juvenile courts and social service agencies are also concerned with the quality of care provided other children in the family. Where one child has been physically abused, other children also may suffer abuse, though this does not always occur. But an abusive parent remains suspect and social service visits to the homes may focus as much on observing and investigating the other children as in counseling the parents.

The social services worker, Mrs Maxey, testified that Marlene had done well in the foster home, but her mother had failed to appear on four planned visitations with Marlene. Further, the mother rebuffed numerous efforts to assist her. The social worker added that the mother could not handle her own life, much less Marlene's, and will not face up to the reality that Marlene needs a permanent home. Since the mother has not rehabilitated herself, it is necessary that Marlene be freed for adoption while she is adoptable . . .

Local departments of social services and, in some communities, licensed private child care agencies carry the primary responsibility for assisting these children and their families. Generally, probation officers are not engaged with these types of cases. The social worker visits with Marlene in the foster home, learns about Marlene's adjustment from the foster family and counsels with them, and attempts to help the natural parents resolve their problems and reclaim their children. Yet, in severe abuse and neglect cases, it is natural that these professionals have a bias that the child's welfare should not again be entrusted to such risks. The social worker, then, may be less than enthused about trying to help an inadequate parent become adequate. A natural parent may not be provided with the name and address of the foster parents. Instead, visitations may occur in the office of the agency. The child protection social worker has one of the most difficult and demanding jobs among helping-services professionals. The worker must confront, daily, a great range of emotions in others and in her/himself.

I've stopped drinking. I'm doing pretty well, though I was sick a couple of times when I was supposed to visit Marlene. But I did see her several times since we were in court. I want Marlene home with me . . . After the mother's statement, the court-appointed attorney commented that Mrs Hartwick had shown progress . . .

The United States Supreme Court ruled in the *Lassiter* case that the federal Constitution does not require courts to furnish counsel to all indigent parents in termination proceedings. Strong dissents took exception to the majority view. Clearly, appointing counsel in such cases is the better policy. The case may involve significant and complex legal issues, negative testimony may shrink under cross-examination, a parent is helped to make a better case for herself.

As the three-year-old Marlene directed her eyes to whomever was speaking, the guardian appointed by the court to represent the child's interests made her report: You will recall that Marlene had sustained a severe subdural hematoma at the hands of her mother. Though she has done rather well in the foster home, her development has not progressed to where it should have. I've talked with Marlene, the mother, the foster parents, the doctors, and the social worker. The mother had been drinking when I last visited her. I am convinced that the threat of further abuse is there. The mother needs Marlene more than Marlene needs her mother.

A growing number of juvenile courts appoint either attorneys or trained volunteers as guardians for youngsters in these proceedings. Their exclusive concern is the child or children; they are neutral as to the agency or parents; they are to be an aide to the court.

I won't injure her again, the mother broke in, I won't do that again . . .
Emotion is common to these types of hearings.

Mrs Maxey, I want to hear more about your counseling efforts with Mrs Hardwick . . .
Judges sometimes ask questions to obtain responses that strengthen the court record in support of the action they may take. An appeal may be taken with such a case. If so, the court would want the record to show expansive evidence of the mother's failure to respond to counseling efforts. Alternatively, the judge may have concern whether the social worker made a serious effort to assist the mother's rehabilitation and whether the mother has had ample opportunity to engage in counseling.

We did talk several times at her house and once at my office. Her home remains chaotic; her life is in chaos. She made no effort to follow through when I offered to arrange an appointment with Dr Goldstein at the mental health clinic. She also rejected coming to the parenting class we offer. She hasn't been working for months so that is not the reason she broke her other appointments with me. When we've met, she refuses to explore what led to the abuse or how to become a better mother . . .
The judge had his record.

Mrs Hardwick, I must terminate your parent rights to Marlene. You have severely injured Marlene. You had a year to show me that you would make every effort possible to regain your daughter's custody. You have not done that, and I cannot wait any longer. I find you an unfit parent who has failed to comply with the court-approved treatment plan. I am sorry, but it is in Marlene's best interests that I free her for adoption . . .

Other termination cases may be more ambiguous and difficult than this one. Here the abuse has been gross and the mother's inadequacies apparent. The natural father has been out of the home since prior to Marlene's birth, though separate proceedings will now have to be brought against him to terminate any legal rights he holds. Though progress is being made in legally preparing Marlene for adoption eligibility, whether in fact this child will be adopted is not yet determined. That the social worker encouraged termination of parental rights and adoption is a clue that the agency considers Marlene adoptable. Social service agencies, juvenile courts, and legislatures have more recently structured proceedings which involve more regular court review and earlier consideration of termination of rights than had been true in the past. There is now a stronger push to assist the parents, promote the return of the child, or, move alternatively toward early termination. These children merit a permanent and stable home. If this cannot reasonably be achieved with their own parents, it is part of the job of the juvenile court judge to see that this is done otherwise.

The court day is over. The judge looked quickly at the next day's calendar, then hurried home to dinner with his wife and children . . .

CHAPTER 2

JUDGE REGNAL W. GARFF, Jr.:
JUDICIAL LEADERSHIP

"When you walk into my courtroom, you have a right to know that I will not say one thing and do another. You can depend on what I say just as I will want to be able to depend on what you say."

Consistency has been a hallmark of Judge Reg Garff's administration of juvenile justice since he first went on the juvenile court bench in Salt Lake City, Utah, on August 1, 1959. His contribution to the children, youth, and families of his community and the juvenile justice system of his district and state has been vast.

He had enrolled at the Law School of the University of Utah when he was twenty-four years old, determined to become a juvenile court judge. Three years later, he initiated graduate social work training at the same university, to further his goal. His field work placement, during this training, was as a probation officer at the juvenile court, at his request. For the next three years, he practiced law part-time and social work part-time. He talks about the latter experience:

"The Relief Society Social Services Department of the Church of Jesus Christ of Latter-Day Saints wanted to initiate a social work program for juvenile delinquents. I was employed to begin this and to work with the youngsters and their families. Most of the referrals came from the police department. Every month I reported my cases to two of the twelve apostles of the Church and to the director of the LDS Relief Society. I like to think my work was instrumental in the Church's expansion of its social services. I thought my work was effective during those three years."

Among juvenile court judges, he was an early advocate of expanded legal procedures in the juvenile court. But his extensive knowledge of social service intervention and his deep commitment to rehabilitation long ago brought his court into prominence for its innovative and purposefully-orchestrated probation services. He knows as much or more about what is needed for good intervention programs as any professional who comes into his court. In no way, however, is his confidence in what rehabilitation can achieve a blind optimism. He is the first to discern the space between good intentions and effective implementation. Aware of the national disenchantment with accomplishing the "rehabilitative ideal", he is convinced that rehabilitation is alive and well in his court. "Otherwise, I would change my profession."

Reg Garff is assertive. He is also clear-thinking. His day-to-day judgments are highly regarded for their soundness and practicality. He clearly fits the description, firm but fair. His off-the-bench judgments are sought out by officials of youth-serving agencies, legislators, and community leaders. The advice he provides is well thought through, though quickly decided. With many of these issues he has "been there before". His recommendations are a combination of common sense, intelligence, and experience. As senior of the nine juvenile court judges in the state, seniority is far from the sole basis for the high status accorded him. The administrator of the Utah State Juvenile Court says of Garff: "He is a leader among the judges. He doesn't attempt to dominate the others, but he is heard to whatever extent he wants to be heard and is usually right. I find, when I seek advice, he's the one I call saying, 'What do you think about this?' He has an amazing ability to sort out problems and get to the heart of them, and then his advice on how to approach an issue is usually sound. It's always been sound. When I go to the legislature, when I want someone to be a voice for this juvenile court, if I had my choice, it would be Reg Garff each time. He is eloquent, forceful, and palatable."

The years of being turned to for advice, the leadership he has demonstrated, the daily decisions he has reached, have all strengthened Garff's confidence in himself and his use of his role. But, he hasn't always been this way. Garff says that no one ever believes him when he says that before he went on his Mormon mission to Holland from 1949 to 1952, "I was really shy. I really was retiring and would not project myself, never took much initiative, always felt like I couldn't do well in sport or any other thing. I was always in the shadow of friends, even though I was about a foot taller."

In the Church of Jesus Christ of Latter Day Saints (Mormon Church), a mission may take place in a foreign country or in the United States. It is not required, but it is expected of Mormon young adults. Garff's daughter, Lisa, participated in a mission to Spain in 1982. The husbands of two other daughters had been missionaries in Ecuador and in California. The mission experience was a turning point in Reg Garff's life. It had permitted him to be receptive to the suggestion of two of his sisters, then graduate psychologists, that there was a need for judges who had behavioral science backgrounds.

Judge Garff elaborates on his mission experience and how it changed him. "In all honesty, one of the reasons I turned my bishop down the first time he asked me to go was because I was afraid of meeting people. A mission is proselyting, and consists primarily of knocking on doors and talking to people on the streets and meeting with them at night in discussions. When you go on a mission, you have what is called a 'farewell' in the church where you ask people to participate and then you have to speak. I had managed to successfully avoid giving a talk in church until my farewell. Six months into the Holland mission experience, the mission president asked me to go to a small town near the German border, Hengelo, and be the branch president. 'President?', I said, 'You've got to be kidding. I'm just learning the language and you want me to go over and take care of a branch?' That experience really threw me into the middle of the soup, and then other leadership experiences followed. When I came home, talking and meeting people were not problems anymore."

When he was thirty years old, Garff sought appointment as juvenile court judge, telling his wife that he was going to get that job, perhaps not this time, but he would get it. He didn't get it then. Judge Rulon Clark, who had presided in that setting for nearly three decades, was reappointed. "The first time I just applied because I wanted them to know I was interested. I knew I was not going to take Clark's place, if he wanted it." But, Judge Clark resigned a year or two later when he failed to convince the legislature to equalize the salaries of juvenile court judges with judges of the court of general trial jurisdiction. Judge Clark had also been concerned that the Utah Public Welfare Commission dominated the juvenile court and held the statutory authority to appoint its judges. The young Judge Regnal Garff also preferred that his initial $7,200 salary instead be the $10,000 salary of the district court judges. Later, parity was achieved.

Several years into his judgeship, when a lawyer advised him he would appeal a particular ruling, Judge Garff suggested that the attorney use, as another basis for the appeal, a challenge to the constitutionality of the Utah Code which then stated: "the Public Welfare Commission shall have the general control and supervision over juvenile courts and probation officers". Other statutory provisions granted the commission the power to appoint, reappoint, or remove the judges and to fix salaries of the judges, probation officers, and other court employees.

These provisions, enacted in 1941, represented an interesting anachronism in an extreme form, the juvenile court as an instrument of welfare department policy. The authoritarian powers of a court were to be harnessed to public welfare objectives. The Utah Supreme Court struck down this law in 1963 as violative of the state constitutional requirement for the separation of powers of governmental departments. The juvenile court had become, properly, an independent entity.

A revamped juvenile code was then enacted in 1965, significantly influenced by Reg Garff's conception of a legally-based juvenile court. This law, together with the relatively few amendments enacted since then, provides the structure and format for the unique Utah juvenile system of today. Expressive of that state's culture and of Judge Reg Garff's belief that children's concerns merit special consideration, Utah is the only state with a separately organized, statewide juvenile court system where all juvenile cases are heard only by specialist full-time juvenile court judges and where these matters are the judges' sole responsibility.

Now, juvenile court judges are appointed or reappointed for a six-year term by the governor from two or more candidates nominated by a Juvenile Court Commission (Garff has experienced no problems in obtaining serial reappointment). The Board of Juvenile Court Judges is the general supervising and policy-making body for the statewide court system, and "the juvenile court shall be of equal status with the district court". The new Code, approved two years before the United States Supreme Court *Gault* decision, contained a number of early due process features such as notice of the right to counsel and detention hearings providing judicial review of youngsters admitted into secure care pending court proceedings.

However, there has been study and discussion in this state, for at least a decade, considering whether the separate juvenile court should be reorganized into the district courts, similar to the trend occurring nationally that is aimed at consolidating and unifying trial courts. Garff knows that where consolidation has taken place, the importance of the juvenile court function has frequently become lost in the shuffle. General court judges reluctantly accept assignments to the juvenile division and tend not to assert a strong leadership role owing to lack of interest or the usually brief nature of this assignment.

Reg Garff strenuously opposes such a structural shift. Garff is the product of a specialized court where motivated lawyers seek this appointment as a long-term career objective. Were it to happen, he would like to see the creation of a family court division of the district court, a blend of divorce and family-related matters with juvenile cases, enriched by a strong family counseling and juvenile probation component administered by the court.

Judge Garff represents the juvenile court's interests as *ex officio* member of the Judicial Council, comprised of judges from all trial courts but the juvenile court. He will not miss these meetings. "We've had some heated discussions there", he indicates. Once he confronted the other judges bluntly as to their modest interest in a people-problem caseload presently within the district court's jurisdiction: "Divorce and custody matters are low on your priority list — just look at who gets the domestic relations cases. It's always the newest, least experienced judge — none of you want to take it." He adds: "I really twisted somebody's tail on that one. All of the district court judges took offense. They denied that it was low-priority, but it really is and they don't want to get involved. Also, they don't think judges should administer staff and they don't want the juvenile court coming into their court and bringing staff with them. But staff are essential."

The youngsters and families who come before Reg Garff each day know nothing of his unflagging efforts to create and maintain a workable juvenile court. What they do see across the courtroom is a tall (six foot, one inch), dark-haired but graying, bespectacled, sensitive man in command of his courtroom. What they encounter is a communicative judge. No one exits his courtroom without having responded to a Garff question or having told the judge what he or she thinks. He has a calm and measured voice, makes clear statements, listens and responds, and punctuates most hearings with a touch of humor.

His eyes move from the record on his bench to the participants, back and forth. A pen is in one hand; his other hand is on his chin. This hand moves towards his ear, back onto the desk, stretches out toward the boy as he asks a question, then comes back to the side of his jaw. He shifts his other hand to the left side of his face as he talks and listens, then lets this hand flow off the side of his face toward the youth. Though he makes all of the legal decisions, he is inviting courtroom participants to help him shape whether and how he should restrict this youth's freedom, and what treatment plan should be erected to provide the supportive strength this youngster may need to stay out of further difficulty. He is, simultaneously, the community's clear symbol for protecting its norms of acceptable behavior, a daily reinforcer of a child's more positive strivings, one whose standards are candidly set forth, and a judge who is personally interested in those ushered into his courtroom.

This is illustrated in the combined detention and dispositional hearing he held with a girl he had ordered into the custody of the state youth correctional agency's community program, following several delinquencies, for placement in a foster home, and who had run away from the home.

Judge: Are you nervous today?

The thirteen-year-old girl nods that she is and the judge smiles.

Judge: Good. Why do I want you to be nervous? So you take this seriously, but not to the point of not being able to talk with me. I need your thoughts to make my decision. I have read your letter and thank you for it. I would like your recommendations. What are the alternatives?

Girl: To go back to my foster home or go to the state school.

Judge: I can't hang you (laughter). But, I need to talk with you about your taking off from your foster home.

Her mother nods affirmatively.

Judge: I need to test my thoughts about your behavior. You've been impulsive — do you know what I mean by that?

Girl: Yes, acting without thinking.

Judge: Every kid gets a wild hair or two. Sometimes you may act like eighteen, sometimes like less than thirteen.

The girl smiles.

Judge: What have you learned?

Girl: People care, you care, my mother does, Sojourn (the agency that arranges and works with the foster parents) does, and my foster family does.

Judge: Another thing I look at is whether one tries to correct past mistakes. Here you turned yourself in. But why should I not send you to the state school?

Mother: My daughter has matured a lot from this program and I was worried when she was on the run.

Judge: Is your daughter past the point of committing crimes?

Mother: No. I want what is best for her, but I understand your concern.

Judge: Usually there is no conflict between what is best for the state and what is best for the child. If the state school is no good for a child, it's no good for the state.

The girl holds her mother's hand; the mother is tearful.

Foster parent: I think she is beyond committing crimes. I don't shy away from a hard line, but she is progressing. She is not the same child she was three months ago.

The girl is biting her fingernails.

Judge: I better hurry this hearing up or you won't have any fingernails left.

The child laughs.

Judge: A week ago, when you came to detention, I was very angry. I probably would have sent you to the state school. But, judges, like kids, need to cool off. I think your advocates have made good arguments for you, not because you have snowed them, but because they do see your progress.

The child is still chewing her nails and holding her mother's hand.

Judge: I'm going to let you continue with the Sojourn program. I see you have paid a little more than one-half of your $100 fine. I will take restitution under advisement. I will order that you remain with Youth Corrections. I will release you from detention, and I'd like to see you again. The Sojourn representative will execute the treatment plan in writing and I will review this three months from today at 9.30 a.m.

The judge leaves the courtroom. The mother hugs the foster mother and the Sojourn worker. The foster father hugs the mother who is still crying as the group leaves the courtroom.

Judge Garff has occupied this particular courtroom since its construction in 1963. It is a part of the Juvenile Court Center, located about six miles from downtown Salt Lake City, in a rather handsome, modern structure. The center houses the three courtrooms for the three judges, a hearing room for the referee, probation and clerical offices, and a mental health clinic. A covered breezeway connects the court building with the adjacent detention center, built at the same time. The architecture is contemporary. There are louvered roofs. Glass underneath the louvred roofs allows daylight to enter. These are one-floor structures. The court's waiting room is airy and spacious; court clientele should sense a certain security from the facebrick walls, while the upper glass provides a lightness to avoid any oppressive feeling.

Soon after his initial appointment to the bench, Judge Garff chaired the committee which successfully engineered the planning and funding for this overall project. The detention center was expanded in 1981 to increase its capacity from forty to fifty-six youngsters. It is not administered by the court but by the Board of

County Commissioners. A group shelter home had also been added to the complex to provide care for six to eight youths who do not need secure detention but who present more problems than are easily managed in one of the shelter foster homes available to court youngsters. The detention center also administers home-detention supervision to youngsters released from the detention center who appear to require close watching and frequent assistance pending court proceedings. The array of alternatives to secure detention that are available here represent as much as any community has provided youngsters at this stage of the juvenile justice process.

The Garff courtroom, with its accordion ceiling and several feet of glass around the perimeter at the top, projects a comfortable, modern ambience. A door leads from his chambers to the courtroom. The bench is one-step-up, placing him about six feet from the counsel tables where there are three chairs, and an additional four feet from the row of chairs in front of the rear wall where children and other parties sit when they have no attorneys. The United States flag flanks the judge to his right, the Utah flag to his left. The clerk also sits off to his left, operating the recording machine. Near her and along the left wall are additional chairs. A non-uniformed deputy sheriff sits there, as does a detention center social worker during detention hearings, and college students when they observe proceedings.

Back in his chambers, Judge Garff sits in a comfortable chair at a large desk — looking to his left through a glass wall into a small rocked patio with evergreens and other trees. On his walls are diplomas, seminar certificates, and a watercolour painting. His two bookshelves contain statutes, bar journals, books and publications relating to juvenile justice, and seminar notebooks. There are also several chairs and a couch. On a table is a radio and cassette player and tape cassettes, such as Beethoven piano concertos. Also on the table are family law journals, a book, *The Brethren* which takes an inside look at the United States Supreme Court, James A. Michener's *The Covenant*, and *The Runner's Handbook*. On the credenza behind his desk chair lay case files which have referee recommendations he needs to review.

Of the judicial chambers in which he has spent so much time since 1963, the judge says: "I love my office. It is my home-away-from-home. I feel comfortable here. I come down here at night to do things I need to do. For years, except to read history and law and juvenile justice journals, I deserted reading. Now, I usually bring my lunch, close the blinds, turn on the music, and read. I've read several books here recently. For an hour, it's my quiet time and no one can disturb me."

As to his courtroom design, he notes that in the old juvenile court downtown he had inherited a judicial bench placed directly on the floor. "I designed my new courtroom one-step-up to make it look like a courtroom. I didn't look like a father figure, like Judge Clark did, and I had given up the idea of a judge as a fatherly person."

The courtroom structure enables Reg Garff to use the authority he wants to use, to build the anxiety in youngsters he wants to encourage, and also to communicate with youths and to have them help share in his fateful decisions, as shown in the following detention hearing.

A sixteen-year-old boy had been placed on probation five months earlier for possession of alcohol and bicycle theft. He had been brought back once since then on a marijuana charge and was now in detention for runaway, a violation of his probation conditions.

Judge: Do you know what a violation of probation means?
Boy: Yes.
Judge: Why did you take off?
Boy: I was with friends.
Father: He does well for two or three weeks, then gets phone calls and takes off out the window. I have found marijuana paraphernalia. He gets phone calls regarding money. I can't control him.
Judge: Do you think he's selling drugs?
Father: I don't know, but only undesirable people come to see him at home.
Judge: Do you know why I placed you on probation instead of sending you to an institution?
Boy: Ug.
Judge: Probation requires you to follow certain rules in order to avoid the institution. Understand that judges are not social workers. They are not like parents. If you don't follow the rules, you'll be removed from home. We're not playing games; this is serious business. And, I don't think you've gotten that message yet. I'm holding you in detention for release by your probation officer and I'm doing this because of your contempt for the court and for your not being under your parents' control. Do you like being in detention?
Boy: No.

Judge: Then make some changes.

Judge (an aside to the probation officer): Release him only when there are agreements between him and his parents as to what his behavior will be.

After this hearing, the probation officer informally mentioned to the judge that the police had other investigations going regarding possible thefts by the boy. The probation officer asked whether the police could question the boy at the detention center. The detention center social worker, present at the hearing, commented that the boy had talked the day before of committing suicide. Judge Garff stated that he did not want the police to talk to the boy until the probation officer checked things out further. The detention center social worker said the boy was still more depressed today. The judge asked whether someone from the mental health clinic at the court should see the boy, and then answered his own question and directed that someone from mental health see him.

After the hearing, back in chambers, Judge Garff smiled and said, "That was my speech Number Fifteen — telling kids, 'You can't do that'." Then he said, with his characteristic insight, "I asked myself whether I did anything different because you were here. I decided I didn't."

Youngsters are able to obtain speedy mental health services from the clinic which is located at the court. Its placement there is a source of pride to Garff. Some years before its establishment, he served as a member and, at one time, chairman of the district mental health committee. He, along with several others, were instrumental in surmounting prohibitive regulations to obtain this service, perhaps unique in the nation, since it brought together staff members from three different district or catchment areas into one court setting which serves children from all three catchment areas. "But, ordinarily, if you didn't have that, you'd have a helluva hassle trying to get mental health services to kids, because you'd have to work with three different mental health clinics otherwise, and you and I both know you lose anywhere from three to eight days just in making a paper referral, at least that." Such an achievement is but one example of this judge's exercise of his "community role" to achieve improved services for youngsters.

The author accompanied the Garff family to an evening wedding reception of a young man who was a friend of the family. The mother of the bride, on being introduced to Judge Garff, commented, "Oh, you're the one who takes care of juveniles." To understand more about how this man, who has taken care of juveniles for so many years, developed his skills and sensitivities, more of Reg Garff's background needs to be chronicled.

He believes that the name Regnal is an adaptation of the name Reginald. He was the second Regnal. His mid-teenage son, Reg, is the third.

Judge Garff's paternal great-grandfather was a convert to the Mormon church in his native Denmark. "They were coming to Zion here in Salt Lake and my grandfather's father brought with him about eight other families who couldn't afford the trip. He had enough money to do that and prepaid for wagons and oxen they were to get in St Louis. But the guy they sent the money to had absconded." The entourage then had to travel across the plains pulling their belongings and children in handcarts. Great hardships were experienced. (An old handcart, one of those used by many Mormon families, is still on display in Temple Square, Salt Lake City.) His great-grandfather died on the trip about "two weeks out". His grandfather, then eight years old, survived, as did a sister and the great-grandmother. Another sister of his grandfather also died en route. This grandfather had had twelve children, giving them all Mormon names, such as Heber, Aaron, Moses, and Regnal.

His mother's parents came to Utah from England in 1879. Her mother, born a Mormon, married a convert to the faith. Reg Garff's ninety-year-old mother, a tall woman with a sweet sense of humor and an alert and agile mind, resides with his family since her serious injury.

The Mormon faith holds to a paternalistic view of the household. Judge Garff's mother describes this as "the husband is the head of the house and the wife is the neck that turns the head." Margaret Wheeler Garff, his wife since 1954, expresses a similar interpretation: "The man holds the priesthood and is the final authority, though our home is a joint effort and we share parenting and governance."

Reg Garff's life, in his words, has been the "epitome of stability". He was born in Salt Lake City on November 9, 1927. Except for a 1946–47 stint in the Army, he's lived in four houses his entire life, all within a radius of perhaps three miles. His father was an insurance salesman and was on the road a lot. Later he was to become the state insurance commissioner. His mother was a stickler on education for their children. Six daughters were born to his parents before the birth of their final child, Regnal, Jr. Two sisters died at an early age. Three sisters hold master's degrees in psychology; the fourth graduated in business administration. His mother's insistence that the youngsters have an education was realized. His parents did not have the money to send their children through college and graduate school. His sisters worked their way through; he did, as well, though he had assistance from the G.I. Bill.

Reg Garff attended a special laboratory school on the University of Utah campus, from kindergarten through the ninth grade. Living near the university was important to his mother, so that her children could have this special schooling opportunity, attend East High School, and then the university. Reg Garff recalls that the school on the university grounds was one with small classes. "It was neat, really a cohesive unit." In his era, high school ended with the eleventh grade. He was to obtain his undergraduate degree in psychology in 1949, his law degree in 1955, and his social work certificate in 1956, all at the nearby University of Utah. "So, aside from the two years at East High, my whole academic life was spent on one campus." His father had attended Utah State University for a short time and his mother never had the opportunity to attend college.

But education was embedded in their children, just as it is now expected of Reg and Margaret Garff's children. His mother lets it be known that she had no trouble with any of her youngsters. She recalls that her neighbors said her children had no decision to make regarding school, that it was always clear that they would go to college. His daughter, Marianne, adds that she never thought of not going to college . . . college was the end of school. On the bench, Reg Garff does not "spin a record" to a child that he or she must get to school, get as much out of school as possible, and prepare strongly for the difficult road ahead. He is concerned with truancy, though, and wants the court to support school efforts to keep youngsters engaged in their education.

His parents had other norms of cooperating with household chores, working hard at what you do, and being home at the appointed hour. Reg Garff laughs and reminds his mother of the time when he was seventeen years old and his father found him several blocks from home in the family car with a young woman at 3 a.m. and said, "Do you know what time it is?" Reg decided to ground himself for thirty days for violating a family rule. As a judge, he wants community norm-violating juveniles to experience some consequences for their misbehaviors.

While Judge Garff, as a child, always "felt very secure in my home", he has sought a different family environment in the home where he has been the head, and a different judge-client environment in his court. His father had been very strict and had a quick temper, though "I was kind of his favorite so there were some soft edges". His mother was easy to talk with, but "she was always in the middle between dad and the kids". He believes there is an appropriate time to be strict, but would hope that court youngsters could see some of his soft edges at the same time. He admits that "the kids" may not be able to see these unless they have been before him several times, since "I think I depict a fairly firm type of judge". He considers consistency a prime value for parents, judges, employers, and others. "Many of the kids we see have always been able to manipulate adults and quickly pick up inconsistencies from them. I'm firmly convinced that kids want consistency, want to know what is expected of them, and how far they can go."

His own education, social work experience, and mission enabled him to be a different kind of parent from his father, and the kind of judge he is. His father did not have the advantages Reg Garff had. "His experiences were hard growing up here. Mine weren't easy, but they weren't hard. Getting into a counseling situation as a social worker really does open you up. It makes you a warmer kind of person and more outgoing." And then there was the mission experience that changed him so much.

When Reg and Margaret married, they moved into a remodeled apartment in his parents' home, rent-free. Margaret went to work; Reg completed law school and social work school. They bought their first house and later built their second, present home, both within three miles of his parents' house.

Their children, except for young Reg, are grown and away from home, though they regularly visit the family nest. Margaret Garff holds a high position in the Mormon church as a member of the General Board of Primary. Primary is responsible for developing religious educational materials for Mormon youngsters throughout the world. Margaret chairs the committee which is responsible for these educational programs for children from eighteen months to five years of age. Primary writes, reviews, and approves these materials and teaching guides; its members serve as resource persons for training programs as to their use in Utah and elsewhere. Earlier, she held a position with the LDS Relief Society in their ward (general neighborhood) and stake (a number of wards comprise a stake).

In her reserved and unassuming way she talks about her husband and their life. "Our values are pretty close. Marriage was not a difficult adjustment. We had been reared in the same neighborhood and with the same religious beliefs. I interpret our religious rules more strictly; he interprets these more liberally. Both families were Republican, though I doubt this influences Reg's judicial philosophy. In part, our children have learned about the world through his accounts of what happens in court, but I've told him I don't want to hear about the serious abuse cases that concern him."

"He's always been close to the children. His busyness as a judge did not negatively affect them. He has always pretty well put his job aside when he comes home. He likes the attention he gets as a judge. He is very good with people. He has a special ability to listen, to point out alternatives, to assist others. Our nieces come to him for his advice and may bring over boyfriends for Reg's approval. He has a strong commitment to the community. True, we took our address out of the phone book after there were some threats, but Reg wanted to have our phone number listed in order to be available to those who need him."

"He's an easy man to live with and it's been fun. I've even learned to endure his sense of humor."

There is a strong affection and close binds between Reg and Margaret Garff. Judge Reg particularly respects his wife's many capabilities and sound judgments. Parenting has been a shared responsibility, though in particular areas one parent or the other has taken greater initiative.

Music is important to the four Garff children as it was to Reg, who had played clarinet in his high school and university marching and concert bands. All four are serious about the piano, and Leslie, twenty-six years old and the mother of three children, continues to work on her master's degree in piano performance. Young Reg takes piano lessons from Leslie, as do Marianne, age twenty, and Marianne's husband, Mike. Daughter Lisa, twenty-three years of age, also teaches piano.

Margaret Garff is the family cook, though her husband assists on occasion and claims expertise in making crepes, a family favorite. Judge Reg sits at the head of the table. Marianne says grace before dinner using traditional language plus improvisation. Leslie jokes about her father's sense of humor. The married daughters indicate that they participate more actively in family decisions than their mother, express certain generational differences with her, but acknowledge that the husband is the final authority. Margaret comments that all three girls look different, are different, but have a number of the same interests. Judge Reg states that he has long believed in a communication model, at home or in court, of being up front, saying here's how I feel and why, of being quite honest in stating one's feelings. He bounces Leslie's youngest child on his lap during dinner. The judge's mother talks of her mission, performed in Chicago when she was nineteen years old. Young Reg expresses interest in a mission in his future. For years there have been "pun fights" around the family table. Each child tries to top their father's punning skills ("After that steak, I would have to say that cows are an udder failure").

Because of their respect for their dad, the Garff children enjoyed being the children of a judge. Some years ago, Judge Reg arranged for the other judges to hear cases involving youngsters attending East High School where his children were enrolled. Leslie had had her hair pulled by a boy from the court though it was nothing serious. "I told my kids that some people say negative things about their father and they should try not to respond or be defensive." Later, he reverted to hearing cases of East High youths.

The family is nourishing to all Garff members. Family members talk and listen about church and community activities, school experiences, skiing, Lisa's letter from her Spanish mission, how grandmother is getting along, all while their short-haired Hungarian dog, a Viszla named Dandy, listens and snoozes. Relationships are warm and vital. There is little hint of adolescent rebellion from young Reg, although his father chides him to push a little harder to get his Eagle scout status and surpass his father's scouting achievements. Father and son go on to talk about planning to ski together on a future weekend.

Reg Garff holds positions of responsibility in his church. At present, he is a counselor to the bishop, who is the chief officer and spiritual leader in the ward of nearly five hundred people. Long active with LDS youth organizations, a current role is for him to meet every six months with senior high youths in the ward to talk about how they are adjusting to life, to discuss the church and its theology, and to communicate the church's interest in them. Also, he is a "home teacher", like many others, assigned to visit three or four families in the ward each month and to help as needed. His church's interest in maintaining a strong family unit carries over to his daily court search of a family's ability to provide stability and emotional support for its children. He follows Mormon precepts in personally abstaining from alcohol, tobacco, and coffee, but does not preach these principles from the bench.

Like many juvenile court judges, Reg Garff accepts speaking engagements from countless PTA groups, church groups, and civic groups. And he is good, very good, in explaining the critical issues of delinquency and what the court is doing about these. But unlike many other judges, he has a special interest and ability in talking with groups, whose members are parents, about how to communicate with their youngsters and how to listen as well. "Often the theme of my talk will be something like, 'What Parents Do that Places Barriers to Communication and Meaningful Discourse with their Kids'. I'm not sure whether this makes me happier or the audience, but I think I have something to share from my courtroom experience. Often, someone will come up and tell me, 'I remember what you said about such-and-such five years ago'. I've learned some things from being a juvenile court judge. If I've been underpaid in this job in dollars, I've had considerable compensation in becoming a better parent to my own children. So, these kinds of things I like to pass on to other people."

In 1973, Reg Garff authored a "Handbook for New Juvenile Court Judges", published by the National Council of Juvenile Court Judges. In this writing he comments first on communication at the juvenile court dispositional hearing, and then on the importance of setting a formal tone with courtroom proceedings. "As much as possible, the court should share the information with the family that will influence his decision. Open communication between the parties, the judge, and the probation officer is desirable and free expression of feelings encouraged. Any suggestions or recommendations the family has should be given full consideration." He continues, "The hearing should be a serious and significant event in the youth's life. It is serious enough to demand the parents' attention and, therefore, they should both be present. It must be kept in mind that the court is treating the family unit, not just the child. The whole aura of the hearing should be one of order, dignity and fairness without excessive formality. There is a great amount of security in orderliness and understanding. Most youngsters appearing in juvenile court have had neither. It should commence in the hearing." Garff's hearings follow his written guides:

Judge: My concern is that this offense took place at 4 a.m. and you had been drinking. How do I know this won't happen again?

Boy: It won't.

Judge: Do you know why I am fining you $100?

Boy: To see how it is when I destroy people's property.

Judge: Yes, and if you are again tempted, you will know there are consequences. Hopefully, you'll think about this before you act rather than after. Are you going to do this again?

Boy: No.

Judge: I hope not. Do you have any other comments you want to make?

Boy: No.

Reg Garff strongly emphasizes the accountability of a youngster for his violation of a law. He also focuses on orchestrating services and suitable punishment for the involved youth. He pushes hard for family participation in the rehabilitative efforts. Reg Garff knows that adolescence often strains child-parent relationships and believes that family counseling can be particularly useful at such junctures. Countless times he has heard a parent say in the courtroom, "I can't control him at home. I can't handle him at home." Too wise to let a parent off the hook and focus concern only on the child, he urges probation staff and collaborative agencies to strengthen parents' parenting skills and relationships with their rebellious youngsters. The Utah statute authorizes its judges to enter reasonable orders requiring parental cooperation. While Garff favors voluntary participation by parents, he does not hesitate to use an authoritarian order when parents question whether they will participate. He will hear out the parents' hesitancy, but then firmly but clearly set out the reasons why their assistance is critical to the court's concern and their own interest.

The Utah cultural climate has unique features which impact upon its juvenile courts. This is a state having both strong public welfare agencies and a strong private welfare apparatus. One does not pick up particularly negative references to the public social services that are common elsewhere. Further, Utah is the only state whose juvenile courts are still concerned with tobacco use violations by minors, nearly two thousand such youths being referred to these courts annually. There is an expectation that juvenile courts will backstop public school efforts to constrain student smoking, and they do. Utah juvenile courts, historically, have been extensively engaged with a rather wide range of status offense violations. Judge Garff worked actively to fashion statutory and rule changes that (1) shifted primary service responsibility for runaway and beyond control youngsters from the court's probation arm to the state social services agency, (2) retained the juvenile court in a back-up role when these social service efforts failed to achieve their goals, and (3) authorized the court to mete out fines for curfew, alcohol, and tobacco violations.

Garff's conviction, underlying his efforts, was that it is a vital state function to provide necessary services as well as necessary behavioral controls. He resisted change until a substitute scheme had been devised; he was concerned that if the court bowed out of the status offense picture, no one would bow in.

Utah, also, reached a policy decision to shut down its state delinquency institution and, instead, to build three small, secure institutional facilities, about thirty beds each, in its three major population centers.

Its juvenile court judges, probation personnel, and other court employees are paid exclusively from state funds. The state juvenile court system has developed, probably, the nation's most effective computerized juvenile management information system. It compiles extensive data for management and research purposes as to what happens in state juvenile courts and prints out individual record information for use at judicial hearings. On his bench, when Judge Garff holds a detention or dispositional hearing, there is a printout of the child's prior record. When Judge Garff holds a review hearing of a youngster earlier placed on probation, there is a printout record of the child's status and the extent to which he has complied with orders requiring payments of fine or restitution or the performance of community service restitution.

In the Utah juvenile court world, Reg Garff is respected for his keen management ability and his good business sense. However, as the state juvenile court administrator explained, "If we didn't have that computerized information system, Reg Garff would be the first one to tell us to invent it. But, let it trouble him one time and he questions its value and gets all over you". Garff knows the value of management information and data, but doesn't want this to intrude upon his judicial prerogatives. Recently, the administrator was directed by the legislature to develop juvenile court sentencing guidelines for use when probation officers make recommendations to judges regarding dispositions. The intent was to obtain more uniform dispositions by the different judges. This bothers Garff, since it impinges on his discretion. He tends to accept the guidelines, but insists on the right to make whatever decision appears best in the individual case. He has told the administrator that, "the tail is not going to wag the dog. That damn computer is not going to run my court."

Numerous juvenile courts experience serious problems in the judges' relationships with administrators and chief probation officers. Judges, feeling they are the accountable functionary, may well dominate the everyday operations of these officials. Elsewhere, judges couldn't care less about the administration and provide little superintending oversight. Garff's perception is that judges should set the policies and free up the administrators to administer, requiring only that the judges be kept informed and be assisted in making sound policy decisions. His initiative helped lead to General Order No. 17, that relinquished extensive judicial authority over court operations and the supervision and employment of staff to the administrative arm of the court.

There are several other noteworthy characteristics of the Utah State Juvenile Court system. One is the long-term use of a fine as a sanction. Judge Garff finds value in the use of fines to strengthen the impact of a court hearing on a child. The youth must pay for his misdeeds and not just receive probation counseling. Further, an arrangement with the legislature enables 20 percent of the fine income to be retained in each local juvenile court in order to administer a community service restitution program for youngsters. This fund also enables some youngsters to be compensated for their community service work for the express purpose of repaying victims through restitution.

Judges may order youngsters to a state youth diagnostic center for the limited purpose of an evaluation. Judge Garff, normally, can obtain adequate evaluations from the mental health unit at the court. But he will order a state evaluation when he wants to see how a youngster responds to the loss of freedom and how he adjusts to a group living situation. In part, this is an evaluation, since the judge wants to obtain a more comprehensive assessment of a youngster's problems as well as guidance as to how this youngster might perform were he to later sentence him, following the assessment, to a boys' ranch or a group home. In part, this is used as a punishment.

In recent years, the state Division of Youth Corrections has made available to the juvenile court judiciary an array of community-based resources, including intensive tracking of youngsters in their homes or different residences, foster homes, and group residential facilities. Again, policywise, Judge Garff helped engineer an agreement whereby the judges retain control over youngsters placed in these community programs. Such an approach contrasts with that in many states where state executive agencies have no duty to return to the court for review of children placed in their care.

There are two other judges in the juvenile court in Salt Lake City. John Farr Larson, earlier director of the state Bureau of Services for Children, was added to this bench in 1963, and Judith Whitmer, in 1971. The district, with a population nearing 700,000 persons, comprises three counties, Salt Lake, Tooele, and Summit. The latter two communities, physically large but sparsely settled, append Salt Lake County. The downtown center of Salt Lake City is growing upward; the environs are spreading outward.

Clearly, not all of its residents belong to the Mormon church. Its primary minority group are Spanish-surnamed citizens. Low-income neighborhoods are clearly apparent though these are not extremely widespread.

Important features of this court include:

(1) *The probation staff*, including the intake arm, is administered by the judicial branch of government. This is particularly important to Reg Garff. He believes that legal safeguards are better protected through court-administered probation and that the court's regulations and potential options at the different processing stages require court control of its staff. Reg Garff recalls "a bad dream I had. I woke up and was really angry. I was in a public hearing and a staff member testified in favor of shifting probation to a state executive agency. I turned to him and told him he was crazy. I was just livid. I was shouting and yelling." He is concerned that this dream does not become a reality.

(2) *Probation services* to adjudicated youngsters are provided from five neighborhood centers. Further, probation caseloads are quite workable, averaging thirty to thirty-five, and there is a relatively uncommon team approach to probation service delivery. The entire neighborhood team staffs each case with the child and his parents, develops the treatment plan, and then is collectively responsible for the execution of the plan, though an individual probation officer is generally the primary agent. Typically, each unit is open from 9 a.m. to 8 p.m. so that probation staff can meet with

youngsters and parents after school or work hours. Judge Garff helped initiate this decentralization concept; his social work background had taught him to take services to the community to increase their effectiveness.

(3) *Review hearings.* There is a required judicial review of each child placed on probation, generally each three to four months. The formulated treatment plan is reviewed; the child and family are required to present how they have involved themselves with this plan. The regularity of review hearings and the concreteness of their focus is unusual among juvenile courts. What is still more unusual is that the judges conduct these review hearings in each neighborhood unit and not in the juvenile courthouse. Of Judge Garff, one probation official stated, "In the courtroom, he may come off a little stiff; in the neighborhood, he comes off really great." Garff comments that he wants youngsters and families to know that he cares about what is happening with them. "If we are trying to treat and rehabilitate, then this is based on relationship, communication, and interest. Review hearings enable this to take place."

(4) *Citizen Advisory Committees.* This concept is not unique to Utah, though no other state has both a statewide citizens advisory committee to the state juvenile court and a district advisory board to each juvenile court within the state. Interested citizens, educators, police officials, business persons and, by design, state legislators, are appointed by the judges to help relate the community to the court and the court to the community. Their full potential is sometimes actualized, sometimes not. They have had their ups and downs. One of the ways they have proved useful has been with informal lobbying for court budgets and funds for building expansions. Reg Garff smiles when he talks about one accomplishment of his district advisory committee. "We were concerned about the kind of care and treatment that juveniles were getting at the state mental hospital. We had been informed that youngsters were being housed at night with adults, contrary to the stated policy. So, after a board meeting one night, we all just piled in cars and went down to the state hospital about ten o'clock, and because we had legislators with us who were on the budget committee we just said, 'We want to see what's going on.' So, the doors were opened, and sure enough there were juveniles in with the adult patients. That visit ended the commingling practice."

The judicial philosophy which Reg Garff applies daily in his courtroom has not changed markedly since his early years on the bench. Its different elements are relatively compatible and he applies this philosophy with consistency and predictability.

One principle is that the less judicial involvement there is in people's lives, the better off everyone is. Such an approach empowers the intake arm of the court to employ informal resolution of lesser delinquencies, inserting rehabilitative services in an effort to achieve repairs with youngsters and avoid formal court intervention.

Second, this judge's stress on a juvenile's accountability for his actions links with his limited intervention theme and his conviction that participation by clients in decisions and plans that affect them engender cooperation and compliance. "It is necessary that youngsters demonstrate to the court that some changes have been made that justify the court's getting out of their lives. We don't want to stay in or mess around with people's lives longer than is absolutely necessary. The only way you can do that is to inform people and involve them in the process and, as much as possible, in the decision making."

A third Garff belief is that state intervention, when it is needed, should be provided to a child in his home and in his community, to the extent that this is realistic.

Fourth, Reg Garff is an advocate of individualized justice. He believes that judges require discretion in order to best deal with individual problems and needs. "Some judges may abuse this discretion and there will always be poor judges despite efforts to improve the selection process for judges. But flexibility should be retained with judicial dispositions." Individualized justice is a higher value for him than equalized justice.

Though the severity of a child's offense, his prior record, and age are important factors weighed by this judge, the youth's potential for rehabilitation, his internal strengths and those of his parents, and other social indicators of his adjustment are balanced in the decision equation. Different children, then, are treated differently, since they respond differently to various orders and approaches instituted by the court. Based on the offense or prior record, no child should automatically be detained or institutionalized, though the more serious the offense and the more chronic the record, the more likely the youngster will be incapacitated. But it follows that more serious and more chronic offenders are in trouble with this judge, regardless of their strengths and potentials, since he sets clear limits and views the protection of the community as a prominent priority.

With an honesty that merits consideration by other judges, he describes that "several years ago I became concerned that I was committing more Spanish-surnamed kids to the state industrial school than other youngsters, or disproportionately so. I asked our research director to study this for me. I wanted to know if I had some blind spots. He came back to me saying that it looked like I did, so I reevaluated my approach and what I was doing and rechecked this again a year later. There was quite a change."

Fifth, Garff views rehabilitation services as of critical importance to youngsters and families and is confident these have been effective in this court. Probation is a blend, here, of intensive helping services and the imposition of controls, made possible by reasonably low caseloads. It involves youngsters and their parents in formulating individualized treatment plans and goals and the careful monitoring of case progress. Probation may well involve services by other agencies as well, but these, too, are subject to judicial review. There is stronger inclusion of parents in probation efforts here than is observable in many courts. Further, many youngsters are fined, ordered to pay restitution, or have their driver's license suspended with a driving-related offense, in order to communicate more tangible sanctions for misdeeds. Such sanctions are viewed as aids to rehabilitation.

Though he concentrates on having the hearing be as meaningful as possible to the child, he believes that his impact is momentary. In his words, "Any longterm effect comes only through more intensive working relationships, and this is not the judge's responsibility or opportunity."

A sixth additional underpinning is fairness. Part of this precept involves protecting children from unjust procedures and practices by police officials, other agencies, and the court itself. Further, fairness requires that a judge do his utmost to see that "youngsters are dealt with fairly in court, that they have been listened to, and their side of things considered."

Reg Garff considers that he is a legally conservative though socially active judge. He does not believe that juveniles should have all the legal rights of adults. And, in general, he functions within the current statute and enunciated appellate court decisions without going beyond these mandates to provide additional rights to juveniles. For example, he does not go beyond a youth's right to counsel to insist that the youth have counsel, except where a child denies an offense and a trial occurs. He also believes that a juvenile has a right not to be represented by counsel if the youth and his guardian intelligently waive that right. He contends that genuinely interested defense attorneys have a responsibility to assist in the rehabilitation process and to explain to youngsters that they need to "shape up". He is unhappy with delays occasioned by attorneys and with what he sees as harmful psychological effects that may occur with youngsters when extremely technical legal defenses are raised. Garff contends that due process needs to be balanced with the interests and needs of children. "Children have a right to stability and security and to not be abused or taken advantage of by more powerful figures."

Finally, Garff is adamant that the court must be a strong advocate for children's needs in the community. "Since children really are helpless, since they have no lobbying groups speaking in their behalf, since they have no one they can pay to argue their interests, the juvenile court must speak for them to obtain the services and the protection from abuse that they require."

The exercise of a "community role" has been a staple of committed juvenile court judges. Probably, Reg Garff has performed this off-bench function as effectively as any. He knows that a judge holds a unique position in the community and "has a lot of clout". Exercising that influence to improve the care of children, he emphasizes, is an obligation of the juvenile court judge. It goes along with the job. In his words: "It's the court's role to motivate and energize the community to develop resources that we perceive as being necessary. That's why I and the other judges are very active in the community. That's why we sit on advisory boards. That's why we're on task forces and ad hoc committees. If you look at my *vita*, over the years it's been a long history of community involvement and I don't get involved in community affairs because I want to run for political office. I get involved because I feel it's my responsibility to orient the community to what the court is doing, to open up communication, but also to make demands of the community as to what our needs are. I can't do that unless I have a good rapport with them."

His *vita* shows several awards and a lengthy list of community activities, present and past. The Utah State Bar Association selected him as the state's outstanding judge in 1975, the first time a juvenile court jurist had received this honor. Three years later the University of Utah College of Law bestowed its highest honorary award, the Order of the Coif, on Regnal Garff. The law school dean cited "professional excellence in his efforts to improve the juvenile court system and for his service and dedication, not only to the legal profession, but to the community at large."

Garff is now a member of the board of directors of the state mental health association, county commission on youth, a special program for emotionally disturbed youngsters, and an international adoption agency. Since 1968, he has been an important force on the region's law-enforcement planning council and its successor agency, where juvenile and criminal justice planning and funding have been the focus. Previous activities are laden with educational, mental health, drug abuse, social welfare, and juvenile justice board and task force roles — often as chairman. The meetings take place at breakfast, lunch, evenings, and weekends.

At a county criminal justice advisory committee meeting, he asks whether this council will respond to the issues currently facing county government of locating a new state-delinquency facility as well as developing a new adult correctional facility within the county? The county commissioner member of the group responds that direction from this committee will be helpful to government officials. Garff asks him to direct what the advisory committee should examine. The commissioner seeks recommendations as to the need for the facilities and suggestions regarding site selection. Another member comments that we need to plan this together and stick together "when the heat comes down". Garff obtains what he was after, an influential group's decision to support proceeding with the construction of correctional facilities that many in the community will oppose.

The next morning, at a 7 a.m. breakfast meeting at the Capitol, he joins state legislators in reviewing possible sites for this proposed secure juvenile institution to be built by the state in Salt Lake County. Legislators representing districts where the facility might be located prefer its placement elsewhere. The director of the state youth corrections agency, who is chairing the meeting, turns to Garff for support. The judge comments: "Our present state institution at Ogden is obsolete. It can't rehabilitate youngsters. The plan to replace this facility with three smaller institutions in three different locations was made with national expert input. You can't lock all kids up. Unless we change them while they're there, the community is in jeopardy when they return. I have reminded the county commissioners that these are our children and they need our help. We're a lot better now in dealing with these problems. Some years ago a group home came into my neighborhood and, after some initial concern, the neighbors forgot it was even there. And, when I chaired the building committee for the juvenile detention center in 1963, that facility was located close to the community."

The day before, Garff had placed a call to the Speaker of the House of Representatives to pass on the judges' support for a legislative appropriation for this regional facility. He also called another county commissioner to encourage sale of county land to the state for construction of this institution. "Despite protests of citizens, children are also citizens of the county and the judges support its location here."

At the end of another court day, he's off to the law office of an attorney who holds the county's contract to serve as the attorney guardian for neglected and abused children in court. The attorney is holding a training session with fourteen volunteers who will assist him in protecting youngsters. Garff explains certain court procedures and emphasizes, "What I don't want is for you to be silent at the hearing and, after I have made my decision, to tell me there was something you should have said." A volunteer asks whether Judge Garff has always been a juvenile court judge. He responds with humor, "I have been a juvenile court judge for twenty-three years, but not always." He is asked what influences him most at dispositional hearings. He responds, "The conditions of the home, the evaluations of the child and family members, and indications whether there will be further perpetrations of abuse." He goes on to help them define their roles as different from the attorney's and as different from a "big brother" or "big sister". "You need a relationship with the child; you must inform the attorney of matters that may be important for the court; you must check out information provided by the child protective agency as to accuracy; you need to provide me with a written report at the review hearings."

An activity he considered especially valuable for the court was his teaching role over a several-year period with state law enforcement officers. Garff's description of what he accomplished is a recurrent theme: "To dispel a lot of myths and misconceptions about the juvenile court, to let them know how we function and how they should function with us."

Reg Garff recognizes that participants at meetings defer to his opinions and judgments. He jests about this but his sensitivity is apparent: "If I speak, everyone listens. I think that's great. But I'd better know what I'm saying. Frankly, I'm never really impressed with titles, mine or others."

There is also a recurrent theme in the statement of Garff's

associates as to the high quality of his representation of the court's interests with community organizations and the value of this contribution. As one example, his co-chairperson on a state-educational task cites his quick grasp of complex issues, his cutting through committee bickering, his earning the respect of the task force for his leadership and guidance.

Reg Garff demonstrates strong skills in his role as administrative judge of the court, a position he has held through virtually all of his tenure. Deliberately, he consults regularly with his other judges as to court administration issues. He describes, "It's kind of a shared gown, the way we function here. Administrative matters are shared with the judges and supervisory personnel. That's the way it has to be in order to work." A fellow judge indicates that Garff is excellent with his administrative capabilities and gets pleasure out of knowing what's going on.

One observes an easy and mutually respectful working relationship in Judge Garff's monthly meeting with the long-term court director. The director advises him that a ramp to facilitate entrance to the court building for handicapped persons will be added quite soon. He advises the judge that a member of the court's citizen-advisory board has resigned. Garff asks about the court's relationship with the schools in the district represented by the outgoing member. They are satisfactory. The judge indicates he would then like to have a representative from the private sector. A revised procedure concerning expungement of court records, following satisfactory performance by a youngster, is considered next. The issue relates to expunging records of cases resolved informally by the probation department. It is agreed that this should be done, but it should not require a court hearing. Instead, a judicial order can be entered following a further record clearance with the police.

The director then asks about the need to publish hearing notices as to unwed fathers. The judge reviews the court's rules and concludes this is unnecessary in certain classes of cases. "Avoiding unnecessary publication will save the county thousands of dollars." The director gives the judge a proposed plan to strengthen in-service training for staff members. Garff indicates he will want to review this and probably add some things. Other matters are discussed. Judge Garff comments that phone bills appear high in neighborhood probation units. The director responds that an additional line has been added and there have been installation costs.

Later, the director relates to the author a statement that is not heard in many courts: "There is no issue you don't dare approach him on." He adds, "If I go to Judge Garff and don't get my way, I know exactly how I will execute his opinion because he has explained what needs to be done in a very clear fashion."

Garff's management ability is also evident from the bench. He notes how long it takes for an offense to get to court. When longer than desired, he requests explanation. He is satisfied if the probation officer indicates the youngster was on the run or that service of legal papers could not be accomplished readily. Probation and prosecution staff know that they have to move cases speedily in this court. When a court petition has been poorly prepared by a new assistant prosecutor, Garff calls the attorney into his chambers for a friendly lecture and separately advises the attorney's boss of the need to review his assistant's work until additional skills are developed. When an agency's report on a child is lacking in specifics, he will not embarrass this official in the presence of the child, but uses a chamber conference to point out the reasons why a treatment plan must be set forth with greater particularity. Agency representatives comment on their more painstaking efforts to prepare for his hearings.

How do others view Reg Garff? His judicial colleague for twenty years, Judge Larson, has had his differences with Garff, but holds considerable admiration for him. "Reg has helped our court administration get on an even keel. He strongly supported the direction to neighborhood probation offices and helped secure funds to reduce probation caseloads. He did a great job in obtaining our mental health unit which is very important to our program. As an advocate for children, Reg is willing to stand up and be counted. He does not just play to the bleachers. We deal pretty openly with each other but I can't match his puns."

Another judge, Judith Whitmer, sees him as very honest, one who makes level-headed decisions and doesn't shoot from the hip, a judge whose legal head is quite well-regarded. This colleague continues that Garff's orientation is not as a politician but as one who is deeply concerned about the acceptance of this court in the community. He is identified as the spokesman for this court and he likes this role.

His long-term court director considers that Garff stands very tall, that he is not inclined toward moralizing, that the staff knows where he is coming from, and that if he challenges them, the challenge has a sound basis. He treats staff as officers of the court and staff reprimands are done privately. This official suggests that while Garff's religious convictions have influenced his personal values, these do not displace his principles as a judge.

A senior probation official indicated that Judge Garff can get angry at staff but gets over his pique easily. "The beautiful thing is that he doesn't hold grudges. His interest that the court be respected has extended to his handing out paper for both youngsters and staff members to accomplish a transfer of their chewing gum. But it was a struggle for him in the long hair days to not comment on youngsters' hair length." He is seen as "tougher" than the other judges in this court and "he does mean business."

A newspaper reporter who has been in the court from time to time sees Reg Garff as a straightforward judge who speaks candidly. Further, "He's not afraid to call someone's bluff at a public meeting one day and the next day have to ask that person for something." He is seen as very fair and concerned about children.

The most critical comments on Garff come from a private attorney whose law firm holds a contract to provide defense representation in this court. He does not believe Garff makes defense attorneys readily enough available to youngsters in delinquency cases. He believes that all detained youngsters and those facing felony charges should have counsel, but this does not happen in Garff's court. Reliance on the probation staff is too strong and prosecutors are more influential than defense counsel. While Garff's legal rulings are sound, "I just don't think I am making any difference here."

Youngsters refer to him as the "hanging judge" or the "hard nose judge". Reg Garff enjoys these references, but believes it is more accurate to see him as both tough and fair. Three youngsters make other statements about him:

Here at the detention center no one wants Garff to be his judge
I was really nervous the first time I went into court
He's been a pretty fair judge so far
He's serious about his warnings
He gets mad when you disobey what he tells you to do
He probably knew I was a halfway decent kid and wanted to scare me hoping, if he came down hard on me, I'd stop offending
He didn't play around. He never raised his voice. But he's got a

look in his eye that's kind of scary. I knew that when he said
something, he would really back it up

His threat really caught my attention

He makes decisions that are best for the kid and the state

He's interested

How has Judge Regnal W. Garff, Jr. changed over the years? "My
judicial philosophy hasn't changed much. In questioning juveniles,
however, I don't probe any more for the reasons behind their actions
or search for underlying personality conflicts. Instead, I want their
responses to help me make better decisions and to lay a foundation
for greater cooperation with these decisions. Also, there have been
significant alterations with how I implement a rehabilitation
orientation. Today, there are more program alternatives to select
from. The court now has better trained, more capable management
and probation staff, so I've receded in what I do managerially and in
trying to change youngsters in the courtroom. I do work harder at
coordinating the different agencies so they don't play ping pong with
the kids. I believe I've become more judgmental, particularly with
abusive parents, and I'm now more conservative when asked to
return a child to parents who have earlier abused him. I've tightened
the legal procedures. First and foremost, I'm a judge and I now
clearly play that role with juveniles. This way, probation officers and
social workers can be more effective. In the old days, juvenile court
judges rarely wore a robe. I've worn out two robes in the past eight to
ten years."

And, how does a committed judge retain his vitality and his
balance when for so many years he has heard law violations and
family problems, large and small, handed out thousands and
thousands of decisions, directions, and suggestions, whose exercise
of leadership and advocacy have stretched on almost endlessly, and
whose task is never finished? His staff, experienced "judge
watchers", watch him for "burnout". One said, "I can catch him in
his slump and we can talk about it. He will say, 'I've judged for nearly
twenty-five years and have still a long time to go until retirement',
and I'll jab him and somehow he finds the way to come back and
recharge those batteries." Judge Garff suggests he is refocusing, not
"running out of gas. Professionals, like trained runners and horses,
need to learn how to pace themselves. My job has never bored me;
kids and cases are never boring. But I take fewer speaking
opportunities, reserve more private time, and handle my courtroom

more to my comfort. Due to my experience, I make decisions more quickly and more soundly. Skilled staff can handle more of the meetings. Refocusing has meant adjusting to a changed court world and judge role."

In recent years, Reg Garff made two serious efforts to obtain appointment to the Utah Supreme Court. He was among the three candidates forwarded to the governor each time by the nominating commission, but was passed over on both occasions by the governor. He comments that he might not have liked being a supreme court justice better than being a juvenile court judge. He would have missed the action, but it would have been different. And long-term judges do need changes.

Reg Garff's family nourishes him, his staff provides support if not idolization, his commitment helps sustain him; skiing, tennis, gardening, reading, and other hobbies all help renew him, and his religious involvement reaffirms his work to build a better world. His recognition of the power and influence inherent in the skillful exercise of his role as a judge and confidence in his exercise of the many features of his role motivate him strongly.

Though serious about his cause, he does not take himself too seriously. His ability to laugh at himself and to see the humor in otherwise serious situations provides a further spark. "I have to tell you about a funny thing that happened. I was working on this kid to get him anxious when outside the courtroom there were voices calling out, 'Kick him! Kill him!' This kid's eyes kept getting bigger and bigger. After the hearing I went outside the courtroom and found Judge Larson and the county attorney chasing after a mouse." This account then triggers another. "One time a girl ran from my courtroom. I sent the bailiff to chase her. The girl came running back in and then went out another door. I came off the bench with my robes flowing and caught her in the hallway with twelve to fifteen people watching, their eyes big as saucers, wondering what was happening." Much happens both inside and outside the Salt Lake City courtroom of Judge Regnal Garff.

CHAPTER 3

JUDGE ROMAE TURNER POWELL: JUDICIAL DIGNITY

"Most children are amenable to juvenile court treatment and are not particularly disposed to going in a wrong direction. They are looking for some kind of supervision to give them the tools they need to make the decisions they should make."

Judge Romae Powell remains an optimist as to the human potential and as to the juvenile justice system achievements. Her positive viewpoint is without naïveté. Her years on the bench reinforce her conviction that the juvenile court is a successful instrument that offers the best chance for protecting community safety and for thwarting the potential adult criminal careers of juvenile offenders. She has banished her fair share of youths to state institutions, but always with the admonishment that a youngster must work out his problems there and must accept responsibility for abiding by the laws or be prepared to face harsher punishment from the criminal courts.

A traditional Powell emphasis has been to teach youngsters accountability for their wrongful actions. Working arduously to strengthen the supervision and guidance provided by parents, probation officers, teachers, and other community agencies, has characterized Romae Powell's performance since her appointment as a juvenile court judge in January 1973.

Her bench is the Fulton County Juvenile Court, Atlanta, Georgia. Citizens of that city and state had paid greater attention than usual to the swearing in of a new judge of this court. Romae Powell is both black and female. She was installed as the first black judge of a court of record in Georgia. Daddy King, father of Martin Luther King, Jr, offered the benediction at the swearing in ceremonies. The event marked a political milestone. It was also a personal milestone for Romae Turner Powell. Now, miles later, her tireless work and patient encouragement is embedded in the hearts and minds of thousands of Atlanta's children, black and white. Today, she is respected in her community as a skilled jurist who happens to be black.

As a promising eighth-grade student in her segregated Atlanta junior high school, Romae Lillyan Turner decided she would become a lawyer. "My civics teacher assigned a research project on different occupations and professions to give us ideas about future careers. Part of my paper dealt with attorneys. I discovered that black people often went unrepresented and were treated unfairly in the courts. And they lacked the money to pay for good attorneys if they were available. My idea was to become a lawyer and provide representation for black people. In junior and senior high school, college and law school, I thought of no other profession."

At home, her father had talked about the injustices that accompanied the notorious case of the Scottsboro Boys. Both Mr and Mrs Turner had stressed the importance of an education to their children. "They kept saying, 'You're as good as anyone else. Education will provide you the opportunity to compete with white people. While you're sleeping, the white man is getting ahead of you.'" And Romae Turner was hardworking in a hardworking family.

She was co-valedictorian of her sixth-grade and ninth-grade graduation classes, and earned high marks in high school, at Spelman College in Atlanta, and at Howard University Law School in Washington, DC. Black students were barred from admission to the University of Georgia Law School in 1947. Her only realistic law school option was Howard University, established as an educational setting for black students in the nation's capital. She opened her law office back in Atlanta, in 1951, as the city's tenth black attorney. In 1954, she became Mrs C. Clayton Powell, marrying the vice president of the Atlanta Branch, National Association for the Advancement of Colored People, who earlier had asked her for assistance with a series of civil rights cases. She carried on her private law practice until 1968, representing her people in a broad range of legal matters, both civil and criminal.

In March 1968, she accepted appointment as the full-time referee for the Fulton County Juvenile Court, the first black referee in the court's long history. The judge who appointed her, John S. Langford, Jr, states, "We needed the credibility of a good black decision maker in our court. Romae had represented some juveniles and I had considered her to be an outstanding trial lawyer. She was my first choice and I was able to persuade her to join the court."

Later that year, when the legislature created a second juvenile court judgeship, Referee Romae Powell applied for this appointive position. She was unsuccessful. But, in 1972, Judge Langford was elected to the superior court bench. Romae Powell was one of thirty applicants for the vacant judgeship. She became one of three finalists nominated by the Judicial Selection Committee of the Atlanta Bar Association. Judge Langford successfully moved her appointment by the entire superior court bench. With her inauguration, in January 1973, history had been made. For her, one personal odyssey had ended, another had begun.

Judge Powell suggests that her first day as a judge was little different from workdays she had served during her five years as a referee. She had worn a robe as a referee and had served as judge *pro tempore*, filling in during judicial absences. She suggests that the court staff had been very supportive of her appointment and seemed happy that she had gotten the job.

A long-term staff member recalls other staff reactions to Judge Powell's appointment. "There was a lot of staff anxiety. The court was emerging from the period in the late 1960s when we had both black and white staff members who were racists. I believe it was a black teacher at the detention center who wrote on the blackboard at this time, 'The white man is through at juvenile court.' Certain white staff members saw her as a threat. But any staff concerns evaporated rapidly."

Racism had been a prominent characteristic of this court during most of the years Judge Powell had practiced there as an attorney. When the building was constructed, in 1960, separate toilet facilities were provided for black and white members of the public and for black and white staff members. Black probation officers supervised only black children; white probation officers supervised both white and black youngsters. In the court's adjacent detention facility, black and white children were housed separately, with separate toilet facilities. Only black staff members serviced detained black youths; white workers supervised detained white youngsters and crossed over to also supervise detained black juveniles. Further, at the state institutional level, delinquency facilities were also fully segregated.

Desegregation of the entire court and detention center operation occurred between 1965 and 1967. Today's Fulton County Juvenile Court is a fully integrated organization. Relationships between different staff members are close-working, relaxed, and mutually respectful. With strong encouragement from Judge Powell, the court has a well-regarded, affirmative action employment program that applies to both race and sex. Members of both races are prominent in different employment categories and in leadership positions.

Judge Powell's background in the civil rights movement reinforced her conviction of the need to protect the rights of all children, not just black children. She comments, "I see no color when it comes to administering the law. The blindfold should stay in place. I considered it an honor to be the first black judge and I tried to conduct myself in a way that showed my competence and also to do a good job for children and the community. But the court's clients and the public had to become adjusted to me as a black judge, and female at that. I only received disrespect once and that came from a black person who said in open court, 'You can't tell me what to do.' I held her in contempt and sent her to jail. When she came back before me later, we had no problems."

The black sheriff's officer who has guarded this courtroom for six years recounts courtroom incidents that indicate racist prejudices remain in Atlanta. "Once Judge Powell had to issue an attachment to arrest a white mother and her son who had failed to appear for a court proceeding. While waiting for Judge Powell to come into the courtroom, this lady complained that she would not have a black probation officer calling her in the morning to make sure her child was going to school, and went on to say, 'All you niggers are just taking over everything. What's this world coming to? A nigger police officer arrests me and there's a nigger probation officer", and then she sees Judge Powell and says, 'and a nigger judge in the court!'" The sheriff's officer laughs and goes on to tell about "the white fathers who would tear into me about the niggers who were running the court and five minutes later they would be bowing low before Judge Powell." He continues with another example where Judge Powell asked a white boy why he wasn't going to school. He didn't respond, but his mother offered an explanation. "He didn't go to that school because there's a lot of niggers there." The officer went on to add that in no way did this cause Judge Powell to lose her composure.

Judge Powell is active in ferreting out whether delinquency incidents may be racially motivated. She suggests that both black and white children are victims of discrimination. There are negative impacts on white youngsters who absorb racist attitudes from their parents. From court observations she notes that sometimes youngsters tell their parents there is a race problem at a school, when there is not, and that youngsters tell lies to their parents to gain approval for staying out of school. She is equally motivated to investigate allegations by black youngsters that their offenses against white youths were the result of racist provocations, as with this example from a dispositional hearing:

Mother: Judge, I wouldn't lie to you. My son only did what he did because of what the other boy said to him.

Judge: Tell me about it.

Boy: I couldn't get along with the white folks there. I was called racial names.

Judge: Did you call them by racial names?

Boy: Yes.

Judge: Suppose the other boy had been black. Would you have gotten off your bike and dunked his head in the swimming pool?

Boy: I don't know.

Judge: You started the whole thing, didn't you?

Boy: Yes. I pushed him.

Judge: Why?

Boy: I don't know.

Judge (to mother): Did you know this?

Mother: This is the first time I've heard this.

Judge: You were the aggressor. We are going to have to work with your attitude to help you not commit further offenses and to help you develop into a law-abiding citizen.

Romae Powell is an ardent advocate of the merits of the juvenile justice system. She believes in the rehabilitative and corrective value of her work with youngsters and the program services provided by the probation department and other social agency services, public and private. She contends that the juvenile court has the critical opportunity to assist youngsters, teach them responsibility for their actions, and dissuade them from law-violating life styles. In her view, the juvenile system, including the state delinquency institutions, is founded on treatment and rehabilitation, the adult system on punishment.

Her unhurried hearings individualize youths, examine background information, set in play officially-directed activities aimed at enriching one's sense of self while teaching accountability for what one does or does not do. But it is also her individualization that prompts her recognition that the offenses some juveniles commit, the manner of their commission, or the chronicity of these violations compel transfer for criminal court handling and criminal court punishments. Still, she retains empathy for those she sends on to the criminal system and regrets that more significant rehabilitation efforts do not accompany the punishments they will receive. While hewing to the belief that these offenders must accept responsibility, she notes that society and family deficiencies have done more to these people than has been done for them.

The Georgia borderline, between juvenile and criminal courts, is one's seventeenth birthday. Prior to that rite of passage, juvenile courts are the arbiters, though juvenile murders may be filed on initially in a criminal court. Also, a juvenile court may transfer to criminal jurisdiction those fifteen years or older for whom juvenile court consideration is contraindicted. As a typical example of both her humanism and her realism, Romae Powell supports the notion of raising the Georgia juvenile-court age to one's eighteenth birthday, but opposed a legislative effort to achieve this when funds were not provided to implement such a change. Her court would have needed additional detention center capability, probation staff members, other support personnel, and staff-training assistance. Nonetheless, she laments that many seventeen-year-old lesser offenders are ruined for the rest of their lives. "They can't get in school, they can't get skills, they have a record that follows them. They were denied the experience that would help them and not spoil or ruin their opportunities for their futures."

She would prefer as policy that all juveniles, until their eighteenth birthdays, receive initial consideration in a juvenile court with the court authorized only to transfer those sixteen years and above who are not amenable to juvenile system rehabilitation. While she does not hesitate to waive to criminal court those youths who have offended with the same design, plan, and attitude of an adult, she deems that the transfer of fifteen-year-old juvenile offenders or even thirteen-year-old murderers is "cruel and inhuman treatment under the United States Constitution."

Romae Power has structured her judicial hearing calendar in a unique fashion. She hears all of her cases the first three days of the week, then uses Thursdays and Fridays for board and committee meetings, conferences, speech preparation, reviewing prepared orders, and reading higher court legal decisions and juvenile justice periodicals. She will hear emergency cases on those days, however. This schedule works well for her despite staff grumblings. Not infrequently, her hearings continue into the noon hour and, on occasions, until six or even 7 p.m. One staff member who appears regularly before Judge Powell smiles and comments, "Sometimes I get very hungry in her courtroom." Powell takes few recesses during the court day, which prompts the suggestion by another staff member that "Judge Powell has a terrific bladder and no appetite. She can sit up there all day."

She usually takes lunch in her chambers. A meal is sent over from the detention center, the same lunch that resident children eat. In 1982, she successfully lobbied for funds to employ a nutritionist to develop more nutritious meals at the center ("We now use honey instead of sugar") and to work with probation officers and parents on ways to further healthier food intake. "Diet is a relatively inexpensive resource compared with other costly approaches. At least we'll achieve a healthier body even if this has no effect on their minds."

Children's cases have been heard separately in Atlanta courts since 1904. The separately organized Fulton County Juvenile Court opened in May 1911. The court's 1960 annual report recites that the first court building was "in such terrible repair it was known as the 'Bleak House' and on one occasion a tub had to be placed in the center of the judge's office to catch rain water which was pouring into the room." Over time, the court moved into different buildings and, in 1960, into its present fifth structure.

Just seven judges, including Judge Powell, have served this court since 1915. It became a two-judge court, in 1969, when Tom J. Dillon was appointed its first, second judge. A juvenile court judgeship has been seen as a stepping stone to the superior court. Judge Langford as well as his predecessor had "moved up" to the superior court by election. Judge Dillon bid, but failed in a superior court election effort. Romae Powell, however, gives indication that the juvenile court will be her permanent home away from home.

Judge Dillon, by seniority, serves as presiding judge. Judge Dillon and Judge Powell alternate weekly as administrative judge in making policy decisions as emergencies arise. Two lawyer referees are employed by the judges to hold detention hearings and other preliminary matters.

The court and the detention facility, which is known as the Child Treatment Center, stand on their own site less than two miles from the Atlanta downtown. They are physically adjacent to Atlanta Stadium, home of the professional football and baseball teams of this city.

The Powell courtroom is medium-sized and dark wood paneled. Her bench sits two steps up from the floor and is flanked by the traditional state and United States flags. To her right is her court reporter. To her left, one step up, is the witness chair, and next to it a ledge which holds a Bible. Also facing the judge is a lawyer's stand, two tables with two chairs each, and four pews of seats. The sheriff's officer, with gun in holster and handcuffs on his belt, sits by the entry door.

Though illuminated by fluorescent lighting, the courtroom is dark and gives off a heavy feeling. It has no windows. Along the wall, to Judge Powell's right are two cabinets filled with old law books. On the far wall she faces is a painting of the judge who served this court from 1915 to 1920. On the wall behind her bench are framed copies of the Declaration of Independence and Bill of Rights together with a replica of the American eagle.

A child, on entering the courtroom, looks up to see a comely, stately, middle-aged black woman in a black robe. Gray is sprinkled through her short, wavy hair. She is strikingly attractive, confident and comfortable — in control. She speaks quite personally to each child, parent, relative, social agency representative, or attorney, as if this were her first year on the bench. Though she has heard thousands of cases, there is a distinct freshness with which she approaches each new case, each inquiry, each advisement, each advice giving. Her calm, even temperament and patience are evident in all hearings. Her questions and her commentaries carry a parental quality in making youngsters account for their misdeeds. She reaches her decisions swiftly. Her experience as a civil rights attorney taught her to anticipate the next question, the next issue. With trials, she senses the cases and arguments that will be offered and is prepared to make quick, well-founded rulings. Her individualized recitations have a teacher-like characteristic as she explicitly sets forth what youngsters must and must not do, what the court will do and why, and the reasons for the actions she is taking.

An example is her regularized and extremely detailed statement to youngsters as to the conditions of their probation. It is difficult to imagine any juvenile court judge in the nation who so richly explains this litany. While this recitation rankles probation officers who consider this explanation as their responsibility, Judge Powell believes in the right to know. She prefers to obliterate the excuse of any juvenile who violates these conditions and says the rules had not been explained to him. The recipient of the statement that follows was a teenage mother found to have committed a delinquent act.

Judge: The first condition is that you must not again violate any of the laws of the city, the county, the state, or the federal government. We do not expect for you to be brought back to the juvenile court by any kind of law enforcement officer or agency, nor referred to the court by any private citizen with a complaint that you have in a wrong way bothered or interfered with other people or their property.

Your second requirement is that you must attend counseling as scheduled by your probation officer. Your third requirement is that you must attend parenting skills programs as scheduled by your probation officer.

Now, the regular counseling program will teach you what the laws are that you must obey and abide by. It will teach you why we have these laws and why you should respect the laws. It will show you about making the decision between behaving within the law rather than outside the law. It will teach you the legal ways and means that you must use to do things that you want to do without committing acts which are crimes. It will work with how you think about committing acts which are crimes. Generally, it will help you in your total development in becoming a citizen in our community.

The parenting skills program is going to help you with your baby. I cannot understand why you carry this baby around on the streets after midnight. By getting you involved in a parenting program, we can avoid your coming back before the court for not giving your child proper supervision. In both of these programs, you must go every week as your probation officer directs and be actively involved.

Your fourth requirement is that you must engage in a vocational or skills developing activity at least four hours a day. You are beyond the compulsory school-attendance age, so I'm not going to order you to go to school. But you have got to get some skills and training not only to take care of yourself but so that you can take care of your baby, also. You are to obey and abide by the rules and discipline of whatever program that you select for enrollment.

Your fifth requirement is that you must pay restitution of $265 for the ring of the victim of the offense. The purpose of restitution is to make you aware of the fact that when your wrongdoing causes injury or damage or loss to another person, it is your duty and responsibility to pay that person back so that the next time the thought comes into your mind to commit an act which will cause injury or loss, that you realize you will have to repay that which you have done.

Your sixth requirement is that you must not carry a knife or any weapon of offense or defense outside of your home. It was obvious from your testimony that when you left the house you had a knife. This indicates to me you had it in mind to do something with the knife. It is our experience that persons who know each other are the ones who, generally, cause the violent injuries and killings to each other. I don't intend for that to happen to you. This is not the first time you have been referred to this court for a violent kind of act. The law requires that you not have a knife on or about your person and we are only ordering you to do that which the law requires.

Your seventh and last requirement is that you cooperate with your probation officer and obey your probation officer's requests and requirements. Your probation officer will have the authority to require you to do other things that will be in your best interest and wellbeing and which will help you reach the goals of probation as soon as possible. Whenever your probation officer makes a request of you, that becomes a specific condition of your probation and a part of the court order.

Now, we enforce the orders of our court. So anytime you decide you want to disobey an order of the court, you decide at that time that the punishment which goes along with disobeying the order will apply. Do you have any questions?

Girl: No.

Judge (to girl's mother): Do you have any questions?

Mother: Only whether she can pay out of her welfare allotment until she gets a job?

Judge: Work this out with the probation officer.

Black youngsters outnumber white youngsters in the Atlanta court by approximately two-and-a-half to one. Their economic class is frequently poverty level. Most typically, it is a mother who accompanies the child.

Judge Powell has a special understanding of the poor black family. These were her legal clients, earlier. She will emphasize to them the necessity to apply themselves at school, her own vehicle for achievement, and vital to these youngsters if they are to escape their present status. Few of these juveniles will go on to graduate from a college, so vocational training and good school, work, and living habits are strongly encouraged. Following are characteristic pro-education courtroom sequences:

Judge: What do you do in your spare time?

Boy: Play basketball.

Judge: Do you ever use your spare time to improve your mind as well as your body?

And with a second juvenile:

Judge: The tests reported you can neither read nor write.

Girl: I can, but not good.

Judge: Then how do you expect to get a job? We have to get you back into a school program.

Her hearings are serious and formal. She does not put youngsters at ease. They know they are in court. Neither stern nor friendly, the message of her courtroom is that she will responsibly enforce the law against the juvenile's present or future irresponsibility. Her tone is measured. She lectures conformity to requirements, not morality. She seeks law-abiding behaviors rather than friendly relationships with youngsters.

She personally swears in each child, each witness, on the court Bible before hearing any statement they make. The children confuse which is the left hand that goes onto the Bible and which is the right hand that is held high. At least one child has been heard to respond "Yes, ma'am", instead of "I do", as to whether he solemnly swears to tell the truth. After ten years as a judge, she is still on her first Bible. While other courts discarded the Bible as the resting point for the swearing-in ceremony years ago, Powell continues its use to solemnize truthfulness and the seriousness of the proceeding.

There is a personal quality about her handling of each case before her. There is no brisk race to get through each hearing to the next. And with black children she will use wording more familiar to them. "Will you listen to your mama?" "Whatcha doing out at that time of night?" "Do you ever get to see your daddy?"

Court attachés marvel at Judge Powell's recall as to the facts of previous hearings when a child appears before her again. "She's got a memory like an elephant." And her courtroom guard worries about her welfare when parents sometimes get very upset and are standing just several feet away from Judge Powell. A child who admits to an offense stands with his parents immediately in front of Judge Powell, just three feet from her, as she rigorously inquires as to whether the child understands what he is admitting to, whether he is knowingly and intelligently surrendering his right to contest this matter, and whether he comprehends the consequences that can flow from the admission. Older boys and their parents tower above the seated judge, which concerns the courtroom guard but not Judge Powell. She responds, "I've never been afraid. I can't afford to show fear. As a lawyer, I was all over town. I would often be in my office till midnight. I never really felt fear going to or from my office or elsewhere at night. And I don't feel any fear in my courtroom."

A pet Powell disposition is to require a youngster to write an essay. Her objectives are several. To further a child's quiet reflection on his illegal act and its consequences for him and for society; to extend the impact of the hearing during the hours the child is engaged in the writing process; to inculcate the recognition that just as the judge must approve the essay at a later hearing, so will the child be returned before the judge for sanctioning if there is a future violation of law or probation conditions.

On return, the child will be asked to discuss verbally with Judge Powell what he has written. Observation indicates that not infrequently, essays fail to pass judicial muster. Their required length varies from 100 to 500 words. The assigned subject matter also varies and is related to the presenting problem: How drugs and alcohol will affect my life; The importance of education; What it will take to make me into a responsible citizen; Why I should not take the law into my own hands; How to get along better with others. An unsatisfactory essay or oral recitation requires a return before Judge Powell in an hour, in a month, or even following a stint in the detention center due to the insufficiency. There, detention center teachers build the essay into the child's daily school program and assist him in thinking and writing through what is necessary. She may also assign book readings and book reports.

Judge: How long did it take you to read the two books for me?
Boy: Two months.
Judge: What did you learn from the books?
Boy: I learned all about O. J. Simpson and what a great football player he was and what a great man he is.
Judge (smiling): Did the books say anything about staying out of trouble? Being honest? Working hard?
Boy: They taught me how to be good.
Judge: Did you learn you could have a good time without getting into trouble?
Boy: Yes, ma'am.
Judge: All right young man. That's fine. I will continue you on probation.

Books and word games and learning to express one's self had been integral parts of Judge Powell's childhood and family experience. She was born August 3, 1926, in Atlanta, the youngest of five children. A sister, four years older, had asked her parents to have another baby, they could get the baby at a rummage sale. Romae was the chosen name, the closest the Turners could invent to approximate the word rummage. It means "of Rome".

"We had a beautiful family. My father was quite a man, and a kind of philosopher. He would shield us from segregated facilities like the movie houses and didn't want me to babysit for families because then I might see myself more as a servant. My daddy was the family leader. He was a homebody and wanted our home completely attractive and pleasant. We used family conferences to resolve things like how to use the family money when there wasn't enough for all five children to get what they wanted. Who should get the shoes this week? My father would tell us stories of his childhood. His family had been farmers, and cotton mill workers. He was born in Crawfordsville, Taliafero County, and mama was born in Mayfield, Hancock County."

Romae Powell reflects backward in time and concludes that her family had been poor, though well-off in comparison with other children. Her father worked at a white-owned laundry and was always taking a correspondence course that helped him know the materials he worked with, the chemicals to use with spotting, how to do better work. His job was a five-and-a-half-day week and the children were all up before their father left for work at 6:30 in the morning. He held a part-time job, as well, with a food distributing company. He had not had the opportunity to attend college, but strongly encouraged this with his children. "He also saw the potential for a desegregated world."

Her mother had attended Payne's Institute in Augusta, Georgia, for two years and had taught school before her marriage. From then on, she was mostly a housewife, mother, and good citizen. Her mother descended from a long line of black educators, two of whom had been presidents of black colleges. She, too, promoted the value of education to her children.

Both of Romae Turner's parents read all the time: history books, literature, newspapers, and magazines. "The games we played at home were designed to train our memories, teach us to think, further our thoughts, outwit others, strengthen our vocabularies."

The Baptist church was another center of family participation. "There was Sunday school and mission work, picnics, church parties at different homes and other parties at the church, candy pullings, and more." Her mother's brother had been a minister, as was her father's cousin, and religious values ran deep in her family. Her family's principles of responsibility, hard work, education, and "a stitch in time saves nine", permeate today's Powell courtroom. "Our parents also taught us logic, and I'm always trying to get the court's clients to see logic in the correctness of what I say." Her parents also required that everyone help keep the house neat. Her father did not believe in debts, wanting to pay cash for anything and everything.

How then do you handle people in court whose lifestyle and home values are often different from those you experienced? "I don't like to moralize, but I do like to use the law and our probation department's efforts to strengthen parenting. I will use the law in commenting on the need for parents to get their children off to school. And our probation officers are constantly overseeing children's school attendance and achievements."

Romae Turner's father died when she was just fourteen years of age. This was a great loss for her. His death also posed added problems to financing her higher education. Her mother lives on today at age ninety-five.

While in high school, Romae Turner entered into oratorical competition, sponsored at different times by her church or by an Elks' Lodge. She won city and state Elks' oratorical contests and was placed second in her region. Among those she competed against in church competition was the sister of Martin Luther King, Jr.

She was to graduate from Spelman College in Atlanta and enroll, in 1947, at Howard University Law School. At Howard, her senior-year class in civil rights law was particularly meaningful. It helped lead her to active involvement as a civil rights lawyer in Atlanta and contributed significantly to her judicial philosophy that is founded on safeguarding constitutional rights. She recounts her two most exciting days at Howard: "Thurgood Marshall, Jack Greenberg, Robert Carter, and Constance Baker Motley, the lead NAACP attorneys, met one night at school with Washington area lawyers to test out the arguments and strategies they would use the next day at the Supreme Court. As students, we were able to sit in on these discussions. The following day we all went to the Supreme Court to hear them argue against restrictive covenants. This was a thrill." The case voided the practice that had allowed titles to land and real property to prohibit later sale to members of specified ethnic or religious groups.

Years later, in this same hallowed room, Romae Powell was sworn in as an attorney authorized to practice before our highest court. All nine justices were present for her ceremony. "This was an equal thrill."

She was to pass the Georgia bar examination on her first try and open her law office in 1951. R. E. Thomas, Jr, now a retired Atlanta attorney, talks about Romae Turner as a lawyer. "Four of us black attorneys were sharing an office and she became the fifth. She was ambitious, energetic, willing to work. I represented a black bank and black real estate brokers and brought her in to do certain litigation and other office work. She was excellent. I worked thirteen hours a day for years and she was there night after night, also. Romae was very diligent in her preparation and would not shirk the legal battlefield. She could be adamant with her position if she felt she was right. She has always been like my little girl. Romae was attached to her family and some evenings one or both of her children would be at the office waiting for her to finish. She took care of her children and her husband, but did not let her law practice suffer."

Prior to her marriage in 1954, Romae Turner handled her "people's law practice" by day and worked on NAACP cases, either as a volunteer or as a "very poorly paid consultant", at night. "Thurgood Marshall and other lawyers from the national office would come to Atlanta and advise us on our cases." Black lawyers did not march in Atlanta civil rights demonstrations of that era; they needed to be available, as lawyers, when marchers were arrested. R. E. Thomas, Jr, her law associate, had been counsel in the first Atlanta civil rights legal victory, a suit to desegregate a whites only public golf course. Romae Turner was engaged in a number of police brutality cases that involved black citizens and in desegregating buses, hotels, and motels.

She is proudest of her work that blocked the State of Georgia from obtaining the membership lists of Georgia NAACP members. And she was heavily engaged in the Atlanta school desegregation case that took place in 1956. She did not conduct the trial. Her role was to interview and prepare all witnesses for their testimony, for handling cross examination, for responses to questions that might be posed by the judge, and on ways to manage any citizen antagonisms that might confront them. Her husband, C. Clayton Powell, then president of the Atlanta NAACP, joined with others to help protect these witnesses at their homes at night against possible Ku Klux Klan violence.

Clayton Powell, today, is a prominent Atlanta optometrist and business investor. His leadership achievements were evident early in his life. He was president of his Booker T. Washington High School class in Atlanta, and president of his fraternity at Morehouse College, Atlanta, where he wrote for the student newspaper and yearbook. His classmate there had been Martin Luther King, Jr.

Clayton Powell states that he had never accepted segregation and has always been mentally free. He was the only black student in his immediate class at the Illinois College of Optometry, in Chicago, during his enrollment. There, he was president of an interracial fraternity and editor of the school's newspaper. He became the first black optometrist to be admitted to the Georgia Optometry Society. His civil rights' concerns led him into leadership positions with the local NAACP. As vice president of the NAACP, he had hired Romae Turner and four other attorneys in 1952 to carry civil rights cases. Later, as that organization's president, he headed a delegation that confronted the governor with desegregation demands.

Clayton Powell did not adhere to a pure non-violent disobedience orientation. Somehow he, like many white citizens, had become deputized as a deputy sheriff, which allowed him lawfully to carry a gun. He carried the gun with him at all times during the tense years. He marched only once, to picket a downtown department store. "If I had marched anymore, I may well have slugged someone who had insulted me." On more than one occasion, threats were made to the health and safety of the Powell family. Once a roadblock was set in place to bar their driving to their home. On another occasion, Romae Powell had bundled their young son up and stood by to leave the family residence if further evidence was received that the bomb threat to their home might be realized.

In 1966, Clayton Powell as a Republican, sought election to the Georgia legislature. He was defeated. It was clear to him that his party affiliation was no asset. He was not to run again. Romae Powell holds no party affiliation. Like her husband, she had been unable to embrace a Democratic Party that for many years, in Georgia, had been overtly racist. She contends, also, that the Democratic Party has excessively accepted and supported a permanent welfare underclass. Nor do her convictions find philosophical consonance with Republican Party tenets and practices. She is an independent voter.

Romae Powell describes her husband as a kind, sweet, generous person. "He's fun to be with but he's stubborn sometimes."

The Powells have two children, C. Clayton Powell, Jr, born in late 1954, and Rometta, born in 1959. Clay, Jr, had followed his father's pathway to Morehouse College. There he was a member of the same fraternity for which his father had served as president. This was followed by his enrollment at the University of Tennessee in a joint law degree and master of business administration program. However, he accepted a compelling job offer from International Business Machines and abandoned his formal education after he had completed his MBA, but with just two years of law school under his belt. He is on a medium to fast IBM track handling large retail marketing accounts in Atlanta. One client is the same department store where hiring policies had been the object of the civil rights march his father had led.

Articulate like all members of this family, he talks of his mother and of his parents' impact on his life: 'She's mom, mommy, babe. We've always been close. I call her my best girlfriend. At home, she was mom. No matter how busy she was, she was there for whatever I needed. We sat up many nights when I needed to talk things over with her. Though, in part, she went to the court to have more time with her family, after several years she was still coming home late, but it was 6 to 8 p.m. instead of 10 p.m. when she was an attorney. She has always worked very hard, but the judge pace is better for her at her age than still going on at an attorney's pace. When she leaves work, she becomes Mrs C. Clayton Powell. Similarly, I want people to see me as Clay Powell and not the son of Clayton and Romae Powell."

He continues, "My sister and I have two very outstanding well-known, vocal, professional parents. This is a burden on any kid, but a special burden on a black kid. Professionals have especially high status in the black community. They're the ones who are listened to, and who are envied. For me, this was a double burden. The black community had extremely high expectations for me and my sister. It took a long time for me to gain my separate identity. My parents' reputation even followed me to the University of Tennessee. People have a way of keeping children of prominent parents from asserting their own independence. Some people believe that I did not have the right not to become a lawyer. Mom wanted me to get both graduate degrees, but had no trouble accepting my vocational choice."

And how did your parents' values impact you? "If I had a cold, I still went to school. If I'm tired and something needs to be done, I do it. Responsibility is instilled in me. I believe I am different from a lot of friends whose parents are doctors or lawyers, but who are spoiled rotten and who put down people who do not have material things."

Clay, Jr, notes that his parents were one of the first black families to move into the neighborhood of their present home. He was the first black enrolled in the sixth grade of the public school he attended. Later, he was to attend a private school where 22 black students were enrolled among the 550 total students. He resides now in the former family residence where the bomb scares took place. Clay, Jr, comments that all four Powells are assertive and strong willed. "This has caused many 'fires' in our house." Visiting with his parents, he looks over to the dinner table and says, "Mom set the Sunday table this Wednesday night. She has out the good china and silverware and the candles are lit. She cooks everything from scratch."

Daughter Rometta, named after her mother, has followed her mother's college and university pathway. She graduated Spelman College and belonged to her mother's sorority there. She is now a graduate student at Howard University, but in dentistry rather than law. She tells of her past, present, and future: "I call her mommie. I had my own key to the house while in first grade and I'd get home first and wait for my brother. Mommie worked long hours as an attorney. She would take my brother and me to her law office at night and even to clients' houses. My dad was busy with his work. She worked long hours as a lawyer, but still spent lots of time with us. We always had a lot of fun together and she's really a great cook. At home we learned to express ourselves both orally and in writing. My mom's the main reason I do so well in school. She used to go over my papers and find errors my teachers had overlooked. She asked the teachers to challenge me more and this helped me excel. I like to talk. So, I would race to get done with the extra assignments so I could talk."

Rometta Powell continues, "My parents wanted me to go to college but I wanted to go on my own as well. They helped me understand that not everyone is able to handle college, but that all people should extend their abilities as far as they can. Yes, my parents taught me responsibility, discipline, self respect, respect for those who are older, respect for others."

She hasn't had the self-identity problems her brother discussed. She was too young to experience much of her parents' civil rights activities. Her parents encouraged her to make friends with those from different races, to neither feel superior nor inferior to others, to stand on her own abilities, and to know that she could do very well as a black person in this society. She plans to return to Atlanta and enter dental practice.

And what do you like about your mommie? "Everything. She tries to be very stern sometimes, but deep inside she's a marshmallow. She's open minded and listens to reason. I'm kind of bossy and I tell her what to do and she listens. She'll hear me out on how I think she works too hard, but then she goes back and works just as hard. I didn't realize how great she was until everyone told me how much they respected her. Then I went to hear her speeches and sit in on her cases and realized how great she was."

Throughout the seventeen years of her law practice, Judge Powell had used her maiden name, Romae Turner, since she initiated lawyering prior to her marriage. On accepting the juvenile court referee appointment in 1968, she also accepted Judge Langford's request that she use her married name. He had believed it would be valuable to court children and families to know that the court officer hearing their cases was married and a mother. The opportunity to expand her mothering opportunities with Clay, Jr, and Rometta had influenced acceptance of the invitation to serve as full-time referee. Quite possibly, Romae Turner, then about to no longer be Romae Turner, recognized that this appointment might someday lead to a judgeship. Quite possibly, the judge who had made this possible also predicted this development and wanted it to happen. He comments, "I never held any reservations about Romae. She was a fine referee and has been an outstanding judge. She was such an easy person to bridge the gap and overcome the suspicions that may have been present in both white and black communities. She could do any job well. She was knowledgeable about the law and quickly grasped what the juvenile court was about. She helped bring our legal procedures into the twentieth century, established a wonderful credibility with disadvantaged court clients, and has represented the court well in national juvenile justice activities. She is a gracious lady."

The plaques and certificates adorning the walls of her chambers tell more of her efforts to be an outstanding judge and of her activities in using her judgeship to make a broader contribution. In fact, there is insufficient wall space for all of these achievements and awards. A stack of them sit in a bookshelf. Some testify to her completion of national judicial training institutes, for example, the graduate session on the law of evidence at the National College of the State Judiciary. Others are certificates from the National College of Juvenile Justice and reflect specialized courses directed to juvenile court judges. One acknowledges her service as president of the Georgia Council of Juvenile Court Judges, in 1978. One recognizes her six-year service as a member of the Georgia State Crime Commission. Another notes her membership on the Judicial Planning Committee of Georgia. Her role as a faculty member at different national juvenile justice symposia is recognized with other certificates. An award from the greater Atlanta YWCA fills another space on the wall. And a prominent space is awarded to her certificate of admission to practice before the United States Supreme Court.

Her personal resumé lists more than forty board, commission, and committee memberships she has held over the years. Her current activities include trustee and secretary of the National Council of Juvenile and Family Court Judges, the steering committee of the Georgia Council for Children, the advisory committee to Parents Anonymous, a board member of the Atlanta YWCA's Project Focus, a member of the liaison committee from the Georgia Council of Juvenile and Family Court Judges to the Georgia Division of Youth Services. The listing includes membership on two Atlanta University advisory committees, the steering committee of the Georgia Alliance for Children, board membership on the Saint Joseph's Center for Emotionally Disturbed Children, and a director of the Fledgling Foundation.

Judge Powell holds to a strong conviction that judicial interest in improving the juvenile justice system is a requisite for this position. She sees the juvenile court judge as the primary advocate to improve what happens to children. She believes the judge can best interpret to legislators, other political officials, community organizations, and community leaders what the system needs, and how necessary changes can best be provided. "If the judge is not the one to take the leading role, then I don't know who will." She has actively lobbied legislators, testified before legislative committees, and has seen some of these efforts result in the legislative changes she sought. She is frequently in touch with county commissioners to interpret court needs and facilitate an appropriate court budget. She utilized her influence to obtain funding for a downtown Presbyterian church to open a medical clinic and counseling center that is used by court children and families, as well as others in Atlanta. She points with pride to her instrumental role in implementing two paid work programs for youngsters that also provide tutoring, counseling, and work skills training.

Powell's comments as to her participation in several national activities reflect her deeply held concerns regarding the handling of black offenders and the stigma that flows from the adult criminal record. At a symposium convened to consider more serious and repetitive juvenile offenders, she reminded participants that if the focus were more on white than on black youngsters, they would be considering treatment and rehabilitation rather than talking so much of incarceration and criminal court handling. She drew for them the earlier parallel with drug abuse. Punishment was the dominant sanction until drug abuse by whites became more evident. Then treatment consideration became more prominent.

In mentioning her lengthy membership on the board of directors of SEARCH Group, Inc., she describes her unsuccessful effort to abort the national project to make each state's criminal histories available to all other states. "I took the position that if you have served your time in jail and completed your punishment, you should have all that behind you. The adult system should be like the juvenile system. Your record should not follow you. It should be like bankruptcy court where you start life anew." Judge Powell was the sole vote in opposition to the plan to proceed further with this project.

She has been a tireless speech maker to myriad local groups where her presentations have certain recurrent themes: That the juvenile court is effective, that more services are needed by youngsters, that schools must accept greater responsibility for their educational failures, that more opportunities must be created to phase youngsters into the world of work, that juveniles must be accountable for their actions. Like other juvenile court judges, she has become more selective over time with speech invitations. For years, she accepted all requests. Now, she selects those that seem to be more important: Ones that hold promise that responsive action will follow. But she has a soft spot with any request from a school or setting where the audience is comprised largely of black young people. She knows she is a good model for them and wants to give of herself to encourage their aspirations.

How has Judge Powell changed her courtroom judgments over the years she has served as a jurist, an era in which there has been relentless public concern about juvenile crime? She responds that she is now more adamant in enforcing court orders. She applies sanctions more harshly on those youngsters who fail to comply with probation rules. It is not just the reoffender who receives the more serious consequences of her authority. It is also those who fail to counsel with their probation officer, fail to attend community programs arranged to build their capacities, and even those who fail to attend school. Her sanctions are related to the specific act of noncompliance. Nonadherence to the school attendance requirement may well result in a sentence to the detention center. There, the youngster must attend the center's school. Delinquent reoffenses now more likely result in commitments to state facilities. Judge Powell resolved to support legislation that now enables her to invoke longer-term confinements in state juvenile institutions for certain more serious offenders. She believes that lengthier incapacitation may be required for these youngsters in order to change them. This is preferable to their handling by the adult system, which to her affords too little rehabilitation and carries with it a more profound stigma and increased difficulty with integration back into the mainstream of society.

Judge Powell adds that she has become more sophisticated in measuring witness credibility, in determining whether people are being truthful or not. Community protection weighs more heavily on her now, as it does on many of the nation's juvenile court judges. Her assessments of each offense examine their deliberateness, motivation, style of execution, anticipated consequences, and actual consequences. She gives short shrift to juvenile offenders who have committed their acts with the same kind of attitude, design, and plan an adult might use, and those who appear so involved with crime that it has become their way of life. She has no tolerance with offenses involving guns or the sale of drugs.

Still, her individualization recognizes that more serious offenses constitute the infrequent cases and are not characteristic of her daily court menu. More generally, she provides youngsters with a reasonably long string and gives them every chance to reform, so that in the end, "a child commits himself to the training school." She allows no room for excuses, but furnishes considerable space for children to "rehabilitate themselves. The court will provide the structure; the child must see the advantages of complying with the rules and the consequences of noncompliance."

A fifteen-year-old boy, serving twenty days in detention under a Powell order, talks of his judge: "The kids don't have any nickname for her, but they say she's a mean judge. I was nervous the first time I came to court and thought she would send me to the state youth development center, but she didn't. She told me the rules of probation, but I wasn't thinking about her when I got in trouble the second time. Then I told her she should let me go, that I would go to school and be better, but she said she would see me after twenty days."

A second boy, serving twenty days for his second offense, thought Judge Powell had been fair with him. He adds that he could not come out and tell her what was on his mind, he just couldn't get this out. He too had listened carefully to Judge Powell's initial statement of probation conditions, but thought he would not get caught on the second round. "She did not understand all the pressures I was under and why I needed the money to buy clothes and pay back the school for the ROTC uniform I had lost." What Powell did understand, of course, was that her rules had been violated, a reoffense had occurred.

Judge Powell is consistent and clear with youngsters. Her sanctions are progressive. She explains this carefully, but generally starts with a less severe sanction, the probation experience. She is extremely positive as to the court's probation department achievements and lauds the staff. She has seen many victories. She believes that she should be accessible to those who need her counsel. Her off-bench time is filled with probation officers coming in to seek advice, workers from other agencies who want to talk over a matter with her, citizen groups that want to discuss juvenile crime concerns with her, and court youngsters who have become law-abiding citizens and have come back to tell the judge about their successes.

She is gratified that her work with any number of community organizations has been helpful to court youngsters. One, the Fledgling Foundation, annually supports fifteen court youths by obtaining a special friend for the child while providing financial support to assist the youngster: For necessary dental work, to purchase needed clothing, to fund nurses' training or a cosmetology school, to provide a camp experience, certain college expenses, or treatment in a center for disturbed youngsters. A fledgling, she says, is a new bird trying to get out of its nest so that it can fly and make life on its own. Former fledglings come back to tell her how well they are flying.

There is unanimity in her state and among the many judges who know her outside of Georgia that Romae Powell is an excellent judge. She seeks to be a good judge, not a good black or good female judge, to all who appear before her. Due to the certain racism in American society, others may not forget she is a black female judge. She is not surprised that whites still make this distinction. Judge Powell stresses that she tries very hard never to bring her race or sexual identity into the courtroom equation or into her relationships with her professional colleagues. It is her perspective, her viewpoints that hold certain differences rather than her judging.

A strong family had strengthened her sense of self amidst a hostile society. Her civil rights activism helped break the back of legalized discrimination, but she sees each day the residuaries of the former slave status whose dejection makes manifest the lingering inequalities of our land. Among her written materials, perhaps the strongest statement of her feelings, in this regard, is her presentation to a national symposium titled, "The Minority Child in the Juvenile Court — The Black Child".

She offers that prior to the legal revolution in juvenile courts in the late 1960s, generally all children were lost in the juvenile court system. But both before and after this development, the black child, particularly, has been lost in this system. Black and white children today are still denied their constitutional rights. Many juvenile court judges still do not accord these rights until they are made to do so, including the right to have a lawyer. Even judges willing to obey the law and accord a child his rights are hindered by budgetary limitations which deny them money to compensate counsel. Still other courts deny children fair and impartial hearings and justify this on the basis of large caseloads, overcrowded court calendars, and insufficient staff. But denial of constitutional rights is not justified by the complaint this would slow down the dockets and prolong the time needed to process a child through the court system. Powell questions whether, in any number of communities where blacks constitute a significant percentage of delinquent youths, the failure to provide counsel, full hearings, and more careful consideration of the child's overall situation is not related to the racial nature of the workload.

She continues, "Consciously or subconsciously, the black child gets the worst of two evils. A white child with an identical record is committed to a training school on his third or fourth offense; the black child, in this circumstance, is waived to the adult court, thus assuring society that he is locked in a criminal justice system for as long as he lives. Also, due to the absence of legal representation, the black child is held off the streets in a detention center when justice could have been better served by permitting him to remain at home. There's no excuse for judges who resist the law; constitutional safeguards benefit all children."

She goes on to note that, in many communities, educational and vocational training, apprenticeships, jobs, foster homes, mental-health services, recreation, and cultural activities are organized on a racial, residential, or economic basis, requiring fees that preclude black participation. When the black family cannot afford treatment costs, for example, the black child is committed to the training school, while the white child remains at home and obtains necessary treatment while on probation. The reasons for these distinctions are not explained in court orders.

She contends that the attitude of the probation officer, rather than his or her race, is the important factor. "Does he present himself as a paternalistic figure, which has been a pattern of black-white attitudes in this country for centuries, or does he present himself as vitally interested in the child, his family, his problems, his well being? Is he snobbish or belittling, or does he convey the feeling of assistance in working through problems? Calling the parents Mary and John rather than Mrs Jones or Mr Jones conveys the paternalistic attitude that makes the involvement totally unproductive. The probation officer's attitude may convey a feeling that 'I'm only working with you because it's my job. I plan for you, not with you. You do what I say or else.' This opens up old wounds. The parents and the child decide they are only being tolerated. Conversely, white probation officers can be very effective with black children when they present themselves as individuals and not as paternalistic white persons, officials who can show the black child how he can become a better person and achieve whatever he desires, rather than how he must live in a white-dominated society."

She acknowledges that today's discrimination is more subtle as well as more sullen, and that this prompts a reaction of hostility toward a society which denies black youths "the beautiful fruits of living and of life." Their delinquent offenses, then, are a consequence of second-class citizenship with unequal opportunity.

How do others view Judge Powell? Her judicial colleague throughout her tenure, Tom J. Dillon, admires her dedication and congeniality. He sees her as courageous, fearless in confronting policies or policy changes that could adversely affect the court's children. She is resolute in her beliefs and he knows she will not fluctuate from her convictions. He cites her courage in vigorously opposing county commissioner efforts to transfer court probation officers to state-agency employment status, because she was convinced court children would receive significantly less service under state employment aegis. This was a politically difficult stand since significant county savings would have been accomplished.

Dillon, the presiding judge, rejects the notion of making any administrative decision of any consequence without consulting Judge Powell. They act in concert. He sees her as excellent on detail, which he says he is not, and this is valuable to the court's administration. He appreciates her forthrightness and frank disagreements with any of his thoughts or suggestions. "A white, tough old legislator and an attractive black woman make a formidable team in any community confrontation, but we haven't taken much heat." He also refers to her as the world's most patient judge.

An attorney who practices regularly in her court echoes the theme that "Judge Powell is tediously thorough, but to the people in there, it's a big deal. There's no way anyone can get out of her courtroom and honestly say they don't understand what is expected of them." The lawyer cites, as Powell's greatest strengths, her knowledge of law, her being a stickler on the law, her willingness to take the time to verify everything, "even though her back may be killing her", her hard work ("probably she works harder than anyone else at the court"), and her participation in formulating policies and juvenile system improvements on both state and national levels.

Senior staff officials mention many of these same virtues, and also repeatedly comment on her genuine concern for children and the consistent dignity of her judicial temperament. They refer to her integrity as a person and as a judge, and to her candor in relationships with staff. In meetings with administrative staff, she will advise them directly if she is disturbed about something. If a probation officer error comes to light in her courtroom, she handles this in private, not in public. She will back the probation staff "to the hilt" and defend them against criticism. One notes that "she hates to admit that an idea she has suggested has not worked out. She's stubborn that way. You have to approach her in the right way."

Some divulge an opinion that court youngsters do not absorb much from Judge Powell's lengthy explanations of probation conditions. "Once they know they're getting probation, they stop listening." Several staff are gently critical of the length of her hearings and suggest that a number of the youngsters receiving her essay requirement can hardly read or write. They may end up being held in detention where probation officers or detention center teachers help write the report.

They note her contribution to improving the court's legal procedures. Children held in detention today receive preliminary hearings that require findings of evidence linking them to the charged offense. Particular reasons why the child is not released must be documented. Greater care is given to the voluntariness of pleas.

The long-term prosecutor in this court considers that Judge Powell gives youngsters too many chances and that the word goes out among youngsters held at the detention center as to how to put things to her to best regain their liberty. He adds, "and I'm not a prosecutor's prosecutor. I'm not here for an eye for an eye."

The public defender does not view her as lenient, but believes her dispositions are fair. He considers that her explanations of the goals and requirements of probation are beneficial to youngsters and their parents, though he exits the courtroom once her decision is reached, as does the prosecutor. The defender prepares youngsters for Judge Powell's statements and questions and instructs them to say, "Yes, ma'am" or "No, ma'am". He appreciates that she provides every opportunity for a youngster to exercise his right to counsel, but observes many youngsters proceed to waive a lawyer because they want to get everything over with as soon as possible. She will hear out a lawyer with his legal arguments or dispositional recommendations and then reach her decision speedily.

Other staff members express high regard for her knowledge of rehabilitation and community resources. They see staff criticisms of her as minor, substantially outdistanced by her many positives.

Romae Powell knows that staff members do not like the length of her hearings, but she doubts this constitutes a weakness. Indeed, she views this as a strength. She wants the parties in front of her to know they have all the time they need to present their cases. Her explanations and admonishments may be redundant to her, but are new to most of the juveniles and their parents. The probing questions she asks youngsters, which bother some public defenders, provide answers that facilitate her decisions. As a lawyer, after a court hearing, she had to explain to her client what had happened, since the judge had failed to, or had to console her client as to why the judge had insisted on such a quick hearing. Now, as a judge, she does not permit such deficiencies to occur in her courtroom. She is also insistent that her decisions be based on the law and on facts, not on race or economic circumstance.

Few lines appear on the face of this small, five-foot-two-inch woman who has carried so much weight on her shoulders for so many years. Cases of child abuse do weigh her down, and she often struggles, with matters involving neglected children, to reach her decision over whether or not to sever permanently a child's relationship with his parent or parents. She doesn't "bleed" when a probationer reoffends. She is disappointed, but long ago learned that no juvenile court can record successes only.

She is naturally hardworking, but has to contend with court officials, family, and friends who for years have told her that she labors too arduously in the vineyard. She still gets up between 5 and 6 a.m., or earlier, to write notes for a talk she will present that day. She gets tired, but not tired of the job. She says she has no burnout problem. Romae Powell's diverse involvement in court-related, community, and juvenile justice issues and activities prevents her envelopment by a burnout syndrome. Not a week passes by but that something new and different comes into her courtroom or office that is stimulating to her. She is refreshed by each child who returns to court to share with her a successful experience or an apparent reformation that follows a Powell sentence. They seek more strength from her, but this experience provides strength to her, in turn. Or the next visitor may be a parent seeking further advice from the judge or to report on progress with a child or with her own parenting skills.

She also relishes national meetings with other judges, to learn of their experiences, to bring back concepts to consider for implementation in Atlanta. She gains other stimulation from reading of legal developments, since this reinforces her knowledge of law, in which she takes pride.

Her own children nourish and enrich her life. Dedicated as she is, Romae Powell still dedicates time to her husband and herself. Hobbies have fallen by the wayside, in the main, and she reads few books these days. She likes to read magazines like Reader's Digest, Redbook, McCall's, and Ebony, sometimes cover to cover, sometimes just articles. At home she puts on records or tapes of symphonies, disco music, or rock and roll. She loves to dance and goes dancing quite frequently with her husband. Yes, they entertain, but less than in the past. She keeps going to her monthly bridge club and makes church about twice a month. The Powells go off on trips with other couples and every weekend do something social or just relax, "and this is important balance with my job."

Nonetheless, Romae Powell worries about the future of the juvenile court. She embraces just one of the three primary directions that are evident with juvenile justice today, that of strengthened legal protections. She regrets the current diminished court role with incorrigible and truant youngsters, the so-called status offenders, and believes that stronger court authority was more valuable for such youths in the past. And she vehemently disagrees with the current direction to process more juveniles in the criminal courts rather than juvenile courts. She notes wryly that placing children in adult jails and prisons motivated the enactments of the first juvenile court statutes and that we seem to be going back to where we were eighty-five years ago.

She remains a true believer in juvenile rehabilitation, orchestrated by a special court, within the context of legal safeguards.

Do you recall, Judge Powell, a hearing that was especially satisfying to you? "Well, I think of one that was particularly funny. This little boy denied he had committed a burglary. He'd given up his right to a lawyer and other rights. I was sure he was lying through his teeth. He kept saying they'd gotten the wrong person and started crying hard. I gave him some Kleenex and told him that since he was claiming an alibi, he had to show he was in school or somewhere else at the time. Still crying, he insisted he had been in school. I told him I would continue this case over so he could bring in witnesses to show that he was in school, and I told the probation officer to set another date and to subpoena in his teachers and the school records. He kept crying. Then I saw him whisper something to his mother. I proceeded to go along and ask him for his teacher's name when he broke out and said, 'That's all right, Judge Powell.' And I reassured him that it was all right to have a second hearing. He broke out again and said, 'Judge Powell, I did it, I did it, I wasn't in school, I'm sorry, I did it.'" Wise to the ways of children and of society is Judge Romae Powell.

CHAPTER 4

JUDGE SEYMOUR GELBER:
JUDICIAL REALISM

"A judge must realize that in all likelihood he's not going to be able to cause any basic changes in a child's circumstances. And sometimes there is nothing that the system provides for the kid, absolutely nothing, and you know it. Then you have a choice. Do you punish the community because it is not providing enough? Or do you protect the community, even though it is not offering adequate social services? Clearly, I make this decision in terms of protecting the community. This is a marked departure from the philosophy I had when I first went on the bench."

Seymour Gelber was fifty-four years of age when, in July 1974, he was appointed by the Florida governor to fill a vacancy on the Dade County Circuit Court, Miami, Florida. A day or so later he met with the chief judge who showed surprise when Gelber asked to be assigned to the juvenile division. Fully aware that new judges, as well as lawyers, tend to hold the juvenile court in low esteem, the chief judge responded that assignment there was not mandatory. Why did he prefer this assignment? Gelber indicated that he had always wanted to work with juveniles and thought he could be most productive in the juvenile court. Despite the rotation system for Dade County judges, he has never left the juvenile court to sit in other divisions, criminal or civil. And he has left an extremely large imprint on juvenile justice system workings since 1974.

There is little rhetoric or child-saving zeal in Gelber commentaries. His initial enthusiasm for rehabilitative intervention with delinquent youngsters faded away early in his judicial career, replaced by a more sober recognition that good intentions do not make good intervention. Still, certain social programs capture his mind if not his heart. He describes himself as a liberal but not a liberal judge. Throughout his life, he has held a deep interest in social justice and a belief that society needs to do far more to wipe away discrimination against those of different colors, creeds, and ethnic backgrounds, and to direct more opportunities to the poor and those with different handicaps.

He knows that the great society is well down the road, if it ever arrives, and on the daily firing line he opts more for locking up and, therefore, temporary community protection than most other judges. The incapacitation of youngsters may take place in the adjacent detention center, at a state institution, or in more open residential facilities available to his disposition. Intuitively, he favors some "immobilization time", but the execution of his judgeship role does not stop with this simple decision. He is a complex man who fully recognizes the old adage that there are no easy answers to difficult problems. Action-oriented, he has worked strenuously on many fronts to make the Miami juvenile court and social agency system function more cohesively and responsibly. He is the first to admit that his demands are high, perhaps too high, both as to juvenile offenders and to juvenile justice system agents.

Seymour Gelber, known to his friends as Si, is not a native of Florida. He was born in the Bronx, New York, on September 1, 1919, and moved to Miami following World War II and more than four years of United States Army service at home and in the Pacific Theater. A number of experiences and interests have contributed to his judicial philosophy and the ways he administers his judicial function. Prominent among these was his more than thirteen years as administrative assistant to the chief prosecutor of Dade County, a position known in that jurisdiction as the state attorney. His boss, Richard Gerstein, was a crusader against organized criminal activity, political corruption, the Ku Klux Klan, and all varieties of crime. Gelber was his eyes and ears, his political advisor, speech writer, office administrator, and assistant responsible for grand jury investigations. He was to attain, in that role, a reputation for political shrewdness, a characteristic which embellishes his judicial reputation today.

Judge Gelber contends that the bench decisions he makes and the rehabilitation programs he sets in motion are far more significant to a youngster than any communication success he may have with this youth. In fact, hearing after hearing may transpire without any questions or conversations between Gelber and the juveniles who appear before him. Communication efforts with youngsters is just not his style. "I don't look on the judge as having great personal influence with the kids, no matter how much he looks like Colonel Sanders. I don't think it makes a damn bit of difference if you lecture these kids. They've had lectures in school, from the police, from their parents, and if I do the same thing everyone else does, then it tells him this guy isn't much different. The judge has a different kind of role and a different meaning. This is a little theater. You have to carry out your role and I do carry out my role. I want them to know they're in court and not in a library. I want their level of apprehension to be high and to stay high. The kids have to believe the proceeding is not cut and dried, that it is fair, that they have a chance in this setting, and that something will happen."

Gelber serves with four other judges in the juvenile court. It is doubtful that he is the favorite judge of the youngsters who appear in this court. They refer to him as "iron balls", hardly a flattering reference, but one that draws a smile from Gelber, and "bow ties", a characteristic Gelber adornment. Nor is he the favorite of the Florida Health and Rehabilitative Services social agency workers. They have mixed feelings about him. In general, they would prefer that he work at building stronger rapport with the youths and be less demanding of them as to the specifics of their plans for intervention with particular youngsters. Their top-level administrators acknowledge even less affection for him. They admire his intellect and astute political sense, but have trouble handling both his bluntness and his humor. The steady flow of Gelber critiques, circulated statewide, are not to their liking.

He gets mixed ratings also from the prosecutors and public defenders who rotate through the court. While Gelber will not hold delinquency hearings without counsel on both sides, he is not a due process judge. In total control of his courtroom, he constantly directs lawyers to get to the point and to the problem, discouraging lengthy hearings and trials. Defenders contend he is prosecution-oriented. Lead prosecutors suggest he operates too quickly and that the law and legal elegance receive insufficient priority from him.

Somewhat unusual among juvenile court judges, Gelber does not need nor seek the affections and plaudits of the courtroom entourage. Rather, he obtains his strokes by keeping his theater's cast of characters off balance, by working at a few more hopeful rehabilitative enterprises, by jiggling the local juvenile justice system toward more accountability, and by his barrage of carefully designed media reports and commentaries. He is extremely well known in his community for the juvenile and criminal justice research he performs himself or orchestrates, and for the extensive newspaper coverage of these reports and of the statements he constantly provides the media. He can also be depended upon to spice his remarks and writing with a wry humor. As a result of the media coverage, observers suggest he is now the best known of all Miami court judges. His hard line on crime has endeared him to the public, though insiders do not consider him unduly harsh. He is a favorite of the media because he understands the nature of this enterprise and of the public pulse.

His chairmanship of the Dade-Miami Criminal Justice Council for the past six years has provided him with a springboard for more broadly asserting himself as the community's expert on both juvenile delinquency and adult crime. Membership on the council includes top law enforcement and justice system officials plus a sprinkling of local legislators and business leaders. The council issues its own reports; further, Gelber utilizes council-derived data for reports he drafts that obtain still more media attention. "Council reports present statistics; my reports analyze these data and point directions for action."

Since becoming a judge, his writings have been directed toward the broader newspaper reader, both local and national. Two articles were syndicated by the Christian Science Monitor and the New York Times. On occasion he is cited as an authority on juvenile crime by national magazines and television specials. His local articles get considerable attention, often stretching across six columns, picturing him with his trademarks, metal-framed half-glasses and bow tie. The articles question present crime control and rehabilitation efforts: "To continue the juvenile system as it is now constituted, in the face of the mounting evidence of failure, is a folly that concedes no hope." They offer redirections: "The few programs that work have been established by private agencies who run them and obtain funds either from private sources or by contract with the government; the answer lies in the private sector to design and implement effective rehabilitation programs."

Gelber, the writer, has come a long way from his first article, written several decades ago. It carried the pretentious title, "Removing Inhibitions through Narcoanalysis in Criminal Investigations". Like others of his articles in the earlier days, he was a commentator on the scene, not too sure of his power or his voice. Today his articles are calls for action, like his latest, "Cracks, Crevices and Caverns", in which he lambastes current change trends in the juvenile system. He cites examples and data showing that large numbers of troubled kids are unattended while the community encourages and demands concentration on "quick-fix experiments" with a handful of the more serious offenders.

He does a lot of his writing on weekends. "I may study the FBI's Uniform Crime report for four or five hours and come up with some information that shows a trend nobody else has noticed. Then I feel like I've struck a lode." Gelber's writings are readable. He frames the issues, buttresses his position with data, communicates knowledge and confidence with his findings and recommendations, educates the community to what is happening, and challenges his readership and the community power structure to take action on his recommendations.

His subject matters cover a wide area. He spotlights the decline in juvenile arrests, debunks popular mythologies about crime, and worries publicly that crime-control panaceas not only may diminish liberty but too often don't really work. Gelber offers panoramic visions for wholesale change but is really more of a piecemeal engineer, seeking to do those things that can be implemented now.

His interest in research and documentation arises in large part from his academic background. In addition to a law degree earned at the University of Miami in 1953, he obtained a Master's Degree in Criminology in 1968, as well as a PhD in Higher Education in 1970 from Florida State University. He complains that too much of what we do in the justice system is based on speculation and intuition. In Gelber's court it is different. His court administrator supplies a steady stream of statistics and each project has to provide supporting data.

On occasions when he feels concern that his well-earned reputation as a more conservative judge threatens his old self image as a liberal, he'll shift gears to write a lengthy newspaper article, such as the recent "Where Have Our Heroes Gone?" In this account, Gelber describes his heroes of thirty years earlier, two black and two white community leaders who took forceful and often perilous stands against racial bigotry in the Miami area. These were Gelber's heroes. With Miami's present quest to become an international trade center, he notes the community has blueprints and master plans and business leaders. But lacking today are the heroes who "brought a spirit to our lives, who defined the highest sense of community caring, whose acts were moments of pride for all of us." When new heroes emerge in this different era, he nonetheless expects that "dissent, non-conformity, unpopularity will be their hallmarks, just as in the past."

Gelber's work day is well structured. Although he says he makes no fetish about being on time, his day's activities can be anticipated. He leaves home each court morning at 7:30 a.m. sharp, after some orange juice and the morning television news. His 7:45 arrival at court is so reliable that a cup of steaming instant Postum sits on his desk, prepared by his bailiff, as he walks into his chambers. Postum and crackers are his companions as he reads the first edition of the morning newspaper. The daily newspaper forms an important part of Seymour Gelber's understanding of here and now. As the state attorney's right arm, he needed to keep extremely well informed. Today, he still reads the early and late editions of both Miami newspapers and wraps up each day with the evening television news and the late edition of the afternoon newspaper.

Gelber generally gets on the bench about 9:30 a.m. Between 8:00 a.m. and 9:30 a.m. there is considerable activity in his chambers. Each Monday at 8:00 a.m., he meets with top staff of the criminal justice council. Other mornings at that time he will meet with high-up officials of the state youth services agency, the court administrator, the lead prosecutor or public defender, or others. He will also schedule 8:00 a.m. hearings regarding dependent children that appear to require a longer trial time. Each morning his secretary brings him the daily population figure at the adjacent detention center, a facility and program for which Gelber several years ago held extensive hearings and temporarily removed the administrative function from the state agency. He signs orders from yesterday's hearings and reviews typed drafts of an article he is developing. On warm Miami days, he will skip the bow tie, placing his robe over a sportshirt when he heads for the courtroom. Gelber is the master of the brief hearing, the short trial, the judge-controlled docket. He will leave the court promptly at 3:45 p.m.

The juvenile court complex is a large, sprawling center. It was constructed in 1975 in an area of Northwest Miami that is surrounded by an expansive Cuban neighborhood. Planners had conceived of a family court concept to house both juvenile and divorce court judges. The idea was to merge these two types of judges and their workloads, since sometimes they dealt with the same family and, fundamentally, they were all engaged with people problems having a legal connection. The experiment failed. The divorce division judges disliked their isolation in Northwest Miami. They wanted to return downtown to the main courthouse and they had their way.

The white-painted structure is built around a courtyard. On one edge is Youth Hall, the state-administered detention center; next to this are offices housing the state agency administration, its intake and social study arms, and the juvenile prosecution office. The large clerk's office, with all of its records, is also on the first floor. Up the stairs are the public defender suite, the juvenile court with its courtrooms and chambers, and other court offices. Field probation staff is based away from the center in several offices around the community. Technically, the generic term of probation officer does not apply to these officials since the Florida legislature, in a symbolic gesture aimed at hardening the juvenile code, substituted the term "community control" for probation.

A few years ago the public waiting room in the Miami juvenile court must have been one of the most crowded and noisiest in the country. Parents, grandparents, and children, lawyers and social workers, trial witnesses and expert witnesses, police witnesses and bailiffs all contributed to the din. The commotion and the confusion prompted studies to find ways to better stagger the case load. Today the waiting-room count at any one time is lower, as is the noise level.

Each day as he walks the fifty yards or so from his chambers to his courtroom, Judge Gelber observes a small mass of troubled humanity. He never takes his eyes off the people as he makes his walk, nodding at a few, but not really trying to make contact. Safety is his concern; he is alert for any disruptive incident that may occur. In the courtroom, he is still more watchful with juveniles he orders into detention or to a state institution. The push of a button under his bench will summon security guards if an incident occurs there. Gelber has had to press the button several times.

Waiting room observers see a tall, angular man with an athletic bearing, six feet tall and weighing about 170 pounds. As he walks, he favors slightly his right leg, due to a hip transplant of several years ago. He is watchful, emotionless, and careful. As always, he knows where he is going and what he is about to do.

The Gelber chair and bench are two steps up in his courtroom, and on a diagonal. From this most important corner of the room, he looks over his half glasses to the clerk who keeps court minutes and the recorder who operates the tape recording machine, both one step below. Beyond, and at floor level, is the counsel table. There, to Gelber's right, sits the juvenile, next to his public defender, with the prosecutor seated across from the defender. At the table's rim is a parent and a staff member from the Department of Health and Rehabilitative Services. At the back of the room are the two rows of seats for the public, one row holding six persons, another five. Three additional chairs are positioned behind the boy and the public defender. There the youngster for the next case may sit, sometimes flanked by a detention center staff member serving a guard function. A nearby door allows the entry and exit of juveniles who are being held in the detention facility. The United States flag stands behind Gelber's right shoulder, the Florida flag behind his left. Private conversations are whispered in Spanish among those waiting. There the black mothers of impoverished youngsters and a few middle-class white families complete the audience.

Frank Stock, Gelber's eighty-two-year-old bailiff, in black pants and white shirt, abruptly calls the first case. "Frank is a retired restaurateur who shuffles people in and out, cafeteria style." Completely unaware of the case at hand, Frank's goal is to move the calendar and to run the courtroom with an iron hand. Lawyers sometimes bristle at his authoritarian approach but suffer in silence knowing that he has the full support of Judge Gelber. Those in the courtroom look up to get a reading on this judge who is reviewing the court file rather than greeting his clientele. They see a self-assured man with a high forehead, graying hair, piercing eyes, and a long nose, wearing a dark blue rather than a black robe. The ambience is formal, neutral.

One quickly notices that Gelber disdains the terminology usually associated with juvenile courts. He doesn't refer to the "detention center" or "state training school" by those more gentle terms. He calls detention "jail" and state school "incarceration", to help establish the tone he wants.

The hearing process is frequently limited to statements that go back and forth between the lawyers and the judge, or the social worker and the judge. Transactions are more a people-processing event than a people-changing event. On occasions, the judge questions a youth. Hearings are brief; advisements of rights are not made since all youngsters have attorneys, court-appointed or private. Dispositional hearings that follow two weeks after a guilty plea and determine a child's fate are neither extensive nor deliberative. If he lacks confidence in a particular social worker, that recommendation often gets short shrift. Psychologists' reports and needs assessment data from school counselors get quick appraisal from Gelber. He speedily solicits views from around the table and is then ready to rule. His synthesis of what has been offered is controlled mostly by what his experience tells him is the correct decision. He decides quite unilaterally. Social work staff have learned that Gelber wants short reports, pointed statements, and recommendations that are specific.

The attorneys recognize that this is a judge who does not discourage trials. In fact, trials occur quite frequently. But the lawyers know that while Gelber encourages the adversary system, the trial will usually be concluded in thirty to forty-five minutes. He makes few notes during hearings or trials. Consistency in his decisions is not a goal. He'd rather keep an air of uncertainty in the court's atmosphere. Gelber doesn't automatically subscribe to the philosophy of sentencing a first offender to the least restrictive sanction and then allowing him to work his way up to the more serious punishments. On the other hand, occasionally he will show more concern over the juvenile's personal problems than with the gravity of the offense. This unpredictability often leaves both the prosecutor and the public defender displeased, which bothers him not at all.

Gelber individualizes cases in his own fashion, short and to the point, as in the following hearing where the first youngster had no previous offense but his co-defendant had a prior burglary. His interest in encouraging schooling as a way out of the delinquency trap is apparent. Another favorite strategy forces social work staff members to work with youngsters by requiring them to reappear in court at a later date with a report as to what has been accomplished. In this case, two teenage Latin boys, driven around in a van by an adult, had been dropped off with cutters to steal bicycles. The two stolen bicycles were later returned. Though the two fathers were present, the communication at this dispositional hearing was strictly between the agency worker and the judge:

Agency Worker: I recommend he be placed on community control and that he perform sixty-five hours of community service.

Judge: Okay. But explain to him if he comes back here I will remember him very well.

Agency Worker: The second boy's elderly father says he can't handle him and he isn't going to school regularly. I recommend placement in a halfway house.

Judge: Yes, but I want a thirty-day written report on how he is doing academically.

Gelber sees no inconsistency between his strong educational interests and his belief that lockup time is worthwhile. He believes that detention time is useful for soul searching. He wants to get the word out to the juvenile community that there is a price to pay. In the following example, two boys had been released to their parents following apprehension and had not been held in detention because they were first offenders. They had climbed up to the roof of a store, gained entry by breaking a glass door, escaped when the burglar alarm went off, drove away, but were caught by the police. Nothing was taken.

Judge: The court adjudicates and will place both boys in secure detention pending dispositional hearing.

Public Defender: I am aware of the court's secure detention policy, but this boy is in welding school.

Second Public Defender: The other boy is going into his final school examinations.

Judge: I'm placing them in secure detention. The boys have other responsibilities than roof-hopping.

Public Defender: When can I move for a release from Youth Hall?

Judge: We'll see.

The public defenders know that Gelber will probably release these youths a day or two later, but the judge keeps that likelihood uncertain so that his "detention therapy" will have a stronger impact. The defenders do not agree with Gelber's theory although the judge has pointed out to them privately that many parents have indicated to him the short stay in detention has often brought about a change for the better.

Judge Gelber acknowledges he is prosecution-minded. He presumes the police have a case and that youngsters are guilty, but he moves to a neutral position with trials. When there is no case immediately following, he enjoys an after trial "post mortem" with the lawyers, discussing the evidence, attorney performance, and his ruling. Gelber does not keep his concerns about lawyer performance to himself. In private sessions he will chide or harangue them: "Sometimes I will give them hell." He will ride a prosecutor for filing a case that had not been investigated thoroughly enough: "These kids were cherubs; they didn't have to come before the judge." Or to a defender: "What you did in that case bordered on malpractice."

If there is a stereotype of a juvenile court judge, it does not encompass Seymour Gelber. Some insights into the nature of this man can be discovered from the penetrating description by a close friend from the old days in the state attorney's office, now also a judge.

"Si is one of the most complex people I have known. He doesn't reveal himself to many. Unlike most juvenile court judges, he has realistic expectations as to what can be accomplished. He doesn't have crazy ideas about the government's ability to change behavior. He knows that kids see through a lot of a judge's bullshit and father role efforts, so he doesn't work for a relationship. That's his realism."

His judge friend continues, "Si is a philosopher who sits on the top of the mountain and can see through the clouds. He selects his intervention carefully. He likes to bring out juvenile justice system problems to a wider audience to build public pressure on a bureaucracy. He has ridden the state agency mercilessly and won't put up with their mumbo jumbo. But his attacks are not with personal animus. He is not interested in being a social worker with a robe on. His interest is in social workers doing the job they're supposed to do. He's the flywheel of the court, the one who tempers a lot of the craziness there.

"But Gelber's real power is the written word. He prefers the distant admiration of the public and the power structure to the admiration of those he works with each day. The media turn to him on criminology and juvenile justice matters more than to anyone else. He writes very well.; he writes what the public wants to read; newspapers rarely edit him.

"Gelber, in court, is impatient with empty formalisms. He wants to get to the point. He applies due process in the way an English magistrate might. But when he wants to use a big case to change institutional practices, he gives a clear message that he wants very heavy-duty lawyering. He is a practical intellectual."

Seymour Gelber's account of his childhood and young adulthood reflects certain intellectual interests, but few intellectual attainments. There are hints of accomplishments that provided a certain confidence and an awareness of his capacity for leadership.

Never a good student in his early years, he, nonetheless, remembers going to the library regularly and taking books home. He recalls a classroom vignette where the teacher asked his class whom they would like to meet if they could go backward in time and meet anyone who had ever lived. "I said, 'the unknown soldier'. Everybody else was saying Moses or George Washington. The teacher was really impressed by my answer. No teacher had ever before complimented me." Emerging from his memory is another example. After turning in a composition in grade school, the teacher asked if he in fact had written it. When he acknowledged sole authorship, his teacher wouldn't believe him. "Although it was a strange way to find out, for the first time I realized that I might have some talent."

Gelber was the youngest of three sons born to Hyman and Rosie Wieselberg Gelber. Both parents were born in Galicia, Austria, and emigrated to New York City where they were married in 1911. He talks of his parents with warmth. A copy of their wedding announcement, printed in both English and Hebrew, sits in a prominent position on the mantel-piece in his living room. His father was a bread baker, as was his father's father before him. His mother had worked behind the counter in the bakery where his father was employed and that was how they had met.

Gelber enjoyed his childhood relationship with his father though he was much closer to his mother. His father was an active trade unionist, liberal politically, but a "fierce anti-communist". He supported equal rights for all except those who spouted a communist doctrine. Eventually his father had his own bakery shop but, "I never helped in the store because my parents wanted me to become more than a baker." Gelber continues, "I was the baby of the family and was considered 'sickly'. My mother took me to lots of doctors who could never diagnose my coughing and wheezing. It turned out to be nothing more than an allergy which they didn't know much about in those days."

His mother came to the States when she was fourteen years of age, went to work and sent money back to bring over other members of her family. "She was a matriarch, the leader of her seven younger brothers and sisters, and of her three sons' families, as well. She reigned supreme until she died at ninety-two. My mother stated with pride that she had taught her sons not to lie, run around, or drink. Her compulsiveness in always telling it like she saw it, kept the family pot in a constant ferment."

When Gelber was six, his family moved to the Brighton Beach section of Brooklyn. "Our family was poor. My mother worked in a bakery all day. Nobody ever told me we were poor and I never noticed the hand-me-downs I was wearing so it never bothered me. I don't recall getting any career direction growing up. All I remember is, that it was fun." Gelber was less than an adequate student. "In high school, I'd alternate between flunking math one term and a foreign language the next term. When I'd repeat a course, I'd pass it while flunking the new course in whatever it was. But I didn't feel that awful about myself for two reasons: my mother pampered me terribly and cared for me so much, and I was the best athlete on the block. I played on the high school basketball team, though not a star, and was a helluva left-handed softball pitcher. A change of pace was my best pitch. Even with three men on base I believed I could get the side out without a run being scored. And I usually succeeded. Our softball team, for our age bracket, won the New York City championship and that was quite a feat."

Gelber recalls some delinquent acts he participated in during high school. With other basketball team members he broke into apartment-house lockers. "We stole very little, but it was exciting." One night they broke into a candy store where the team hung out and were almost caught. The next day they saw the police conducting an investigation. "That was frightening. Our common sense of morality told us all that this was wrong and never again did we do anything like this." But his group did sneak into a synagogue kitchen to steal the food prepared for the reception while a bar mitzvah ceremony was going on upstairs. This delighted their juvenile sense of humor because there wouldn't be enough food left for the celebrants. "But we had our 'built-in thermometers' and knew when to stop. Maybe this all makes me more tolerant as a judge of certain lesser delinquencies."

Gelber had to make up some math credits after high school graduation to get into night school at the City College of New York. He worked days at the garment center while struggling with his college program. College report cards support his contention that he was a mediocre student: D's in accounting and speech; B's in two business law courses; permission to resign from readings in modern French.

At age twenty, while waiting for the pre-World War II draft, he entered government service for the first time, going to work with the Farm Credit Agency in Washington, DC as a clerk-messenger for a year. Entering the Army two months before Pearl Harbor, he was to spend more than four years in this next governmental role. He trained in Tampa, was assigned to the Signal Corps in New Orleans, moved up to the sergeant level, and spent sixteen months in the Asiatic Pacific Theater watching radar screens for advancing Japanese aircraft. "The military experience had many positives for millions like me. I saw new and strange cities, found out what a real restaurant was, went to a concert for the first time, traveled half way around the world."

His sports interests continued in the Army. He was constantly organizing athletic programs and managing and coaching basketball and softball teams. "We won the championship in Guadalcanal. In Japan, with the Army of Occupation, I found a gym, brought in my 6'4" and 6'8" players, and winking at General McArthur's non-fraternization rule, we whipped a good smaller team representing Tokyo University."

Gelber's scrapbook from that era contains a letter to the editor of a New Orleans newspaper that he authored from the Pacific. His sense of humor and social conscience were also apparent then as he described the New Orleans of the 1940s where he had been stationed. "Living close to the library made me a frequent visitor. Invariably, though, my books would be overdue . . . New Orleans isn't all crêpe suzette and gin fizz. There are the dirty streets that can't be blamed on a manpower shortage. The war must accept the blame for juvenile delinquency and inadequate housing. However, war in most cases brings out existing faults rather than causes them."

Several postwar years in Brooklyn were uneventful, so he moved to Miami, got a job in charge of workers loading furniture for delivery, and went regularly to the Young Men's Hebrew Association, nights and Sundays, to play basketball. Shortly thereafter, he was hired as a physical education teacher at a private residential school on Miami Beach and substituted for English teachers when they were absent. He also held a summer job at the YMHA, leading groups of youngsters. "I liked working with kids. I had an affinity with them." Colleagues in both settings encouraged him to continue his education. He took a history class at the University of Miami and learned he could get into law school there by using his earlier college credits and the course work he had taken while in the Army.

Gelber enrolled in law school at age thirty-one, taking morning classes while teaching physical education in the afternoons, dorm fathering in the evenings, and studying at nights. Shortly before graduating law school, in 1953, he met a fellow teacher at the private school who was to become his wife. Throughout his legal education, he thought far less of private law practice and far more of using law in a government service position. He had long thought that government service was the highest career aspiration, that "through government you could change the world." Gelber's own late development parallels his oft-quoted theory that in the long run, maturation does more for juveniles than all motivational and rehabilitation theories put together.

Seymour Gelber did proceed to open a private law office, found it dull, and "was scared to death in the courtroom". He handled a lawyer friend's unsuccessful campaign for city council. Soon after, he immersed himself in the successful campaign of Dade County's state senator. The senator invited Gelber to be his aide during legislative sessions at the state capital in Tallahassee. "We hit it off very well.

He was more conservative, moving toward liberal; I was more liberal, moving toward conservative. He liked my not being a yes man and that I would speak up when I thought he might be making a mistake." The senator controlled extensive patronage in Dade County. Asked by the senator what position he might desire, Gelber, interestingly, asked to be a juvenile court judge. Presumably, Gelber had the next vacancy in this court, but none occurred. Gelber's next priority was the state attorney's office and the senator got him this job in October 1957.

There is probably some truth in Gelber's statement that "assigned to traffic court, I was terrible trying cases; assigned to criminal court, I don't think I ever won a case." What he lacked in trial skills he more than compensated for with his administrative abilities and political acumen. Soon after, he was inserted into what was to become his long term niche: administrative assistant to the state attorney, office administrator, and counsel for the grand jury. Full-time with this office for thirteen years and part-time for another three, Gelber was to become very well known for his handling of important grand jury investigations and for his views concerning crime and criminal justice reform.

His boss all that time, Richard Gerstein, known nationally for the activist office he directed over a long span and now a prominent private attorney, remains Gelber's closest friend today. Gelber oversaw the indictment of synagogue bombers in 1963, the 1964 investigation to determine whether the Clay-Liston heavyweight championship fight in Miami had been rigged, the bombing of a newspaper editor's home, a Ku Klux Klan investigation, a possible Miami connection to the slaying of President John F. Kennedy in Dallas in 1963, and the uncovering of direct links between the Watergate burglars and the Nixon White House through tracing money "laundered" in Mexico. Newspaper references to Seymour Gelber during that era describe him as thoughtful and honest, the theoretician in Gerstein's office, and a realist.

In 1966, Seymour Gelber again resumed academic training, commuting from Miami to Tallahassee three days each week to work on a master's degree in criminology at Florida State University while continuing his role with the state attorney. He resigned this position in 1967, moving his family to Tallahassee to become an assistant state attorney general, heading up a new statewide grand jury project to investigate criminal activities in parts of Florida that had deficient law enforcement practices. He left this position to re-enroll at

Florida State in a PhD program, while teaching university courses in juvenile and criminal justice and law. His doctoral dissertation assessed security operations at 254 college and university campuses, a warm topic at the time. The dissertation noted the dilemma that, "the failure of school administrators and the campus police to deal with campus disorders leaves the door open to intervention by local police even though 'overreaction' by outside police agencies is considered the occurrence most likely to change an orderly demonstration into a campus disorder."

He returned to Miami in 1971, went back to work full-time with Gerstein, and was to gain both local and national prominence while "on loan" as legal advisor to the Miami Beach police chief during the Democratic and Republican conventions held there in 1972. He was key to the concerted effort to avoid the turmoil and uprisings that had marked the Democratic National Convention four years earlier in Chicago. A newspaper account refers to Gelber as the "witty and urbane gentleman . . . his inevitable bow tie unstrung, overseeing Flamingo Park and its tentcovered Protest City, the groups opposing the Viet Nam war, Yippies, Students for a Democratic Society, a Communist Party tent, and more."

Another newspaper report criticizes public officials who had "weasled" in their public statements about what would be done "when 500 angry anti-Nixon demonstrators were closing in on convention hall for a night of trashing and tear gas. But not Gelber. 'We can give 'em Collins Avenue', he said, which was precisely what the police eventually did. Gelber was equally frank in expressing his opinion about the high-priced, super-secret convention intelligence system which was supposed to provide advance information from police spies and other confidential sources. 'We got briefed every Friday', Gelber said. 'Most of it was worthless. We got better information when we just went out and told the demonstrators who we were and asked them what they had in mind.'"

In late summer 1973, Seymour Gelber was named director of the Master's Degree Program in Criminal Justice at the University of Miami. He continued as a consultant to the state attorney's office while directing his larger energies to reorganizing this degree program, teaching, and research. A year later, he was appointed by the Governor to his judgeship.

Gelber lives in a comfortable but far from ostentatious Miami Beach home with his wife, Edith. Married for twenty-seven years, they have had a very good time together supporting their respective careers, raising their three children, and enjoying friendships and community and cultural activities. Edith had gone on from the private school where they had met to teach Spanish, French, and Latin at Miami Beach High School, later heading up the foreign language department. Her husband also defers to her English language skills, asking her to edit his writings "and to spot excessive verbiage, an affliction most prone to judges." She is his sounding board for ideas and directions.

Gelber talks of life at home, with some tongue in cheek. "Edith is commander of activities in the household and handles all important decisions. The last decision I was consulted on was what our family policy should be in the war between Iran and Iraq. My cases do not have any special priority at the dinner table. If what I am doing in court or in the community seems to fit in with whatever we are talking about, then I get the floor. My family as a group do not permit pontificating. You can be certain that in every family debate in which I prevail that I have earned it. Our family laughs a lot and argues a lot. We don't take each other or our arguments too seriously. We have different stars on different days but everybody gets to be a star sometime."

The Gelbers belong to a synagogue but attend only on the high holy days. "My rabbi is my good friend. We talk politics or whatever, but not much religion. The rabbi may call for advice when one of his congregants is arrested."

On retiring from teaching, Edith became a real estate saleswoman though her husband had preferred she open a bookstore or art gallery. Afternoons, about 4:30 p.m., they can be seen golfing together on a nearby nine hole course, a sport Judge Gelber took up a few years ago after a hip replacement ended his paddle ball activity. Edith does the cooking and sets up the meals. But there is only a partial tradeoff. Seymour Gelber does the dishes but refuses to scrub the pots and pans. Word games have been a family bill of fare for years. Despite Gelber's obsession with the daily crossword puzzle, his wife trounces him and other family members regularly when they play Boggle, a word game.

Edith Gelber talks of her husband and his judgeship. "He's still not tired of his work. After nine years as a judge, he loves going off to court each morning. He's made the job creative and constantly finds new aspects that challenge him. Si rarely brings his cases home with him, but does bring his studies home. When he does bring a case home, it's because it might be interesting to us, not because it's a painful decision to him. He's more objective; I'm more emotional. He sees problems from many angles, and his pragmatic mind is always searching for a different kind of approach. Si appreciates the workings of government and is always trying to explain to people that the very nature of our system requires compromise and that we must be more tolerant of our public officials. He gets a bit upset at often having to defend the actions of public officials at parties we attend."

Eldest daughter Judy, twenty-five years old, married a lawyer after her own graduation from George Washington University Law School and now practices law in the Washington, DC area. She comments: "If anything, both our parents were lenient. They let us make our own mistakes. Unlike many of my friends, I had few complaints about my folks. My views were listened to. My brother and I were both high school debaters and we had lots of dinner table debates about public policy, education, integration, and crime. You couldn't get away with anything that was not well thought out. We had big, heated discussions and my brother and I would fight back with Dad. He didn't cringe when we used four letter words. He was fun, but could be exasperating. My friends found him warm but it took them a while to get used to his wry little jokes. After that they all adopted him. Those debates were a good training ground for my legal career. After Dad, I'm not cowed by senior lawyers in the firm."

Son Daniel, twenty-two years old and a law school freshman, is more brash than his father, but demonstrates a lot of his dad's interests, such as basketball, writing, law, and yes, humor. He jokes, "I never knew there was a Sunday newspaper. My dad always sent me out for the Saturday night edition of the Sunday paper. Then on Sunday morning he'd pick up the Sunday edition." He continues, "It was pragmatic for us not to be bad kids, with a juvenile court judge as a father and a teacher at the school we attended as a mother." Dan goes on to talk, before a prideful father, of how, during his senior year at Tufts University, he had organized a basketball game with a team at the Walpole prison in Massachusetts, and of his role, just before graduating, in raising money to publish a critique of the university administration which left the college president somewhat aghast. He leaves to take a twelve-year old neighbor boy to a movie. The youngster had attended a camp where Dan was a counselor. The boy's father had recently died of leukemia.

Daughter Barbara, twenty years old and a junior at George Washington University, recounts that her largest problems in adolescence related to the telephone. "I inherited long-time talking on the phone from my mother. Judy and I had a private phone so we wouldn't tie up our parents' line. If my grades weren't good, they'd blame the phone. Once, about 3 or 4 a.m. on a school night, I was on the phone with a boy, and my father appeared in my room and pulled the wires while I was talking. I never saw the phone again." Barbara tells of another incident: "Even though my brother and sister are great speakers, I was scared to death when I had to make a speech in high school on the issue of providing students with birth control information. I got confidence when Dad told me how tough it was for him to make his first speech and that even today, he's still a little nervous when he has to talk before a large group. It gave me courage and I did all right."

Having a father as a juvenile court judge presented no special problems to the Gelber youngsters. In fact, they liked it. They achieved well on their own, but had a special status due both to their father's position as well as their mother's. Seymour and Edith Gelber have passed on to their children qualities that have been important to them, such as the importance of education, the use of the opportunities a community provides its citizens, and a responsibility to participate in enriching the lives of others through community service.

It takes a little deeper digging to more fully understand Judge Gelber's viewpoints regarding rehabilitation, his appreciation for community safety, and his perceptions on the exercise of the power of the judicial role. He believes that rehabilitation can work, but that it cannot accomplish the expectations the community demands. Alternatively, he tries to lower community expectations while improving agency performance, hopefully to reach a level of acceptance to both.

He doesn't believe the juvenile system can save or even help every child. "But I think we have to take risks. It's almost like a crap game and you're gambling with the community's chips. You throw these chips in a pot called community safety. So you put a kid in a rehab program instead of locking him up in 'state school'. Then you nurture the program or his role in the program and three weeks later he is rearrested. So, you've lost that chip. Then you throw out another chip and try with someone else. You have to have faith that the system can succeed, otherwise you can't really do any good in the juvenile court. But if you use too many of the community's chips unsuccessfully, you pay the price of losing your credibility and maybe even your job. So you gamble less with a violent offender and gamble more with the repetitive, nonviolent offender."

Seymour Gelber, like the overwhelming majority of juvenile court judges, advocates individual justice. He believes he is reasonably consistent with his detention and dispositional decisions, but prefers the fewest constraints possible with his discretion. Typically, he believes judges should have wide latitude, extensive resources to choose from, the opportunity to consider the individual characteristics of the youngster before him, and the authority to make a decision based on the total picture. Sometimes, in making a decision, he will transpose the race of a person in front of him to make certain he is not allowing race to become a factor in the decision. On occasion he may even be harsher with middle-class white youngsters because of the privilege and opportunity they have been afforded.

Despite his emphasis on community protection, he is continuously pointing to the recurring declines in the frequency of juvenile arrests both nationally and locally. This prompts him to reassure the public that juvenile delinquents are not taking over the world and that profitable redirections can be undertaken. His article, syndicated by the New York Times in 1982, cites these data and faults the "hysteria displayed by state legislatures, eager and ready to emasculate the juvenile justice system". He goes on to propose a restructured, two-tier system that would change the image of the juvenile court. Its judges would be authorized to hand down tough up-to-five year sentences for juveniles between fourteen and eighteen years. "Hardcore juvenile transgressors would know that even at their age crime is a very serious business." For those below age fourteen, traditional rehabilitation measures would be applied. He would de-emphasize counseling programs, reduce the mandatory school attendance age to fourteen years, strengthen vocational training "outside the regular school system", expand neighborhood remediation centers, and add forestry and conservation camps to the rehabilitation enterprise. He doesn't expect too much of this to come about soon but feels it would make the juvenile court a more realistic forum in which to operate.

A few years back, Florida legislators authorized prosecutors to file directly on sixteen-year- and seventeen-year-olds in the adult criminal court. Gelber seeks to reclaim some of these youngsters by encouraging prosecutors to retain more such cases in the juvenile court and to have criminal court judges return more of these youths to the juvenile system for better informed sentencing. Experience in

Miami and other courts reveals that some juveniles handled in the adult court suffer tougher sentences but that many receive sentences of a fine or probation and others get lost in the shuffle.

Since becoming administrative judge in mid-1982, Gelber has sought to strengthen the judicial oversight opportunity. Unlike many juvenile courts elsewhere, Florida judges do not administer either the probation or detention center function. Gelber hasn't allowed this restraint to stand in his way. He has initiated judicial review hearings thirty to sixty days after a grant of probation status, so that both the child and the agency worker will need to return to court to explain their activities. A similar double-edged strategy was introduced with all youths at the point of their return from the state school. A judge must now approve the specifics of the aftercare plan.

It is Gelber's view that the monitoring role is the most important function that judges possess. A judge needs to insure that intervention and rehabilitation programs are taking place, otherwise there is offender and bureaucratic "drift". His experience has led him to an engaging view of the nature of bureaucratic systems and the exercise of the judicial potential. Though he lacks direct authority over state agencies, he often asserts such authority, shrugging off any criticism of judicial imperialism with the acid comment that "The bureaucrats' main interest in life is to avoid problems, not to provide services for their clients. They will do whatever is necessary to avoid conflicts. Most of the time, they're happy to be ordered to do something, even though they may not agree with the order or its validity is questionable. Now they have a reason why they must do it."

He sees the bureaucracy as a willing participant but too involved in departmental minutiae and inertia to perform at full capacity, absent a jolt. He moves in on these agency workers when their performance seems to lag, frequently sending their reports back for more details and will direct them to provide certain treatments outside their plan or preference. Generally they comply, even when Florida law does not require it. Gelber doesn't overdo this, not because he's afraid they might appeal but because he recognizes that he must work within the system. "Push an agency hard on an issue and they'll bend", he says, "but being a hard-ass on every case will cause a breakdown, hard to repair."

Several years ago he conducted broadly-based hearings on deficiencies in the adjacent detention center. Without challenge to his actions, he temporarily transferred administrative responsibility to a blue ribbon citizens' commission he had appointed and set a population cap. The press joined in with a series of supporting editorials, as with one in the Miami News: "Slowly Judge Gelber is tightening the noose on state officials who stubbornly and arrogantly refuse to provide badly needed additional staff for Youth Hall." Gelber never attempted to enforce the cap but his action spurred expansion of the non-secure, home-supervision detention alternative, a formal medical treatment program was established, the school board enlarged its teaching staff, and the next session of the Legislature appropriated funds to double the detention center capacity. When it was questioned whether he held the legal authority to take over the operation of the detention facility, he responded simply, "I interpreted our statute to grant me that authority and, since no one appealed, I do have the authority."

Gelber went to the mat with HRS, the state agency, in 1982 in a test to determine whether the judge or the agency had the authority to determine a particular treatment plan for a damaged and dangerous fourteen year old. The boy had been engaged in knife assaults, armed robberies, armed burglaries, was used by drug dealers in making deliveries, and any number of thefts. His criminal history began at age eight. Mental health evaluations had urged long-term intensive therapeutic treatment. The youth had earlier been institutionalized in a state delinquency facility and had reoffended shortly before the time of Gelber's hearings. Expecting recommitment to the state, the agency planned two sessions a week with a psychologist and one hour every two weeks with a psychiatrist. But Gelber wanted the boy in a special Texas treatment center which would require a quarter of a million dollars over four years. This care would cost one fourth of all monies available for the purchase of residential psychiatric treatment for emotionally disturbed youngsters in this district. Though other states had ruled against judges who had directed costly out-of-state treatment, Gelber did not back away. A Miami News article on this case preempted most of page one and all of page seven. Judge Gelber had taken this issue to the people: "What do we do about 'Shorty', age fourteen, who has lived a life of violence?" There, Gelber contended that the state was obligated to provide necessary treatment, that the community had a probable killer on its hands if effective treatment were not achieved, and that unless total treatment were obtained, the state would assuredly spend vastly more money incarcerating Shorty, quite possibly for the rest of his life. At the last moment, the agency withdrew its appeal and agreed to fund longterm treatment in the out-of-state residential center Gelber had requested.

Seymour Gelber expresses and implements the belief that a judge has the authority both as a judge and as a political figure to cause change. The catalyst role applies both within the internal court setting and outside with the broader community. He indicates that he is not a fighter by nature, but an agitator and aggravator. In his words, "I go for the soft underbelly of an agency hoping to find some muscle. I push until the muscle shows. The Health and Rehabilitative Services agency has very little muscle. With the present state attorney, I'll make my point, find some muscle, and leave it alone." Gelber never goes for the jugular vein in his infighting, recognizing that "We must live together. There's no point in destroying each other. Today's opponent may be next week's ally in another struggle."

He smiles when he tells the story on himself of how he once tried to impress an audience with a picturesque description of his version of a juvenile court judge. "The judge needs to have the spirit of Don Quixote, the role-playing ability of Marlon Brando, and the toughness of Vince Lombardi." There was a moment of silence until a voice called out, "Judge, you might be taking yourself a bit too seriously there."

Gelber doesn't let overstatement bother him too much so long as he makes his point. He feels that his job is not to come up with some great program or piece of legislation that will forever mark his service but rather to instill community confidence in what is being done and to maintain the credibility of the system so that his successor doesn't have to start all over again from scratch. He suggests, "if in the process I overact or overstate a bit, so be it."

Inside the courthouse, he calls daily for more thorough reports, more speedily delivered rehabilitative intervention, and more comprehensive programming for youngsters. He strokes competent HRS social workers and attorneys and counsels his court administrator on ways to expedite and smooth caseflow. Other judges falling behind schedule always find him available for assistance since Gelber's courtroom management style gets him through his daily workload before his colleagues.

He innovates approaches for monitoring performance and conducts his own research both on court caseflow and delinquency characteristics. Distribution of his studies to the press puts added pressure on agencies whose efforts he has found lacking. Several years ago, Judge Gelber conducted an investigation of 120 cases dismissed by the court because of the prosecution's failure to be prepared for trial within required time frames. The Miami Herald retitled his study with this heading, "Missing Witnesses Botch Youth Cases". Staff turnover problems in the juvenile prosecutor's office and inadequate internal monitoring procedures were subsequently remedied and the office initiated a project to contact victims and witnesses prior to the trial date. A related problem was that state agency intake officers were unable to complete their inquiries and bring cases before the prosecutor in a timely fashion. Staff shortages were blamed. Gelber's locally famous response was, "I don't care if you have to parachute more workers in here, you get them here and process those cases." HRS staff members were brought in from other regions of the state and the agency caught up with its work.

Gelber's background as an educator influences his effort to bring the local colleges and universities into a closer relationship with the criminal justice system. He's had only limited success in getting criminology and sociology departments to offer faculty and students for research and monitoring purposes. Despite what he considers only a half-hearted response, he says he's determined to bring academia into a more active role.

His own research efforts are produced regularly. These are mini-studies on issues of interest: juvenile crime and drugs (few juvenile crimes were found drug-related); burglaries and truancies (there was a high correlation between household burglaries and juvenile offender truancy); necklace snatching (this offense was found to be twice as frequently committed as purse snatching). He produces a major study every three years, titled, "Profile of Juvenile Crime". This compares juvenile crime rates, including racial-ethnic dimensions, with preceding years and additionally each compilation studies an area of special concern. The 1977 Profile looked at the relationship between school attendance and juvenile crime. The 1980 Profile examined the economic and social conditions of juvenile delinquents' families, and the 1983 Profile assessed conditions surrounding dependent and abused children. These triennial profiles are regularly quoted as data sources in newspaper articles.

Another area where his effort to involve community leadership has been rebuffed relates to his dealings with religious leaders. He brought together the heads of various religious denominations to encourage development of neighborhood programs that would directly involve individual churches and synagogues in servicing delinquent children. He offered staff assistance to design special programs to fit the needs for each religious institution, but the religious leadership declined. He says he hasn't given up but he's not optimistic. Privately he is deeply disappointed over this failure, contending that the church hierarchy offers more rhetoric than action.

Like other juvenile court judges, Gelber has held membership on myriad boards, committees, and commissions. Unlike others, he has not been one to testify before legislatures where "you do your little minuet and the committee performs in kind and that's the end of it." A favorite activity has been his chairmanship of the Dade-Miami Criminal Justice Council. This vehicle has furthered his contributions to both education and action as well as his own influence. As part of the council's examination of the value of establishing a citizens' review board to assess complaints against police brutality, the Miami Herald cited Gelber's balanced commentary. "The law enforcement community should recognize that citizens have a right not only to participate in the grievance process, but to oversee it. Of equal importance, the day-to-day field activity of the police is so dangerous that action warranted under circumstances of the moment looks quite different in the calmness of another day. None of us ought to forget either of those facts."

Along with his efforts to paint a realistic picture of juvenile crime Gelber, mostly through the council, tries to make certain all crime trends are accurately portrayed to the community. While not directly critical of the press, he fills in what he perceives to be their shortcomings in reporting crime trends. It was a Gelber study that first publicly stated that the crime wave attributed to the arrival from Cuba of the Mariel boat refugees had subsided and was likely to continue to decrease. Similarly, in his analysis of the council's 1981 year-end report of crime, he suggested that statistics showed Miami turning the corner on crime and predicted a downtrend in the offing. Reported on the front page of the Miami Herald, at a time when Miami was being characterized as the crime capital of the nation, the report was the first of many similar statements to be made by criminal justice officials and other observers.

Gelberesque political sensitivity and direction are evident in his weekly conference with council staff:

Judge: I want to know about your investigation of rapes of juveniles in the adult jail. Are jail officials covering up by not filing incident reports?

Staff: We have a committee, but we haven't called our first meeting yet.

Judge: You have a hot potato, and you better do something about it.

Staff: We are collecting data and interviewing people.

Judge: You are vulnerable, particularly until you have the first meeting. Don't sit there waiting for the bomb to explode.

Staff: We'll call the meeting.

On another subject:

Judge: The Chamber of Commerce got the legislature to increase the sales tax to fight crime and now everybody has a different priority on how to use that money. The Chamber of Commerce wants to spend $8,000,000 of this money on 800 "take home" police cars and another big chunk for more jail space. I want the money to save our juvenile rehabilitation programs and the county manager wants the money for general purpose use. The first thing to do is to find out if any automobile dealer connected with the Chamber might make a lot of money from the sale of these cars.

Staff: O.K. The Community Relations Board is supporting us.

Judge: But will they go out and fight for us?

Staff: We can encourage the programs that would be terminated to lobby the county commissioners.

Judge: We've been offered $900,000 which isn't enough. We need at least $2,000,000 to keep those programs alive. The county manager has assured me privately that we'll probably get close to that amount. Let's continue to seek the four million we are asking for and oppose the Chamber's request for "take home" police cars. They got the tax money but that doesn't mean they should decide how to spend it.

Staff: How do we do that?

Judge: I think we have to play it tough. I'm going to appoint a community-wide committee to work on this. I've already arranged for the state attorney to be chairperson and I want to get some powerful police officials and business executives on the committee.

Gelber's other favorite community activity has been the Miami Boys' Club educational remediation program he orchestrated. He brought together the Boys' Club that wanted to do more with delinquent youths and a corporate donor who indicated an interest in funding a project that could enhance future opportunities for hardcore, impoverished, delinquent youngsters. Each morning, staff counselors deliver the seventy participating boys to public school, and at the end of the school day transport them in vans to the Boys' Club for a special four-hour program. There, staff teachers work with the youngsters, using a ratio of one teacher to just two youngsters, for several hours of math and reading. Dinner is provided along with recreation and a daily group counseling session. All the boys come from the Liberty City ghetto area and have highly repetitive delinquency records. The program expanded to a second Miami site in early 1983 to serve an additional thirty youths. Although Gelber is on many youth boards, this is the one he gives particular attention to. "Too often public agencies only want kids likely to succeed so that they'll be funded for another year. Here the private sector goes out looking for tough cases and is not afraid to fail."

Earlier, Gelber served on the Dade County Mental Health Board. He was the first president of the Dade Marine Institute, a private agency that works with delinquent youths in an educational and adventure-at-sea model. For some years, he has been an active member of the American Bar Association section on criminal justice. He has chaired its terrorism committee, served on another committee that reviewed the then proposed FBI charter, and an ad-hoc committee that was invoked to alter and strengthen the nation's criminal justice system. Currently, he chairs an ABA advisory committee to assist with the implementation of ABA approved national juvenile justice standards. Judge Gelber enjoys the stimulation of these national activities, the broader perspective this affords him, the professionals from other states with whom he interacts, the reading preparation he must do, and the diverse ideas he absorbs. He prefers the action orientation of these committees to meetings of judges. In fact, he declines participation at Florida judge meetings, since "all they do is sit around and talk about their cases."

Seymour Gelber does less public speaking than many juvenile court judges. This is not his forte. He prefers committee work that is action directed. He uses the written word to get his message out to broad audiences. Still, he accepts some public speaking invitations. His favorite format in recent years has been to hand the audience his eleven question crime quiz, ask them to complete it, and then together go over their answers. For example, true or false, juveniles committing serious crimes like robbery and burglary usually end up with only a slap on the wrist? Other questions deal with the perceptions regarding comparable crime rates in several Florida communities, the extent of juvenile crimes committed by Cuban boatlift refugees, and others to which he provides unexpected statistical answers. He jokes with his audience: "If you had them all correct, you cheated." If someone indicates as many as six out of eleven correct answers, Gelber may respond: "That's great, that's about how well juvenile court judges do." His overall interest is in furthering a more realistic understanding of crime and delinquency problems and court practices.

How do other professionals view him? With admiration, sometimes ambivalence, occasionally with dismay. His close judicial sidekick for the past nine years says of Gelber, "The hallmark of his work is his common sense. He is a great place to turn to for both professional and personal advice. Some see his in-court style as too abrupt and others are afraid of him. But Si likes being the heavy. And he is extremely efficient and well-organized."

Another judge lauds Gelber's program ideas for delinquent youngsters and his writing ability. He sees him as extremely sensitive and compassionate, though Gelber appears to avoid the image. The judge adds, "Si has always been more interested in public service than lawyering. If he'd been in private practice, he wouldn't have made a living."

A third judge sees him as the stabilizing force in the court, a leaning post, a guide. "He gets to the point. He calls it straight. The handful that may not like him are this way because they've been told by him how it is."

Although he wouldn't win an election based on votes by HRS personnel, his best relationship exists with the middle-level supervisory group who look upon him as the friendly bear who has invaded their lair. "They accommodate my growl and try to avoid my bite." One of these officials and a close friend has been an inveterate Gelber watcher for years. "Si likes people to believe he's punitive, but he's not. He's difficult to anticipate — he doesn't want you to anticipate him. Staff like him because he's fast and fair, and if they have credibility with him he'll take their recommendations. If they're late to court or late with their reports, he'll nail their rear ends and that's good for them. He's got a mind like a steel trap. Some say he is arrogant and cranky. He is arrogant but it comes with his confidence. He's also funny as hell."

Another middle level administrator clearly has a love-hate relationship with this man. She lauds his intellectual abilities, his command of language skills, and his political acumen. "But he prefers theories and systems to dealing with people individually. With his bigger efforts he will start off in a good direction but not see them through. He is always playing cat and mouse with us; his hearings are too fast; he is too sarcastic; and kids don't think he cares about them. I get bitterly disappointed because he could make this system one of the best. Yet, he's fascinating, and despite everything I've said, I love him dearly."

Gelber, not unexpectedly, also comes in for some slams from the chief juvenile public defender. Defenders suggest that he is prosecution-minded, insufficiently attentive to law and legal procedure, and summary in some of the things he does in the courtroom. They believe he overuses the detention center lockup and hasn't followed through sufficiently in the big case to make enough changes there. Staff attorneys have problems when he lights into them after a hearing, but nonetheless find this instructive. "Yet of all the judges, he has the most respect from our staff. And if you're upset about what he has done, you can see him later in chambers and he's friendly again. He makes you laugh a lot and usually you're laughing at yourself."

Predictably, prosecutors are more positive. They see large merit with his ongoing effort to help the community understand crime and delinquency issues and develop problem solving directions. They also see him as a ready ally with any effort they undertake to make case processing more efficient. Senior prosecutors rely on Gelber appraisals of more fledgling staff to assist their own training and supervising efforts. Yet Gelber's interest in quickly getting to the point has consequences in that staff attorneys do not need to know all of the laws or rules of evidence to get by in his court and this can develop poor work habits. Nonetheless, they find him extremely instructive to young attorneys and a judge they can learn from in the many informal conferences they hold with him. They contend public defenders fail to understand that the more serious the case and the more likely the incarceration, the greater will be Gelber's requirements as to tight legal procedures. It is with lesser cases that he is less meticulous. They know he will run his court the way he wants to and they have little problem accommodating to this.

Gelber is bemused by his critics. He considers his tough image to have been carefully nurtured. If he is "iron balls", that's all right with him. He indicates this makes it a lot easier to go before the Chamber of Commerce to get support for rehabilitation programs "when you don't have that 'soft on crime' label". As to his failure to establish better personal relationships by more open communication with juveniles and their parents, Gelber's response is that "the secret for success in the juvenile court is to get the system to work, not in a personal commitment to each individual. If the system works, then everything else falls into place. If it doesn't all the feeling tones won't make any difference." Besides, Gelber feels that burn out, ulcers, and heart attacks come more quickly with judges who take each case home. He brags that when he walks out of the courtroom he immediately forgets the name of the last defendant. But he doesn't forget what went wrong — why the system failed.

The experienced professionals in this court find Gelber remarkably lacking in defensive qualities. He dishes it out but is willing to take it in return. He loves to go on the offensive, but his attacks are impersonal. His apparent anger is carefully controlled. He creates an environment where those he complains against can come back and retaliate in kind. In fact, he likes this. This is some of the muscle he is looking for. And his toughest critics, those who get angriest with him, find their anger melts away when they meet him in chambers and he spices the discussion with his clever wit while sipping his Postum or buttermilk and munching his crackers.

Gelber's wit, if not his wisdom, merit collection in an anthology. In one case hearing he mulled a staff recommendation to place a youth at Dade Marine Institute. The public defender opposed the plan.

Judge (to boy): Are you interested in boats and snorkels?
Boy: No, I bake doughnuts.
Public Defender: He has worked three years at Dunkin' Donuts.
Judge (spoofing): Can you dunk doughnuts with a snorkel?

At the end of another hearing, Gelber directs state HRS staff to arrange mental health counseling for a youngster and adds, "I don't think you should have to go all the way through the United Nations to make these arrangements."

And there is vintage Gelber talking about a judge's need to deal with the realities of his job. "A guy wearing the dress up there has to mix up the different factors and come up with a recipe that responds to a kid's problems and the community's requirements. The judge has to be the chef to determine the ingredients and decide how much salt should be added."

Then there is Gelber providing yet another university student an interview in his chambers: "The big outcry is why there's delay in executing people on death row, as if it's a picnic sitting there waiting to die. The public seems to prefer that jails be places where inmates brutalize each other."

Also, there is Gelber commenting on the frequent turnover of prosecutors in juvenile court: "They come here for a cup of coffee and are in adult court before dessert." Then there is Gelber's lack of due process concern over psychologist intervention with detained youngsters prior to their adjudication: "Any time you can get at a kid with anything that might help, get at him. It's like chicken soup; it can't hurt."

Seymour Gelber's humor, writings, and interest in provoking action as well as attention have brought this soft-spoken but cantankerous person a long way. They have maintained his vital interest in his judgeship during the nine years he has walked down the hall and climbed up and down the two steps. He thoroughly enjoys his role and his opportunities. He doesn't need personal adulation. He doesn't even mind getting reversed by the appellate court. He looks upon the juvenile court judgeship as a superior calling, far different from the role assumed by judges in other divisions of the court system. He perceives that the others function best in the background, keeping things in order, while the litigants flail each other about. The juvenile court judge on the other hand needs to be in total charge. "He's the main actor with the responsibility to see that all others in the case do their very best." If the law doesn't give that authority to the judge, Gelber thinks he must assume it. Absent the judge, there is no part of the bureaucracy able or willing to assume this leadership role. If the judge oversteps his bounds, he can be restrained by public opinion, by the ballot box, and by the appeals court. But he sees no room for timidity or judicial standoffishness in this business.

He has made it clear that he will not seek another term of office when his present term expires in 1986 and suggests that this fact may enable him to take more unpopular positions in the public realm. He understands well his present influence but realizes few will recall his achievements ten years from now. Declining interest in immortality, he wants no "public slab of granite", no building in the juvenile court complex named after him. But something has been named after him, as reported in the Miami Herald of November 19, 1982. "A two-year-old greyhound named Judge Si Gelber won the fifth race at Biscayne Kennel Club this week, paying $5.60. The dog, owned by lawyer Max Kogen, was named for Dade County Circuit Court Judge Seymour Gelber. Kogen, who owns 120 greyhounds, named all the puppies from one litter after local judges. But Judge Si is the best of the lot, he says."

CHAPTER 5

JUDGE EDWARD J. McLAUGHLIN: JUDICIAL LITERALISM

"The most important obligation of a juvenile court judge is to be scrupulously careful to assure that everyone involved in the proceedings is accorded his rights guaranteed by the law and the Constitution. The judge who disregards the law to do what he believes is good for people gives scandal to the child and the family. He is abandoning his position as a judge and gives the worst possible example that he can disobey the law if he's got the power to do it. Even if some children benefit from this extralegal treatment, the real lesson they've learned is that might makes right. This is precisely the lesson we are trying to dissuade them from learning."

The legal literalism of Judge Edward J. McLaughlin may well have provided sleepless nights to local law enforcement officials, social agency representatives, and other judges of this court since he took office as a family court judge in Onondaga County, Syracuse, New York, in January 1973. But it is doubtful that this caused nocturnal restlessness for Edward McLaughlin or the children and families who appear in his court each day.

His classical education in an Irish Christian Brothers' academy and college, and at a Catholic law school provided him with a special understanding of the relationship between society and the state. He treasures the United States Constitution that he suggests was written under the hand of God. The oath he swore to administer the laws of his state and the Constitutions of New York and the United States translates itself to compel that the judge, police officials, lawyers, social agency representatives, and yes, children and families, adhere to legal requirements.

But McLaughlin's world view is anything but cloistered. Growing up in New York City with a father who was a lieutenant of detectives and with four uncles who were policemen taught McLaughlin a lot about the nature of crime and police operations. He learned from his father that corruption takes place within government and the criminal justice system, to be distrustful of good intentions and of what others suggest is the truth, and to recognize society's need for a fair administration of justice. It was natural for McLaughlin, as a judge, to insist on a legal regimen and traditional courtroom processes that test the credibility of witnesses and the proof that is offered.

His bright red hair as a youth, and certain qualities derived from his Irish background led him to test rules during his childhood; quite possibly, this has made him more understanding of those who come before him for failing to observe society's rules. Conversely, his youthful experiences with urban street life influence his conviction that some youngsters are beyond treatment by the juvenile justice system and require criminal court punishments.

Edward McLaughlin grew up in a family that was linked closely with working for government and through most of his life he has worked in one or another public service role. But becoming a family court judge was not his long-nurtured career objective. The criminal court bench would have been a more predictable seat for him. He had prosecuted organized crime groups for the federal government. For two years he had served as associate general counsel for a state commission to revise New York's penal law and criminal code. Also, he had been a principal assistant district attorney in Syracuse for two years, and for another six years was general counsel for the New York State Joint Legislative Committee on Crime, Its Causes, Control and Effect on Society.

It was from this latter position that he became slotted for a family court judgeship in Syracuse. The chairman of the joint committee was a state senator from the Syracuse area who headed the county's legislative delegation to the capital in Albany. It happened that the senator held a high regard for McLaughlin's legal, political, and personal relationship skills. It happened, also, that the senator and McLaughlin were both Republicans in a Republican-dominated county. It was also true, at that time, that the Onondaga County Family Court was seen as a judicial system embarrassment and a political liability to the state senator. A blue-ribbon investigating commission had found serious fault with court procedures and administration in the aftermath of a notorious case that involved the death of an abused child. The senator asked McLaughlin if he wanted to become a judge of the family court. McLaughlin had never been inside this court, either as a lawyer or citizen, but he answered affirmatively. The senator paved the way for his nomination and then for his election in November 1972.

It was during McLaughlin's trying military experience in the Korean War that he had decided on his preference for the Republican Party. He was awarded the Silver Star for gallantry in action in Korea and the Bronze Star for heroism; battlefield wounds also prompted his receipt of the Purple Heart. He perceived that the Democratic Party had been unable to keep the country out of a series of wars, but "Eisenhower got us out of Korea, and, later, Nixon, got us out of Viet Nam." In no way a pacifist, McLaughlin's views of both foreign affairs and judicial system affairs respect the threat and the backup use of force. The courts need to resort to legalized muscle to carry out their purposes.

A cardinal McLaughlin tenet is that society makes its rules through law. Accordingly, judges, above all, must play by society's rules. He is a stickler for the law and a leading advocate of the legal regulation of juvenile courts, organizations that remain conflicted as to how much law should constrain their rehabilitation enterprise. Unequivocal adherence to the law dissolves any conflicts McLaughlin may have. The issues, then, involve interpretations of ambiguous statutes. And to resolve statutory uncertainties, Judge McLaughlin, probably more than any juvenile court judge in the nation, undertakes the writing of legal opinions. More than forty such trial court judgments have been published in official New York State court report volumes. He teaches the law, by these written decision, in his colloquies with attorneys in courtroom and chambers; further, he has been incessantly engaged for years in college and university teaching.

He is also a literalist with judicial ethics. In an election bid, he returned all contributions received from attorneys, asking that they redirect these moneys to the party. He did not distrust lawyer motivations in contributing to a judicial campaign; he only wanted to be free of knowing which lawyers had helped finance his effort.

When Ed McLaughlin talks about the roles of the judge and court issues, his content is different from that of other juvenile court judges. There is virtually no discussion about protecting the community. He speaks very little of the need to have additional resources to facilitate the rehabilitation of court youngsters. He has no pet rehabilitation programs. He does not describe youngsters in psychological terms. There are no complaints about the growing legalization trend, adversarial lawyers, or the number of trials he conducts. Nor is he heading off, constantly and chronically, to meetings.

The New York Family Court Act, except for a 1976 amendment that was concerned with particularly serious offenses, does not direct its judges to consider community safety with delinquency cases. Rather, judges must find juveniles to have committed an offense and to be in need of treatment; then, they can order youngsters into the care of an organization that will provide necessary treatment.

McLaughlin speaks little of the need for additional resources since, in general, he believes his community has been generous in its provisions to children and that other resources can be obtained around the state. Some specialized, costly programs are missing, but there is much that is available.

New York judges administer neither the probation nor detention function. He has little to do with these programs. He insists that he is a judge and not a master's degree social worker, psychologist, or institutional director. He has helped a few new community services become organized, but maintains no intensive continuing relationship with them. He weighs courtroom evidence as to the need for treatment; the professionals determine the type of treatment to be implemented.

McLaughlin has deliberately made his court into an adversarial forum and rejects appointing lawyers for children who will not be unswerving advocates. He loves trials, which to him are akin to reading novels, though he encourages agreements and settlements. He believes that court orders are more successfully enforced when the parties in interest concur with recommendations for the court to approve.

McLaughlin presides in a family court. A family court has significantly broader jurisdiction than a juvenile court. Juvenile delinquency and status offense petitions comprise just 8 or 9 percent of the overall 12,000 petitions filed in this court annually. There are also the usual, some of them very unusual, child abuse and neglect petitions. There are hundreds of petitions alleging the paternity of a child, and asking that the court ascertain fatherhood and order fathers to pay child support. These are the early steps in a process that is often accompanied by nonpayments and further hearings regarding support delinquencies. Interstate support orders are also enforced here. Offenses within a family, particularly assaults between husbands and wives, are a regular bill of fare of the court.

Large numbers of petitions concerned with the education of handicapped children are considered here, since county financial support for this care is contingent upon court approval. These matters are more routinized than individualized. The adoption of children is legalized in this court. Contested child custody and other disputed matters growing out of divorce or dissolution cases, heard in another court, are transferred to the family court for determination.

Yet, this is not an unlikely setting for Edward McLaughlin. He is a family man. He and his wife Arden have delighted in raising four children. McLaughlin can be useful to families in his judicial role, though he sees virtually irreparable family disintegration on many court days. From his police lieutenant father he absorbed a feeling for the disadvantaged; a half-hour observation of the McLaughlin courtroom tells any observer that the poor represent the bread and butter of this family court. He has a passion for due process of law and the court's clientele are a daily reinforcement to him that everyone, but particularly the ill-informed, requires protection against the state's powers. He loves the law and, because he has insisted on contentious legal advocacy, his agile legal mind encounters regular stimulation.

Since 1975, as administrative judge of this court which became a five-judge court in 1983, McLaughlin has had strong visibility in his community. The administrative role also connects him with local and state judicial hierarchies. All this strengthens his base if he chooses, in the future, to seek election to a higher judicial office. His reelection victory, in 1982, may have whetted his appetite to bid down the road for the state supreme court. The supreme court, in New York, is not the highest court as it is virtually everywhere else. It is, rather, the general trial court, though a powerful bench seat.

McLaughlin, as a personality, is forceful and colorful. He constantly reads history. Historical references lace his language. He has deeply held convictions. He spices his *credo* statements with vibrant phrases and illustrations. He has energy to burn and looks forward, at the end of a rigorous workday, to working with his law clerk on legal writing projects for a few hours before going home for dinner. He is an acute observer of the relationship between law and society. A number of these characteristics emerge during a lively interview with a Syracuse University student in his chambers:

Student: What are the frustrations in your job?

Judge: I'm not frustrated. I like the job. It's warm and nice in here.

Student: Is the court used by the parties to harass each other?

Judge: Less so since we have speeded up the process. Ten years ago, a large percentage of parties used the system to harass each other. Not now. It's not as much fun to annoy someone when it's all over quickly. We used to average eight or ten appearances per petition. Now it's just two.

Student: What is the most frequent type of case you hear?

Judge: Support.

Student: Is it a hindrance to carry out the law as it is written?

Judge: Always. The whole idea is for the law to get in the way.

That's the way it's supposed to be. You need laws to protect you from the state. The judge represents the state. If you keep asking why, at the end you will find that laws protect the weak from the strong. The strong don't need the protection of the law. Did you read Lord of the Flies?

Student: Yes.

Judge: Well, there the strong made the laws. In the early days, the state imposed laws for its purposes, but even then the laws protected people from the state. If the king said he would take 10 percent of your harvest, you knew he wasn't to take 20 percent.

Student: Do people sometimes want things the state cannot do for them?

Judge: Yes. For example, a woman comes to court asking that we stop her husband from beating her. What she wants is that he love her. We order him out of the house. So, he finds another woman and there's a divorce. Or, with a paternity case, a woman asks the court to order support for her out-of-wedlock child. We order $20 a week and visitation. Five years later she is married, but now has to contend with visitations by her old boyfriend. It's best to stay the hell out of court.

McLaughlin elaborates his treatise on the role of courts in an early morning lecture to a marital therapy class composed of graduate psychology students at Syracuse University. He begins by saying that every society has some form of court system, even the Vietnamese boat people established courts on their boats. He then comments on the report by Martin Frobisher, the sixteenth-century English navigator, who encountered Eskimos on his search for a Northwest passage to India and the East. McLaughlin paraphrases Frobisher, who had observed tribesmen pushing over a cliff a tribal member who had taken another's tomahawk. "This we call 'self-help'. But if you use self-help, the tribe is in jeopardy. The tomahawk is what we call jurisdiction. The way to determine the truth is called procedure. The first rule of procedure is that only one person talks at a time. The way to determine truth is not who is strongest in combat. The contract in giving up self-help is to submit to a court and to use the force of the court as a substitute for self-help force. The court's force is necessary, as with the parking violator who will not pay his fine because he believes that government is a communist conspiracy."

McLaughlin jokes that there is a Chinese saying that it is better to walk into the mouth of a tiger than walk into a courtroom. He goes on to discuss family offenses and the court's use of force. The husband strikes the wife violently. She comes to court and gets a protective order. He assaults her again, but the wife tells the judge she doesn't want her husband jailed. McLaughlin suggests if she didn't want to use the court's forces, she should not have come to the court initially.

He provides another example. A customer gives a prostitute a check and subsequently stops payment. The women then claims rape. Will the court enforce the rape charge? No, because prostitution is an illegal act. He goes on to discuss rules. In football, the rules permit tackling, but a lineman cannot use a knife to help him get to the running back. With a husband and a wife, it is all right to fondle, but not to assault. The problem, he indicates, is where does license begin and where does it end? In a contested divorce, the court will determine the custody or possession to a child. If the mother obtains custody and remarries, her new husband may wish to adopt the child, but cannot unless the first husband relinquishes his title to the child. He quips that the students are getting the fastest law course they'll ever have in their lifetimes.

McLaughlin lectures without notes and with frequent recourse to the blackboard. He describes how the courts determine child support amounts and proceeds to discuss the limits that confront court efforts with family problems. "If the parents agree on joint legal custody but never resolve their feelings, the father and mother take the kids to different churches and different doctors and the kids become hypochondriacs." And with other custody problems, what are the court's remedies if the mother denies visitation to the father? If the court agrees with the father and orders a moratorium on his support obligation, the mother will deprecate the father to the children, telling them he doesn't care. If the court puts the mother in jail for violating its order to provide visitation, the kids may have to go to a foster home. If the court indicates it will give custody to the father, the father says no, I'm on the road five days a week. "No remedy is any good."

He makes an aside to the class that some day in the future, we'll have no jails, just different amounts of drugs injected by the government depending upon the severity of the crime committed. For theft one receives 10 cc's; for assault, 100 cc's. He wraps up his lecture with the principles that guide judges in custody determinations: Custody to a parent, keep the siblings together, provide the least disruption to children's lives. He departs with a question. Is it a denial of civil rights if a husband tells his wife to shut up? He answers, no, the First Amendment constrains only government's abridgment of freedom of speech. He is on his way back to court.

The family court is in the historic county courthouse in downtown Syracuse. A variety of courts are housed in this structure; the family court is on the first floor in quarters recently remodeled at McLaughlin's suggestion and with the help of the Family Court Citizen Advisory Committee. The probation agency and social services department are officed in adjacent county government buildings. The juvenile detention facility is six or seven miles from downtown.

The sheriff's deputy, who serves as his bailiff, and also has the name of McLaughlin but is no relative, calls the courtroom audience to its feet as the judge enters. What they see is the black-robed judge attorneys refer to as "the lawman" and court youngsters refer to as "the big red-headed judge". They notice a six-foot-one-inch, heavyset, ruddy-faced individual who looks younger than his fifty-three years. McLaughlin gives off the energy of one who intends to be the governor of the proceedings that will take place. But this is a modulated tension. He wants participants to feel comfortable in his courtroom, does provide the time that is necessary to advise them fully as to their rights, yet needs to march through his docket to wrap up the morning by 12.30 p.m. and the afternoon by 5 p.m.

There is a quiet dignity that surrounds his large courtroom. The judge sits off to the far corner in a high-backed leather chair, one step up from the floor. Behind him are the flags. Oak paneling runs a third of the way up the courtroom walls. Pale yellow paint then carries the walls to the ceiling. Enclosed fluorescents bounce light off the white acoustic ceiling. On the wall to his left, two large windows permit more light to enter. Also to his left a clerk enters minute orders; to his right is the witness chair and the court reporter's desk. Three tables, each with two chairs behind them, face the judge's bench. Behind these tables during the course of the day, sit the parents and their attorneys, children and their law guardians, the public prosecutor, and probation and social service agency staff members. There is a row of seats in the back of the courtroom that holds parties who wait for the next case. Hearings tend to be brief in this court, trials somewhat prolonged. For the former, everyone tends to stand behind their tables.

In New York and just three other states, juvenile offenders must be handled in adult courts following their sixteenth birthdays. Further, 1978 legislation in that state permits initial criminal court handling of thirteen, fourteen, and fifteen-year-olds charged with more serious law violations, though these juveniles may be transferred back to the family court for handling. Also, New York permits delinquent processing with one's seventh birthday.

In testimony before legislative commissions and in his writings, Judge McLaughlin has suggested two extremely divergent approaches to restructuring how the judicial system encounters juvenile offenders. The first is a more traditional enlargement of a juvenile court's jurisdiction. Juvenile offenders would be handled by family courts until their eighteenth birthdays. He accepts the treatment rationale of juvenile courts with this model, considering that most youngsters can make gains through rehabilitative offerings. He asks, however, that policy makers increase the minimum age of the court's jurisdiction to the tenth or twelfth birthday, believing that non-coercive community agencies should be responsible for lower-age youngsters. Since a small percentage of youngsters are genuinely criminalistic and beyond the reach of rehabilitative intervention, he would authorize family courts to transfer such juveniles for criminal court punishment. Presently, New York State is virtually alone in not authorizing such transfers. With this approach, he likes kids.

A radically different view is presented in his late-1982 law review article, "Completing the Cycle: Reality and the Juvenile Justice System in New York State", co-authored with his law clerk, Lucia B. Whisenand. Here, a proposal is made that the time has come to abolish juvenile courts. All juvenile offenders would be handled in the criminal courts. With this recommendation, he still likes kids. He believes that the criminal courts are the only forums where juveniles will receive all of their constitutional rights.

The proposal is based on certain perceptions. The noble juvenile court experiment has lost many of its attributes. Its promise of rehabilitation has been shown to have as many myths as realities. "Punishment has surreptitiously gained respectability; its treatment doctrine has eroded." Other developments have obfuscated the original juvenile court construct. Juveniles have some rights but not the full panoply. Some juveniles are criminalized at the whim of a prosecutor while similar offenders remain in juvenile courts. Child care bureaucracies frequently have replaced more personal helping methods. Treatment is least available for the child who is most antisocial. For the more docile and perhaps more treatable juvenile, long periods of freedom deprivation are used, but without scrupulous protection of constitutional rights. Most judges lack behavioral-science skills and the concept of the judge as a "super social worker" is both harmful and dangerous. The private nature of the court insulates its processes from public examination. A more honest approach to juvenile rehabilitation and punishment by criminal courts would demythologize judicial system handling of juveniles. Juveniles would better understand that society takes their law violations seriously. Deterrency would be increased. The rights of both the juvenile and the public would be more effectively protected. Respect for the courts would be enhanced.

This has not been the first espousal of this view and will not be the last. But others have suggested that this type of cure is worse than the present disease. However, pandering to an angry public is not a McLaughlin stratagem. Nor does he desire simplistically to recycle a discredited arrangement of juvenile atonement. Rather, he views that a court system should enforce society's rules without the confusion of the proffer of help that is accompanied by the judicial hammer.

Unlike many judges, McLaughlin acknowledges the contribution of his law clerk with his published writings. They share authorship and alternate the lead author position. They approach writing as a team, with debate and lively discussion of an issue prior to any attempts being made to formalize a view or opinion. First drafts are read aloud, edited, and often redrafted.

Back in his courtroom, McLaughlin's concern for a youngster's welfare and legal rights is evident.

Judge: (to a blue-eyed, blond-haired, fourteen-year-old boy charged with a burglary): How're you doin' today, Tiger?

Boy: Okay, Judge.

Law guardian: We deny the charge. Neither parent is present.

Boy: My mother and father got separated.

Judge (to law guardian): Let me know later if he is not big on his parents; I can appoint him a guardian *ad litem.*

Judge (to law guardian): Where do you want your client?

Law guardian: He . . .

Judge: Well, you're his lawyer.

Law guardian: Keep him at the Hillbrook Detention Home till his parents can be brought in.

Judge: They might be in Tahiti. I'll only hold him two days. He's entitled to a fact-finding hearing within seventy-two hours. I will appoint a guardian *ad litem* for the hearing due to the uncertainties about the parents. (And then to the boy): I know you've been living at this private children's institution. Is there anyone there you like?

Boy: No.

Judge: Do you have any aunts, uncles, cousins, anybody?

Boy: I have an aunt, but I don't want to live with her.

Judge: Okay, William. Is that what they call you?

Boy: No, Billy.

Judge: Billy, be a good boy and give my regards to Mr Harmon (the director at the detention home). Did you get seconds for dinner last night?

Boy: Yes.

McLaughlin insists that all he does is try to treat kids fairly. He doesn't give kids breaks. He doesn't give anyone breaks. Everyone, especially the judge, must obey society's rules. He will not tolerate a lawyer saying, "Whatever you think is best, Judge." He is demanding that "no law guardian I appoint will sell his kid down the river."

Edward Joseph McLaughlin entered the river of life on May 12, 1930, in New York City. He attended parochial schools and that's where his bright red hair got him into trouble. "I got kicked out of the parish school because I didn't like the nuns touching me and my red hair. Red-haired people are expected to test the rules and I did." He was reenrolled in an Irish Christian Brothers' academy in the Bronx. He was late the first day in the new school. As discipline, he received a ruler strike on his hands. This he saw as fair discipline. He had not complied with the rules. The Christian Brothers' Order was to become the greatest influence on his life. The Brothers stimulated and advanced his thinking regarding the history of man, the relationship of mankind to society, a range of issues related to morality, and one's responsibility to contribute to a more just society. A different order of Christian Brothers was to educate his three sons later in Syracuse.

The other powerful influence on his life was his father, a tough but fair New York City cop who was to command the detectives in the seventeenth precinct that encompassed 42nd Street, Grand Central Station, and the Waldorf-Astoria Hotel. McLaughlin's father was guided by a sense of "rough justice". He opposed reliance on beating confessions out of people, a not uncommon practice in that era, but did use occasional force on police characters he was certain had committed serious law violations. "Still, among detectives, my dad was a due process guy." His father, who believed that the upper classes had advantages that were denied others, retained an identification with the under-privileged. "He taught me never to take advantage of poor people and that, if you have power, carefully use this to help balance the scales, assisting those less advantaged."

Policing and crime were daily talk around his family dining table. Ed McLaughlin talks about his father's "phenomenal intuition" as a police investigator. "His powers of observation were unbelievable. He would take gigantic leaps into space and be amazingly correct. A wealthy Connecticut woman came to the state to report the loss of $100,000 in jewelry. He asked where she had stayed the night before and received the name of a fancy hotel. He asked where she had left the jewelry that night and she said in the trunk of her chauffeur-driven automobile. My father was thinking about the case at home that night and decided the woman knew who took her jewels. It had to be her chauffeur with whom she was probably having an affair. So he called her back to the station and asked where she had slept one night earlier. My father did not accept her statement that it was with a lady friend in Westchester County. She soon admitted she had slept with her chauffeur and her chauffeur had taken the jewels."

Judge McLaughlin credits his father with helping him become more cynical. He learned that government officials can be bought. He absorbed the old police saying that "cops are not too concerned about prosecuting the rap, but they do want the guy to have the ride downtown." Later, as a prosecutor, he found one of his father's admonishments to be true: Never try a case on eyewitness testimony alone. Eyewitnesses are not sufficiently dependable; miscarriages of justice may well be the consequence. His father was to serve as bodyguard to presidential candidate Wendell Willkie during the 1940 campaign.

On completing high school, McLaughlin entered the Marine Corps at age seventeen. A year later, he resigned to become a Naval midshipman. Three years later, he resigned to enter the Army. He wanted to get into the Korean War and he wanted to fight. He obtained both wishes. By age twenty-one, he had earned a commission as a second lieutenant in the infantry and was a company commander. A year later, he received a battlefield promotion to first lieutenant. McLaughlin says that since age eighteen, "I've always been in charge. I need to be in charge."

But felled by a charge of the other side's ammunition, he was returned to recuperate at Walter Reed Hospital. At the time, he held a career interest in the Army, but set this aside to enroll in Manhattan College, a Christian Brothers' school. There he was intrigued by some of the ultimate questions. Who made you? Why are you alive? What are you doing in this world? He read deeply into Irish, European, and American history and retains this passion today. He still reads histories far into the night, including an array of works on the history of torture. He is a combination of the practical man who functions with a perspective of the nature of man over the long evolution of society.

Edward J. McLaughlin was also a cop. During his senior college year, he graduated from the New York City Police Academy. Sworn into the department with badge no. 8822, he took an immediate leave of absence to continue his college work. He was not to pursue a police vocation. Instead, he followed the suggestion of the Christian Brothers and enrolled in law school in 1955. Awarded scholarships to Notre Dame, St. Johns, and Villanova law colleges, all Catholic schools, he accepted the full scholarship, room and board, and $120 per month from Villanova. There, he was on the editorial board of the law review, won an academic prize, and was an honor graduate. He had anticipated picking up his Army career following graduation, but instead, was successfully recruited by the United States Department of Justice for assignment to its organized crime and racketeering section. For two years he was involved in the investigation and prosecution of these matters in the federal courts in Rhode Island and New York. He was a trial attorney in a difficult and complicated arena, "but I've always done things just to prove I can do them."

Transferred to the federal attorney's office in Syracuse, in 1960, he continued to specialize in organized crime prosecutions for a year, then switched to private law practice, deciding to make Syracuse his permanent home. But the non-public field of law was never to fully claim him. Together with his part-time private practice, he was to double as associate general counsel for the penal law commission, as principal assistant district attorney, and as general counsel for the Joint Legislative Committee on Crime. It was in this final role that he worked closely with the state senator who "became my rabbi".

McLaughlin also began teaching on a part-time basis, a role he continues today. In 1963, a time when a series of United States Supreme Court decisions impacted significantly on police search and seizure, interrogation, and other procedures, he volunteered to teach a course on constitutional law to policemen at the local community college. He notes, "It was funny. I was told it would be on their time and no one would show up. Amazingly, 400 officers took that first course. The next semester, I taught a course on penal law with the same enthusiastic showing. I repeated these courses a second year and then I had to drop out because of time pressures."

His courses led to the development of the police science department at the college, still in existence. His teachings stood him in good stead with law enforcement officers who, today, still try to puzzle out his judicial philosophy. The county sheriff says, "He was the best teacher I ever had. The classes were packed. He was a great, lively lecturer. He tossed in the right amount of anecdotes. He taught us hard, sharp law. I feel affection for him because he helped us when we needed it. A year later, I watched McLaughlin prosecute probably the most notorious criminal case Syracuse had experienced. It was a bitch of a case to try. Mac put on the best criminal prosecution I'd seen till then. But the police today have a hard time figuring him out. They don't know whether he's liberal, conservative, or what."

A present police lieutenant also took a McLaughlin course. "His nickname was Red McLaughlin. He knew you have to teach cops differently. They fall asleep if you just give them the facts. He was lively and got along very well with us."

In 1970, McLaughlin began teaching criminal law and procedure classes at John Jay College of Criminal Justice, City University of New York. For some years, he would commute to New York City to teach an evening class each week. After six years he called this quits.

He has also taught continuously at the Syracuse University College of Law since 1974. The first several years he worked off of his strength, criminal law and procedure, transferring to teach family law and procedure once he had developed this expertise. In 1978, he began teaching a class on children's rights at the University College, Syracuse University, and, in 1982, initiated his class in forensic social work at the university's School of Social Work.

Teaching, McLaughlin says, is in his enlightened self interest. By instructing police officers, lawyers, social workers, and others, a constituency is developed, so when the court is criticized for some reason, other professionals can explain or defend court procedures and decisions. "They may not agree with what I did, but at least they can say, 'Well, maybe this is what happened.' People don't know what goes on inside a family court. It's like a shaman, it's magic or something. At least the star chamber was public. If a judge returns an abused child to his parents because the case is not proved and the parents proceed to kill their child, the newspapers, quite appropriately, will inform the public of what has happened. The people will know the result, but probably not the reason for it. The court is criticized, but judges under their code of ethics are not permitted to aggressively respond to the criticism. This is a good rule. Judges should not get involved in public controversies of that type. Therefore, they must depend on attorneys and others who know about the court to defend them."

Edward McLaughlin handily won election to the family court in November 1972. McLaughlin's Republican affiliation and his influential party support carried him to an easy victory. Franklin Delano Roosevelt had never carried this county during his four presidential campaigns. It was not McLaughlin's nature, however, to sit quietly on his bench, rock no boats, and simply be the community advocate for better services to children and families. Instead, he provoked the professionals who process and service children and families with his insistence that they adhere to the letter of the law. Nor did he espouse a judicial hard line on juvenile crime.

Instead, he stressed his duty to administer present public policy under present law. Later, as administrative judge, he carried at least his proportionate share of the court caseload despite the additional time required to perform this role. He gained prominence in statewide judicial circles as he moved up the hierarchy of the Family Court Judge's Association to become its president in 1981. He was appointed to the state Family Court Rules Committee and is an official delegate to state conferences on law and the press where he advocates his belief that the family court should be a public court. He brought certain national recognition to this court when he taught several classes at the National College of Juvenile Justice in Reno, Nevada, and served on several national advisory commissions that assessed proposed national juvenile justice standards and other juvenile justice system developments.

His 1982 reelection race was complicated by the authorization of a fifth judge for the court. McLaughlin's seat was up, together with the new judgeship. His Republican running mate obtained the Conservative Party endorsement and was backed by the Right to

Life Party that supported anti-abortion candidates. McLaughlin was a nominee of the Republican Party and the Liberal Party. One Democratic candidate, a woman who was to become a winner, also held Liberal Party support. She was certain to receive strong support from women voters. The bar association preliminarily voted not to recommend McLaughlin for reelection, some attorneys disliking some of the changes he had instituted as administrative judge. McLaughlin's calculations indicated that he could be squeezed off the bench. Though an incumbent, his campaign would have to be an active one.

So McLaughlin had 100,000 cards printed with his picture on the front and his attainments on the back and began handing them out at the farmers' market on Saturdays and at shopping centers. He wore a campaign straw hat with a Vote-for-McLaughlin band around it as he did his hand-shaking tour. His attitude was, "If you guys are going to make me run, I'm going to run." He invited speaking engagements and accepted those offered him. He issued a special administrative report on his court which helped to reverse the bar association's position and to obtain a newspaper endorsement. In supporting his candidacy, the Syracuse Herald-Journal noted he was a "hard-working, up-on-the-issues judge, who found time to reduce the huge backlog in family court cases while building a national reputation for his work on the bench. Legislators and other courts seek and quote McLaughlin's opinions and rulings."

With the assistance of neighbors, he made a batch of four-foot-by-four-foot lawn signs and with the help of his family put them up on a variety of sites around the county. His wife, Arden, a party vice-chairperson in the ward, speaks about the election drive. "I took a leave of absence for a month and went campaigning with Edward. When he was at court, I would drive around and when I would see a corner home where a lot of traffic passed by, I would knock on the door and ask permission to place a lawn sign. No one turned me down. The party handed out Edward's cards door to door and other friends gave them to people they met. Edward is a fascinating candidate. You should see him in action at meetings. It's his sincerity, honesty, and dedication that goes over so well. People like him. They believe in him. A lot of our friends were at our home on election night. Returns from early reporting precincts were not positive. We lost the city, which is more Democratic, but won the county and won the election."

McLaughlin was front-ranking among the four candidates. He

topped the other successful candidate by about 1,800 votes and the third ranking candidate, the Republican nominee, by about 10,500 votes. His 1972 electoral margin had exceeded 40,000 votes. His electoral apprehensions in 1982, that he might get lost in the crossfire of five political parties and the national pro-Democratic direction, had been based in reality.

McLaughlin had married Arden Mary Shaughnessy in July 1958. He says of her that she is half Danish and half Irish, but has a stronger Danish cultural identification. There are Danish ship captains in her ancestry. Her grandfather had written a book about his fifty years as a master mariner. Inside their wedding bands, engraved in Danish, are the words, I love you. She has been an operating-room nurse, but now works three late night shifts a week at a nursing home. He says of his wife, "She's a great lady. Arden is my flywheel. She has common sense. I'll throw out an idea at the dinner table and if Arden reacts negatively, I know I can't use this."

Arden keeps the family financial books. She is the primary cook for the family. The judge's specialty is to prepare the Sunday brunch that frequently includes an Edward J. McLaughlin cheesecake.

Arden McLaughlin glows as she recounts her life with her husband. She loves him as a husband, father, and judge. He chose the names for their first and third children, she for their second and fourth. The work ethic is strong in this household. "At one time the six of us held eleven jobs."

Roderick, born in 1959, graduated from Notre Dame University and is a law student at Syracuse University. He was named after his father's dad. He had thought of coaching swimming, but finally decided on a law career. He had to decide this for himself. He looks to the head of the table, to his father, and half serious, half joking says, "My father would have been happy if I had gone to West Point and become a military chaplain. He would not have had to pay tuition." Rod goes on to talk about the values he absorbed from his parents: "Education, hard work, and verbal qualities. If you can't defend yourself around here, you're dead. And if you ask him a question about history, he gives you overkill. Frequently, dad will get up and get the Encyclopedia Britannica or a history book and start reading it to us."

A moment later, in a discussion about a judicial friend who had lost re-election for another term, Judge McLaughlin departs for the family library to return with a copy of Shakespeare's Merchant of Venice. He thumbs to the page and reads out how Portia, dressed as a magistrate, is importuned to do a small wrong in order to achieve a great good. Portia responds that, if she attains a great good, she will have done a greater wrong.

Six-foot-six-inch Ted, named for his father by his father and officially another Edward McLaughlin, was the third born child. He attends Slippery Rock University in Pennsylvania, in large part because of his water polo skills and the university's emphasis on that sport. At the moment, he plans a career with the FBI. He looks like his father. People stop him and say his name must be McLaughlin. Well, have you had any problems due to your father's position? Ted responds that when he was sixteen, while working at an inner-city swimming pool, six young people approached him, one of them with a knife, and slapped him around. "One boy said that my father had put him away. Eventually they let me go, and I arranged to work at a different pool."

Ted continues on about the family: "You can talk with our father. He won't give you a hard time. He'll give you options. He doesn't talk much about what happens in court, but we can all tell if he is preoccupied about something. Our family is really close." He looks at his mother with a smile and adds, "And if Mom hadn't become a nurse, she'd have been a nun. She's a very moral woman."

Fourth in line, Christian, age sixteen, joins actively in dining table discussions. He reports on his earnings from the paper route and a landscaping job and his proximity to being able to buy a home computer. He reports on school progress and water polo.

Then there is Betsy, named Elizabeth by her mother, but known to the family as "Fav", short for Favorite, the only McLaughlin daughter. Age twenty-two, a graduate of Boston College, and like Rod, a first-year law student at Syracuse University, she enters into a more private conversation about her father. "Dad and I have always been very close. He's always helped me with decisions I've had to make, offering options and letting me know his thoughts. Two or three times a year we have a very long talk about my present and future. I look forward to this. He knows so much about so many things and if he doesn't know something, he'll get a book and read out loud about it. His natural style is to lecture. When we talk, he leads and does more of the talking. Dinner together was always important. Dad wanted us all to be here at dinner. He would always open the conversation to ask each of us what we had done that day. It was always understood that whatever was said at the table would not go beyond the house. I could always tell when child abuse cases were weighing on his mind. Dad's even more in touch with our family because of what he experiences in court each day. He always insisted that I be like others, and not be different because he was a judge. In part, I always try to do my best because I want him to be proud of me."

The final member of the family is Licorice, ten years old, and a big black dog.

The McLaughlin workday begins at 9 a.m. and ends about 7 p.m. He rarely eats lunch. The last two hours of the day usually involve legal writing in conjunction with his law clerk. He reads his history into the night. He may well experience a 4-hour, 4-hour, 4-hour, 6-hour, 13-hour sequential nightly sleep pattern.

McLaughlin answers questions differently from other judges. His responses are founded on legal principles, the rules made by society. The judge's most important role in improving the juvenile justice system is not to make the system more accountable or extend rehabilitation offerings but to accord youngsters and other parties their constitutional rights. Do you see juveniles as responsible for their offenses? If they prove it. Do you see as more prominent your responsibility to the community or your responsibility to the juvenile? My responsibility is to my oath of office. When do you commit a child to the state? When the evidence is sufficient. How has your administration of sanctions changed during your ten years as a judge? I'm not authorized to administer sanctions. How, then, have your dispositions changed over time? They haven't changed because I always rely on the evidence. How do you exercise your discretion as a judge? In New York, family court judges have no discretion. How should punishment fit the crime? There's no punishment. But isn't confinement in a delinquency institution punishment? Not under our laws; it's for treatment.

McLaughlin's judicial philosophy and administration of hearings conform to a strict legal literalism. He will wink at the children who come before him but will not wink at the law. He hews to sturdy beliefs as to the responsibilities of all judges and the more particular functions of the family court judge.

Judges should administer society's rules in an impartial way. Constitutional safeguards are to protect the minority against the majority. The minority includes those charged with crimes or delinquent acts. Due process of law requirements and lawyers safeguard court clients from judicial error and judicial arrogance. Public trials and jury trials are protections against judicial corruption. The results of court hearings should be predictable. Broad judicial discretion denies predictability. His own descriptions are more engaging than these statements.

"A judge's oath is to the Constitution and not to the mob. Judges might not like certain laws, but their feelings are unimportant. What society says by its laws is important. If a judge thinks it's morally wrong to impose the death penalty and refuses to impose it, he should resign from the bench. Society doesn't care what he personally thinks. Either the judge obeys the laws or gets the hell off the bench."

To McLaughlin, judicial ethics mandate that judges reach decisions only through legal reasoning. They must give no appearance of prejudice in any direction. Judges should have exacting guidelines, by statute, rule, or case decision precedent, in conducting their offices. "Like the ship in the channel, precise buoys should guide the judge, otherwise the public will see the court as a capricious and arbitrary institution used for punishing the poor. Within this ship's channel, the judge should have some reasonable discretion. But if confronted with a choice of clear guidelines or discretion, I'd go for the guidelines."

For McLaughlin, the function of the jury and the public courtroom is to keep judges honest. "Sure, the jury is there, so they might as well judge some facts, but their real function is not to judge facts. Their real function is to protect citizens from corrupt, incompetent, and drunken judges." McLaughlin loves the judicial function, knows its vulnerability to abuse, demands that it be checked by lawyers and established legal procedures. He also discerns that society's laws change over time.

"The public decides what's a crime or what isn't a crime. Take abortion. It used to be a very serious crime. Today, at least in the first trimester, society considers it neutral. Within our lifetime, it's going to be a positive. They're going to be offering women rewards. Now, if I told you in 1965 that I thought abortion was bad, and in 1982 I told you I was neutral about it, and in 1990, I told you I was in favor of it, you'd think I was a whacko. Or, here in New York, we're against gambling casinos and when I drive to New Jersey I'm in favor of them, and when I reach Delaware I'm against them, and when I get to Nevada I'm in favor of them. You'd think I was a nut. But crime has no relation to tomorrow."

Edward McLaughlin believes that there are special perils associated with judges of juvenile courts. He is mindful of his readings in juvenile court history, its paternalistic assumptions, and its negation of constitutional protections. Obviously, he prefers a due process model juvenile court that is grounded in law and whose rehabilitative measures fit tightly within legal parameters. He worries publicly about judicial colleagues who evade the law to accomplish what they believe juveniles require. He opens up his courtroom to the media and court-watcher groups so that what he does in court can be watched and he can obtain external assessments of his procedures. "As soon as I hear there's a courtwatcher group in town, I call them and ask them to sit in and review my court." In his writings, he has urged that jury trials be authorized for juveniles as an additional protection against arbitrary judges and overreaching prosecutors. He embraces the treatment purposes of juvenile court laws, but acknowledges some youngsters are untreatable and merit punishment by the criminal courts. The humane New York Family Court Act, he suggests, does not say it will be enforced primarily against the economically disadvantaged, but this occurs.

McLaughlin extends judicial ethics on one score. He contends that, in dealing with children, a judge must affirmatively go out of his way to establish there is no prejudice one way or the other. So he will explore matters that would be passed over more quickly in an adult court.

Lawyers form his brigade for protecting children's rights and achieving their entitlements. Not any lawyer, but attorneys who will challenge the judge and the system to do what the law mandates. "Before I came here, there were few attorneys. The family court was a roulette wheel. No one could predict what would happen. When a lawyer would say to me in the course of a proceeding, 'Well, whatever you say, Judge', that was the last time he got appointed by me. He was trying to make me into the lawyer. But he was the lawyer, not me."

To McLaughlin, due process means fairness and fairness starts out with requiring a lawyer for every child. The cost to government in paying lawyers for the indigent is of no concern to McLaughlin; this is part of the governmental duty to insure justice. "Providing lawyers enriches a child's belief that he has been respected by the court." McLaughlin also contends that juveniles are more likely to comply with court orders when they feel they've had a modicum of justice provided.

In his court, the law guardian's function does not end when the judge has transferred a juvenile's custody to an agency for placement in a private or public facility. McLaughlin carefully instructs each child of his right to petition the court to modify or terminate this placement if he feels the setting is inappropriate, fails to provide him with the treatment he needs, or if he considers himself rehabilitated but is not allowed to return to his family. The child and his parent have the law guardian's card. McLaughlin's law guardians know that they must make themselves available to the child and have a duty to investigate and petition the court for relief upon the child's request. At such hearings, he has found sufficient evidence to transfer a juvenile from one institution to another, from an institution to a group home or foster home, and from a foster home to a group home.

Soon after he went on the bench, a private institution approached him and urged that he not advise the youngsters of their right to return to court. Juveniles would tell staff members that if they didn't do what they were supposed to, they would go back and tell Judge McLaughlin. McLaughlin countered that his purpose was not to interfere with the treatment of the children, but to provide them their rights under law. He asked that they check out the children he had placed against those committed by other judges. The staff returned to acknowledge that all of McLaughlin's youngsters had successfully completed the program. "The kids had done a lot of bitching. They had done a lot of threatening. But maybe this did some good."

McLaughlin has some trouble with the law that requires, as requisites for court intervention, that a youngster be found in need of treatment and that treatment services be available. He knows some youngsters are not treatable, and there is no statutory handle for him to transfer this youth to criminal court for punishment. Divergent cases illustrate his contention.

In one, he dismissed his own manslaughter adjudication of a child who had killed his father because at the dispositional trial there was insufficient evidence that the youth was in need of treatment or supervision. "This was an awful tragedy, but the mother fully supported her son under the difficult facts of this case, and the juvenile justice system operated properly. The boy did not need any help by the time the disposition occurred. This was not McLaughlin's idea of the way the system should work, but the people of the State of New York saying to me how it must work."

In the other case, McLaughlin placed the custody of a confirmed delinquent youth with the state youth agency. He escaped from the institution three days later, was recaptured, escaped again by stealing the superintendent's car, was returned again to the institution, stayed one night and left. Still at large, the state agency advised the judge it had discharged him from the institution's responsibility because he was untreatable. "This, too, was done by society's law. Untreatable juveniles should be transferred to criminal courts where society's right to punish depends on only one consideration, whether a crime was committed. Being untreatable was not this boy's fault. It wasn't society's fault either. It's like a very communicable disease for which society lacks a cure. That's unfortunate, but we can't let someone walk around in the community with such a communicable disease." McLaughlin has pressed this issue in extensive testimony before a legislative commission.

McLaughlin opts less than many juvenile court judges for asserting jurisdiction over status offenses, the non-criminal misbehaviors, such as runaway, incorrigibility, and truancy. He estimates that about half the runaway and ungovernable youngsters are desperately looking for help and will accept any help offered. "So why label them as ungovernable to give them help?" The other half includes those wanting everyone to get out of their lives. "They reject treatment. You put them somewhere and they'll run. They've got problems, but won't accept treatment. So why give them another burden to carry?"

He is chary regarding the effect of court labels. He suggests the worst label he gives out is abused child. Years later, this person may have graduated from teachers' college, goes for a job interview, and tells the superintendent she was an abused child. She doesn't get the position because the superintendent thinks previously abused persons will now abuse children. Ungovernability is another disadvantageous label. Years later this person has her earlier status interpreted by a potential employer as one who was sexually permissive, or in seeking a job with General Electric, will be rejected because of concern she will "foul up the computer paper". The least harmful label he hands out is juvenile delinquent. One can always say later that he had stolen a car when he was young. The potential employer's response may well be: "Boys will be boys."

McLaughlin is apprehensive about separating children from their parents for even brief stays in the attractive pre-trial detention facility. "Regardless of the sign over the door, if the key turns, it's a jail. It may be a nice jail, but it's still a jail. I don't want kids there. I want them out of there. My biggest hangup is that I will not permit detention unless there is proof under the statute. And New York's detention statute is the toughest in the country."

He is constantly in a cold war with the county commissioner of social services, "my biggest delinquent. They built the Panama Canal with less trouble then I have getting services for kids from him." With this and other executive agencies, he uses two primary strategies. One is his counter-irritancy program. The other is his recourse to written opinions.

The first approach involves inconveniencing the bureaucracy. "If they irritate me, I'll irritate them more." Soon after he came to the bench, he discovered a girl who had been held in the detention center for 245 days. He spoke with the agencies involved. They all provided excuses as to why they had not found a placement. "Since I don't eat lunch and civil service people like to eat lunch, I called a meeting in my chambers every day at noon time with between ten and sixteen people present, including the law guardian. I would call for progress reports. They would say there's no point in coming back tomorrow, they will not have responses to their letters. And I'd say you never can tell, you can make a phone call or something. Everybody came back and I'd make them sit there each day until two o'clock. It took just five days to get her placed. And you know what? That's the last time I ever had that problem, because they know that's exactly what I'll do."

A variation of this approach may take place when the social services department requests ten more days to find placement for a detained youngster. To force action, McLaughlin will set a hearing in two or three days, advising the department's attorney he will need to present his evidence at that time. "The law requires both that a child be in need of treatment and that treatment be available. If you have the treatment program, fine. If not, I will need to discharge and dismiss this case."

His more than forty published trial court opinions are the contact point for clarifying the law and procedures these agencies must follow. He knows, of course, that court decisions are not universally implemented by agencies affected by them. This is a further reason for his interest in developing a cadre of aggressive law guardians. One decision that undoubtedly alienated police officers and explains some of their antagonism toward McLaughlin was his holding that juveniles could not be interrogated except in the presence of an attorney.

Another McLaughlin ruling held that he could not constitutionally commit a youngster to restrictive placement under New York's tough 1976 Reform Act. Since the law mandates that minimum incarceration periods must be served as specified, no child can petition back to the committing court to modify the placement if treatment, in fact, is not being provided, or to terminate the placement because he has been rehabilitated. Judge McLaughlin concluded that such determinate sentencing is akin to criminal court punishments and that family court judges are precluded from administering punishments. Further, in his view, punishment can only be meted out constitutionally if there is a jury trial provision and the whole array of rights that accompany the criminal process. New York law denies juveniles the right to have a jury trial in family court. Accordingly, McLaughlin placed this youngster with the state youth agency under regular indeterminate provisions and not by the harsher, restrictive placement authority.

A ruling also took exception to the state youth agency's requirement that institutionalization be made a condition of probation. McLaughlin's analysis included a finding that probation in New York State is a voluntarily accepted status. Since the boy had rejected the probation offer, since the law requires that treatment be available for a youngster, since the state agency refused to accept the youngster for treatment purposes without a probation accompaniment, McLaughlin found it necessary to dismiss the case. McLaughlin's legal reasoning was reinforced by statements concerning the impact of a court label. The provision of treatment, presumably, outweighs the negative aspects of judicial intervention. In the absence of treatment, it is harmful to label a child. Since no evidence showed treatment would be made available, "the court will not countenance the official imprimatur of judicial action upon Anthony J.'s life." Standing on the law, McLaughlin forced the agency to bring its policies into compliance with law.

Ruling after ruling has coerced police, prosecution, and rehabilitation practices to conform to the letter of the law. He has consistently voided the informal approaches that for years went unchecked and those that had used the court's authority to fulfill what agencies thought was right for youngsters rather than what the law said was right. His decisions acknowledge there are consequences to his holdings that will pose problems; he may well suggest legislative changes in his opinions.

Judge McLaughlin believes that one of his most important rulings assessed the boundary line between reasonable and excessive corporal punishment administered children by their parents. Two separate cases were folded into this decision. His listing of factors to be weighed include a child's age, sex, physical and mental conditions, ability to understand or appreciate the correction, the means utilized, the degradation involved, and the purpose of the punishment. He then had little difficulty finding excessive parental discipline for the following: Twenty-six criss-cross lesions on a seven-year-old's back caused by striking with a branch, the child stripped to his underwear; requiring that children bend over and hold their ankles while keeping their knees locked for up to half an hour, one youngster screaming and another vomiting during the three or four times this method was used.

Juvenile court judges appear, today, to hear a growing number of cases involving the sexual abuse of young children. These matters, along with the brutal physical abuse of children, are particularly disturbing to judges, and not only to judges. One McLaughlin opinion details the cold written facts involving a sixteen-month-old girl who lived with her mother and her mother's boyfriend. Physician examinations found that a laceration had been made that extended from the child's vagina to her anus. Sutures were required. In addition to the 'episiotomy-like wound', part of the hymen was not intact, there were bruises on the labia, and old scar tissue from a previous trauma was noted in the vaginal wall. The mother's boyfriend, at the time, was on parole from prison where he had been incarcerated for raping an eighty-four-year-old legally-blind woman. McLaughlin entered findings that the child had been wounded by an act beyond her control, an act that occurred when no one other than the mother and the mother's boyfriend had access to her person. They had inflicted the injuries or allowed them to be inflicted.

Two guards stood behind the boyfriend during the hearing, and two other guards stood nearby. Still, McLaughlin asked whether there was any good reason the boyfriend's manacles could not be taken off? A guard complied with the judge's request. Before the hearing continued the next day, the sheriff came in to tell McLaughlin he was concerned that someone would be struck because the manacles were removed. McLaughlin responded, "I don't want him manacled as it is not human."

After the hearing, in chambers, Judge McLaughlin indicates this was probably the most bizarre sexual abuse case he'd experienced in ten years. He recounted other cases he could not forget: The nine-year-old girl who had gonorrhea occasioned either by her father, stepfather, or grandfather, or two or all of them; the sexual intercourse between an adolescent son and his mother; father and stepfather cases involving oral fellatio or anal intercourse with children.

But there are happier moments in his courtroom. There are the parents who benefit from counseling and parenting classes, reclaim their previous neglected children and do well by them. Other youngsters, legally freed from neglectful parents, succeed with adoptive families. Delinquent youngsters abandon law-violating patterns and proceed into productive young adulthood. There is satisfaction in the courtroom report of a foster mother who reports progress with her foster child and a strong interest in continuing with care until the child's parents are better able to reassert parental custody. There is a sweetness to McLaughlin's greetings to the foster parent and a warm cordiality expressed to the parents of a retarded youngster who have a question to ask about their child's care in a special educational setting. He busily makes notes in his record book during all of his hearings, sometimes holding the black pen in his mouth as he underlines a note with a red pencil, switching pen and pencil at a later moment to continue his record. Rather than use a gavel occasionally to call for order in his court, he will thump his desk with his ring finger that contains both his wedding band and college ring.

In chambers, he holds meeting after meeting with attorneys, exploring whether agreements are possible and, conversely, discussing the law that will govern a hearing. He often stands for these conferences, pushes to bring out the unresolved differences, reads out his earlier case decision along with other rulings and statutory provisions that will be relevant.

His chambers is also his workplace where he does his legal writing, oversees court statistics as administrative judge, holds numerous conferences, and is the dispatch and receiving center for each day's flurry of telephone calls. The New York Times is on his oval desk. There are the usual law books and other materials on the bookshelves and the diplomas and certificates on the walls. There are also framed photos: A boyish, crew-cut Ed McLaughlin as a soldier in the Korean War; Wendell Willkie on the candidate's podium with his bodyguard, McLaughlin's father, watching over the audience; the state senator who had opened the door to McLaughlin's judgeship.

How do you assess the effect you've had on this court over ten years? McLaughlin believes he has brought fairness to all parties. He has made lawyers as lawyerlike in this court as they are in other courts. He has brought court dockets to their best state of currency since the family court was initiated in 1962. He has uplifted the image of the family court within the overall court system. He is egotistical enough to believe that other family court judges are more observant of due process safeguards as a result of his insistence on these standards. He may have contributed to an accelerated construction of the new detention facility. "And by being a pain in the ass" to the department of social services and the division for youth, he has reined them in to better follow the rules. His legal decisions and their use by attorneys and others check bureaucratic inertia. The state is now represented by attorneys in all cases. They prepare the orders rather than the court. The attorneys must initial all draft orders they submit as a further step to accountability.

And how do other officials view McLaughlin's judgeship? Predictably, there are mixed readings. Criticisms or admirations tend to relate to whether one's organization or function gained power or lost power as a consequence of McLaughlin's administration. The views also speak from the particular bias of the observer.

The commissioner of the county department of social services, frequently in running battles with McLaughlin, was surprised McLaughlin would encourage that his viewpoint be solicited. He has "no great working relationship with McLaughlin and, no real communication." He also notes there is little communication between the administrative judge and the other judges of the court. "So even if McLaughlin's door were open, which it isn't, it wouldn't take care of issues with the other judges." He doesn't quarrel with McLaughlin's standards for his agency, but finds them unrealistic. The department is unable to consistently deliver services at the level and speed that McLaughlin demands. Regulations, civil service requirements, budget limitations constrain department performance below McLaughlin's standards.

Later, in response, McLaughlin asserts that he has to deal with constraints, too, the Constitution and the law.

The commissioner of probation is less negative about the administrative judge. On a personal basis, McLaughlin is "super". But the commissioner, as a professional administrator, is frustrated with the family court. He cannot recount a single meeting between all judges and his management staff since 1969. He regrets the judiciary's "benign neglect" of probation. There is not the joint policy development he prefers. McLaughlin makes unilateral decisions that impact upon probation administration. But the commissioner likes much of the McLaughlin approach: He treats probation officers as professionals, he's the only judge who will go to the county legislature and support the probation budget, he looks after kids' rights, he's interested in kids, he puts agencies on the spot to serve kids better, he doesn't overdetain, and he's not afraid to stand up in front of police groups and tell them he's opposed to what they're doing.

An experienced juvenile probation officer rates the McLaughlin years a net plus, but emphasizes there has been no picnic. McLaughlin's more contentious law guardians had overwhelmed county prosecutors who had been used to law guardians being "buddy buddy" with probation officers and social workers, allowing them to do whatever they wanted for children. Law guardians now fight for their clients and the lazy ones have gotten off the panel. This has prompted other judges to be more responsive to law. McLaughlin has made probation officers sharpen up their acts. Social studies are better prepared. A stronger case must be made in requesting placement away from home. Because McLaughlin is so insistent on following the law, a lot of cases are thrown out, the police are pretty upset, and the probation department has been bothered. He crammed the changes down everyone's throats. For a long time everyone thought he was crazy. That is no longer true, but they still think he's soft. He's certainly forceful in pushing everyone into the roles they're supposed to perform.

The sheriff likes McLaughlin from the old days when McLaughlin was his teacher. When issues arise, he finds McLaughlin cooperative and sensitive to departmental problems. "It was his knowledge of the law that burned up the cops. He would show them the law they had ignored for years."

The police lieutenant also holds a soft spot for McLaughlin from classroom days. He suggests that police officers used to get up in arms about juvenile crime, but now take this more for granted. He acknowledges that it's difficult for family court judges not to get in wrong with the police. Law enforcement officers want a kid put away, but fail to understand the judge often has no opportunity to do this under law. McLaughlin's smart, he quotes the law, he's never been wrong. And he is very strict about not talking with police about a case that's coming up before him.

Another family court judge appears to resent McLaughlin's aloofness from his judicial colleagues. He fails to join them for morning coffee, communicates mainly with them by memo, and holds no more than three *en banc* meetings per year. "I can go weeks or even months without seeing him. We don't question his intellectual, legal writing, or administrative ability. But we may read the statute differently as to the procedures required." The judge suggests that lawyers may be concerned with the way McLaughlin manages his own calendar and schedules too many sittings, but never question the quality of his trials or knowledge of the law. He holds admiration for the way McLaughlin has whipped the court's administration into shape.

A former family court judge, who now appears frequently in this court as an attorney and law guardian, expresses strong reservations about McLaughlin. It is obvious there is a gulf in their respective judicial philosophies. He suggests that McLaughlin hesitates to detain youngsters and never wants to put anyone away. He believes McLaughlin gives attorneys more leeway than they should have, does not hint to attorneys what his disposition might be if they fail to settle, and all this "screws up his calendar and forces more trials than necessary." Lawyers complain his hearings are often delayed.

The former judge sees McLaughlin as knowledgeable and hardworking. He will let reporters into the courtroom if they want to come in. He's obtained extensive publicity from his legal writings. And he's a pusher. He got the administrative judge appointment and pushed his way up to be chairman of the Family Court Judge's Association. "But don't think the police are not upset with his decisions at the detention stage and at disposition. He is known for putting kids back out on the streets, which he defends on a basis of law."

A private attorney, frequently appointed as law guardian, admires McLaughlin. He sees him as magnificent on the law, as one who enters decisions that are well reasoned legally but are equitable, and as a judge who doesn't need to please attorneys. Lawyers become irritated waiting for McLaughlin hearings. But this is a McLaughlin stratagem: To encourage settlements so as to conclude more readily the day's calendar, but also because McLaughlin believes that it is inherently better for parties to settle than for the court to rule. The attorney, who is law guardian for a number of Vietnamese children placed in foster homes, says that "McLaughlin truly loves kids. He will come down off the bench to talk with the children. He talks in a fatherly fashion without being patronizing. He explains everything to the kids in court. The youngsters are both respectful and relaxed with him."

Another law guardian praises McLaughlin's due process safeguards for all parties. His written opinions are useful to lawyers. McLaughlin is warm and friendly to youngsters and explains court processes to them; McLaughlin reached out to one boy, asking where he had gotten that wild T-shirt? His only shortcoming is that he schedules too many trials on the same day. But she would quickly trade that shortcoming for all of his positives.

The detention center administrator is a McLaughlin fan. McLaughlin convinced him of the importance of due process and the difficulty in obtaining its enforcement. McLaughlin administers the law with no exceptions; other judges find exceptions. McLaughlin forces proof that the high barrier to detention admission has been met; other judges believe a little dose of detention is good for a youngster. He makes decisions on the law and has no worries about the consequences; agencies complain because he forces them to do what the law requires or to do something speedier than they want to do. But he gets results despite their gripes. No kid has ever complained about McLaughlin. They know he likes them and will stick up for them.

A citizen volunteer who has worked with Ed McLaughlin on Junior League, court watcher, and other projects views him as "our primary professional and political ally." McLaughlin worked closely with the League in the development of a dispute resolution service project. He welcomed court watchers into the family court and met with them to review any questions they held or problems they had observed. Any number of citizen groups welcome his encouragement and support with their efforts to improve services to children and families.

A newspaper reporter notes that McLaughlin is always searching for ways to augment the court's ability to meet people's needs and to use the media to help interpret these needs to the broader public. Newspaper people see his court as a jungle, as a private court that is not to be examined, particularly with its large number of lower and lower-middle income people wandering about and whose cases do not excite an average reporter. But McLaughlin seeks out the press to publicize administrative changes and the new projects he always has going. Newspaper features that McLaughlin has stimulated have increased the court's visibility and reduced its cloistered nature.

McLaughlin is seen as energetic and ambitious, with a voracious appetite intellectually and in regard to the law.

His secretary, who carries a particularly heavy workload because of McLaughlin's position as administrative judge and his prolific writings, says, "It's never restful here, but it's never boring either."

Finally, his law clerk states that McLaughlin is absolutely dedicated to the concept of due process of law. He's got a fantastic memory as to cases, holdings, details. He understands nuances. He is extremely hardworking and a very good boat rocker. He has an ability to approach old problems from new angles. He creates an impression of energy wherever he goes.

And how does Judge McLaughlin sustain himself and retain a freshness under the demands of a relentless daily workload? He responds there is no boredom at all. He has no trouble with the job's demands. No, he never gets sleepy on the bench, but occasionally he likes to play a little game with the attorneys. He will close his eyes. They may think he is asleep. Then he'll ask a question that relates to the evidence presented half an hour earlier.

But if he confined himself to the minimum requirements of his task, "It could be a crummy job, like shoveling coal." He finds challenge in making this court work the way it should. He likes to uncover the legal issues that propel him to his research and a publishable trial court opinion. He enjoys being what he calls the yeast that facilitates the efforts of community groups to enhance the services his county provides its citizenry. And he enjoys the opportunities he has to educate, advocate, challenge, and cajole.

His written opinions are scholarly, logical, and follow the usual style, though his arguments and conclusion may seem unusual to some. His oral language is more picturesque. He talks of a person who is so thin you can hold a light up to her and read a newspaper through her. He tells of a case where both parents were so inadequate he would not give them a canary to care for. He prefers settlements with sexual abuse cases to avoid youngsters going on the witness stand where they must think they're sitting in the Gobi Desert all by themselves. He contends that judges are so enamored with removing children from their parents, that if you gave every family court judge in the state an armory, he would fill it. As to the consequences of court actions that result in forms of punishment more than treatment, he notes that punishment is seen as a bad word, but in his opinion hypocrisy is a worse word. He sarcastically faults the commissioner of social services for being keyed to take care of little children, but who sloughs off responsibility for those "teenage barbarians". He observes that the public rejects prison reform directions, "People feel better when they see an offender come off a chain gang, weak and chastened."

More of his mixture of knowledge, history, the role of courts, and humor are blended into his public presentations, as with one to a group of educators that asked for more answers from the court with truancy and school discipline cases. Here, McLaughlin starts again at the blackboard. He jokes that he does not spell very well and gets around this with his scrawl, obtaining the benefit of the doubt. He goes on to say that if a child is under sixteen and is ungovernable, parents can go to the state and have the state beat up on the kid for them. But if a seventeen-year-old girl is sleeping with her boyfriend, you've got to beat her up, the state won't. You've got to grab her, take her home, and chain her in the basement.

He goes on to describe that parents are liable for the willful negligent acts of their children, unless the children are emancipated. The upper amount used to be $1,000, then $2,500, and will someday go up to $10,000. No one ever pays this, but it makes legislators feel good when they raise the amount each year. Has anyone ever collected a nickel? If you bring suit, the parents say I gave up on Charlie three years ago, he's emancipated. McLaughlin adds there's an old saying in the law, you can sue the Bishop of Boston for bastardy, but there's no guarantee you'll collect anything.

He continues to disarm his audience as he comments about present laws that prohibit locking up truant and ungovernable children. A court is society's mechanism for using force instead of self-help. But since you can't lock up these youngsters anymore, children get the wrong idea about how society enforces its rules. One could make a persuasive argument that since force is now removed, jurisdiction over these children should be totally withdrawn from the court. He tells of difficult decisions he must make and obtains laughter when he says he would like to use dice, but they make him use rules of evidence. He places delinquent and errant youngsters into perspective. Just 2 percent of kids come to court for any reason. Last time I checked, 8 percent of congressmen had been indicted! He recommends a statute authorizing earlier emancipation, but cautions that if the bill's title is "Children Can Divorce Parents", the proposal will fail. He hasn't given the teachers what they expected, but they have experienced a man who understands their frustrations and whose bottom line is law.

To this judge who answers questions differently from other judges, there is one final question to ask. And what, Judge McLaughlin, is your advice to new juvenile court judges as they prepare to take the bench? First they should go to the bathroom.

CHAPTER 6

JUDGE JAMES S. CASEY: JUDICIAL RESPONSIBILITY

"Judges who handle child abuse and neglect matters need to learn at the earliest date how the social service system really works. One way they can find out is to appoint attorneys who are good advocates to represent the children and the parents. After a while, judges will see deficiencies that will disturb them. They will learn that the state oftentimes is a more neglectful parent than the actual parent. Judges need to follow up not only with an individual case, but to try to better the system by being advocates for children, for changes in the law, for programs in the community."

James S. Casey has specialized in the hearing of child abuse and neglect cases through most of his tenure since appointment as a judge of the Probate Court for the County of Kalamazoo, Kalamazoo, Michigan, in February 1976. Judge Casey hears other juvenile cases as well: delinquency, status offenses such as truancy, incorrigibility, and runaway, and the cases that make Fridays different from other days of the week — the adoption of children. But early on, he decided that abuse and neglect matters needed to become his priority.

He wanted to bring order into the complex social service system that works with these youngsters, their parents, and foster parents, and involves different agencies that offer a range of assistance in these cases. He believed that improved court procedures were necessary in establishing the proper relationship between the state and the family and that substantially more judicial time was needed to oversee case developments once evidence of abuse or neglect had been proven. He had a fascination for the law that governed these proceedings and a deeply held concern for the welfare of the children who were victimized by parents or others charged with their care. Today, despite his quite massive engagement, he remains dissatisfied with his impact on the social service delivery system. With other components of the court, for which he has been chief judge since January 1977, and for which his leadership has engineered any number of productive changes, the numerous attainments still fall short of his high goals.

Judge James S. Casey is a man with an extremely strong conscience. His perfectionistic need starts with his own labors. The court he directs is regarded as one of the better juvenile courts in Michigan. He needs it to be the best. But were this to be achieved, however this might be measured, the restlessness that characterizes Jim Casey would not yield to relaxation. He would then be beset by a new agenda to advance the court to greater heights.

Certainly, the responsibility of this office weighs heavily on many juvenile court judges. But Casey's drive is particularly acute. For him, the juvenile court is a personal possession. Behind the warm twinkle of his eye is a person preoccupied with obtaining the highest level of respect for this court.

He dearly loves his wife and six children, but carries the court's problems home with him. He will go each Monday to the Rotary Club luncheon to meet friends, old and new, and to hear a talk on something other than juvenile justice. Yet, he is there as Mr Juvenile Court, prepared to interpret why the court cannot order parents to pay for their youngsters' delinquency damages, since this is not authorized by law, and to respond to other questions regarding court achievements and limitations.

Quite frequently, he arrives at the court at 7 a.m., the first court employee to initiate the workday, and he may well be the last to leave the court. His evenings with the family are punctuated with court-related telephone discussions. He sits with his youngsters while they watch television but he is reading case reports in preparation for the next day's review hearings of children in foster homes. He is fond of writing out lengthy case rulings, no small amount of the writing occurring in his home study, but laments that he has been unable to take a legal opinion writing course that would help him shorten these tasks.

In strong demand as a teacher and lecturer at Michigan judicial institutes and legal seminars, and as a speaker in and about Kalamazoo, he periodically decides to reject such invitations then, invariably, is unable to say no. In a superhuman way, he accepts responsibilities and is an easy target for groups that solicit his participation. In his human way, Judge Casey has made a mark for himself and his court.

Casey first developed interest in a judicial career during his two-year service as a law clerk to a judge in the United States District Court in South Bend, Indiana, following his graduation, in 1961, from the University of Notre Dame Law School. In helping draft a number of published court opinions, "I saw the loneliness of being a judge, but I also saw that one could have quite an impact on the community."

He tucked the judgeship idea away for a while, went back to Kalamazoo, opened a law practice, began teaching business law part-time at Western Michigan University, then shifted to teaching fulltime and lawyering on the side. He handled some complicated estate cases and was appointed fiduciary in one matter that required unraveling extensive claims against a lawyer who had misappropriated funds entrusted to him by clients. He served, quite often, as guardian to persons in whose interest mental illness commitment proceedings had been initiated. He also served as guardian or attorney for children in the juvenile division of the probate court.

Jim Casey then made his decision about the future judgeship. Nine years into his full-time teaching career, he decided to resign his position in a year, enter full-time law practice, then run for the probate judgeship position when a current judge was expected to retire and create a vacancy. This scheme did not have to be put into effect. The judge retired earlier than had been anticipated and Casey was appointed to the opening by the Michigan governor. Jim Casey was intensely excited with his selection. He had been attracted both to the human side and the technical side of this particular court. His wife, Joan, recalling the family's delight with the judgeship appointment, says, "It was like he had become President of the United States."

Probate courts in Michigan may be unique. They administer the estates of deceased persons, and are responsible for proceedings concerning mentally ill and retarded persons and for safeguarding the assets of those persons. They also handle the range of juvenile matters from juvenile delinquency to child abuse and neglect, and they place the legal stamp of approval on adoptions. In recent years, these courts have also had to consider whether an abortion should be ordered with a pregnant girl who is a ward of the court, as with a child who had earlier been found neglected. In jest, but in reality, probate judges describe their courts as carrying responsibilities from pre-natal to post-fatal.

The Kalamazoo court then had a complement of two judges. The estates division was on the first floor of the downtown courthouse, the juvenile division on the fourth floor. During his first week on the bench, Casey sat with the senior judge to observe, make notes, and begin to learn the craft. Casey was to handle the juvenile division four days a week, the probate division one day. The senior judge did the reverse of this. Casey recalls an early problem that occurred in handling his first waiver case, a very serious decision as to whether a youngster should be transferred to a criminal court for adult holding. The problem arose not because he was perplexed with the facts in the case or the law, but because, in moving from chambers to courtroom, he had not fully buttoned up his robe. He closed the door on his robe, and continued walking into the courtroom only so far as this constraint would permit. "This was very embarrassing." Nonetheless, he became totally immersed in juvenile court work.

Jim Casey was unopposed when he was elected, in November 1976, to complete the two-year unexpired term to which he had initially been appointed. The senior judge did not seek re-election. His seat was filled also in a November 1976 election by the chief prosecuting attorney. Casey had quickly become the senior judge, empowered with the authority to determine his workload and that of the other judge. His mind was drawn to the probate procedures with its interesting legal questions, its oversight of estate matters, its guardianship of the rights of disabled persons. This involved interchanges with the trust departments of banks and one set of lawyers.

His heart was drawn to the juvenile division, a different set of interesting legal issues, lawyers who generally were appointed by the court at nominal fees to represent its typically indigent clients, the oversight of the court's probation agency, detention facility, and other social service programs, the opportunity to have quite a different impact on his community.

At first, Casey handled juvenile matters three days each week, probate matters the other days. His colleague took the reverse assignment. But Casey then became involved in what was to become an important achievement of his judgeship, resurrecting an old plan to build a new juvenile court center. The idea had been given up four years earlier when probate judges rejected the idea of asking taxpayers to underwrite a new building by way of a bond issue campaign. Case had discovered that federal funding might be available in the form of a direct grant to the county. He worked with other officials to revise the architectural plans, selected a different site, this one adjacent to the court-administered detention center, and finessed the $1,788,000 needed to build and equip the handsome new center.

With its dedication, in early 1978, Judge Casey and the probation staff abandoned the fourth-floor, downtown courthouse setting for the spacious site three miles away. No longer would it be necessary to turn off the air conditioner on summer days so that tape recordings of juvenile court hearings could be audible. No longer did three probation officers have to share one office. During the planning and building process, Jim Casey had decided that, as chief judge of the probate court, he would dedicate his basic efforts to the juvenile court division. A judge friend from another county refers to the Kalamazoo juvenile court center as "Casey's Castle". While his home is his castle, "Casey's Castle" is his home away from home.

The newspaper announcement of the grant award included a statement by Judge Casey that is characteristic of his sensitivity, certainly genuine, but also politically skillful. He expressed gratitude to the county commissioners for their forethought in applying for funding and to the two previous judges who had worked for several years and experienced great frustration in developing earlier plans for this facility. Prominent, also, was a recurring Casey theme, the need for coordination between social service agencies. The new building would facilitate a better-coordinated working relationship between the court's administration, its probation arm, and the detention facility and special child-care residential unit housed adjacent to the court center.

The Chief Justice of the Michigan Supreme Court spoke at the building's dedication. The public was invited to tour this new county resource. The two-story brick structure provides two courtrooms, three referee hearing rooms, probation and clerk offices, meeting rooms and lunchroom, and a Casey pride and joy: a nursery for young children. There, children are cared for while they or their parents await hearings. One of many grants he has obtained from the Kalamazoo Foundation furnished the nursery.

The new court center clearly meant specialization between the two judges and Jim Casey had made his choice. But he finds stimulation and relaxation in substituting for his downtown colleague during the latter's vacation or an illness. Casey seeks recognition not only as a juvenile specialist, but as one who is knowledged in estate and mental illness matters as well. In typical Casey fashion, he keeps abreast of legal developments with probate matters that are not juvenile in nature, putting in innumerable hours to build and retain expertise in this component of the court's work. Presenting a 1982 lecture to the Probate and Trust Section of the Michigan Bar Association, a prestigious group, furthered Casey's reputation as a more generalist probate judge.

The Casey judicial philosophy is not a complex one. It stems from the statute he works with and his own practical experience in knowing the court cannot do all things for all children. The Michigan code guides its courts to retain children in their own homes, wherever possible and to secure suitable care for youngsters who must be removed from parental control. Casey cites other statutory references in commenting that the first role of the court is to protect the community from serious juvenile offenders and to protect children from abuse and neglect.

A further responsibility is to help make sure that children who need services get services, offered by community agencies or by the court. He portrays schools and voluntary, non-coercive agencies as the first line in a community service network. Juvenile courts should back up this first line, but must resist being merely a dumping ground for cases that should be handled outside the court, but are not. A juvenile court cannot be effective, indeed, it is set up to fail, if high volume leads to mere court orders that are unable to bring about a difference in a child's life. Regularized legal procedures and lawyer advocacy are critical ingredients of the Casey stance.

Periodic court review of the extent court orders are, in fact, implemented is Casey's key to making the juvenile justice system function the way it is supposed to. For review hearings to work, court orders must be specific so that a judge or referee can determine one, three, or six months down the road whether the plan has been carried out, and, if so, have the anticipated results been realized. This review scheme seeks to force accountability with agency workers, youngsters, and parents.

Too often, however, a well-conceived and structured treatment plan is not executed as ordered and the easygoing Casey becomes perturbed. A probation officer has failed to file a school report. A social services worker has shortcut a counseling effort with a natural parent. Probation department deficiencies disturb him because the court administers this program and, as chief judge, he has worked arduously with probation managers to both improve and tighten how this unit functions. He refuses to discount county social services department failures, though they are administered by the executive branch of government, because he insists that he is a necessary party to information as to what happens with youngsters who have been made wards of his court.

Two case situations pop out of his memory in this regard. With one, he and the attorney were reviewing a late-filed report prior to a hearing to determine the disposition the court would enter for two neglected children. The report contained information that the children had been abused in a temporary foster home where they had resided pending the court's disposition. "The social worker had not conceived the idea that those children are wards of the court and had not reported this to me earlier. I had to order a complete written report for the next morning on what had occurred and why it had not been reported to me."

A similar case also found the judge the last to know, though this involved other foster children that had been abused by foster parents, rather than the child in question. More than five days of hearings had transpired without the agency advising the court that this child was being removed from one foster family setting to another. "At the same time we are intervening and taking children away from their parents, the state is unable to have this child in a setting where he can be raised properly."

Yet, child abuse and neglect matters can be still more complex and result in still more egregious consequences. It happens, in juvenile courts, that a judge returns a child to a parent and a more serious injury follows. Judge Casey has not escaped this painful scenario. True, the law directs judges to return children to previously abusive and neglectful parents at an early date unless a likelihood of significant danger awaits the child. Judges are also beholden to enter decisions based on the evidence presented to them in open court. The case of a child, given the pseudonym Terri by a Kalamazoo newspaper, continues to haunt Jim Casey and others who are interested in the intricacies of the law that surrounds the preference awarded families to raise their own children and the measures of proper state intrusion into the family home. A retrospective view, following the occurrence of a tragedy, often simplifies what happened and too quickly raises the finger that attributes blame.

Terri, in today's vernacular, is now a vegetable. Following her return to her mother's care under a Casey order, Terri fell down a flight of stairs at her mother's apartment, was blinded, and her vocal cords were paralyzed. Several surgical procedures offered no hope that she could be restored to the condition she experienced before the fall. A police department investigation determined that the fall was an accident, not a result of abuse.

Earlier, Terri had been abused by her mother. A hospital treated her for multiple bruises, her out-of-wedlock mother had admitted to abuse, she was placed in a foster home and later adjudicated a ward of the court. Terri was one and a half years old at the time. The abuse was severe, there had been broken bones, the mother had been biting the nails of the child to punish her because the mother believed she was behind schedule in completing toilet training. The child's nails were filled with pus.

The prosecutor did not ask to terminate the mother's rights to Terri. The county social services agency did not request this of the prosecutor. The case was a civil proceeding before Judge Casey. Because of the mother's admission, adjudication of wardship was entered and Terri was entrusted to the county social services agency. Casey ordered the mother into parenting classes, to undergo a psychiatric examination, to follow agency recommendations for counseling, and to be entitled to visit her child under the agency's direction.

Six months later, at the court's review hearing, the social worker recommended return of Terri to her mother. Casey was uncomfortable with this recommendation and called for more comprehensive hearings that took place over a two-month period. All experts recommended return. Only the foster mother expressed concern. She had suspected that Terri had experienced further abuse during visits to her mother's home. Clearly, the evidence favored return, and Casey entered this order. He also required a daily visit by the agency with the mother. Within a month, a sorely injured Terri was back in the hospital.

Social workers were later to report they encouraged the mother to put up a gate on the second floor so the child would not fall down the steps. She pledged to do this. No one had insisted this be done immediately. A lie detector cleared the mother. She had not pushed Terri down the steps. From the hindsight view, Casey contends the agency should just not have allowed this to happen. Caseworkers were also to acknowledge that on visits they had noticed the mother withdrawing from Terri, as she had done earlier before the initial abuse. The court knew nothing of this either. Casey learned of the trauma in the middle of his family's Thanksgiving Day dinner. He was to visit Terri a number of times in the hospital.

The press asked Casey to open the court record and he complied. The record and his notes indicate that he had prolonged the request to return Terri in order to hear four or five days of additional testimony. The social services agency was angry with Casey for opening the court record. They doubted whether in the future psychologists or social workers would provide reports and testify, were records to be open. The record did not seriously fault the social services agency.

Through a press account, which disguised Terri's name, the public better understood what was happening behind courtroom doors. The press talked with the attorneys and others who were involved, including the foster mother and the maternal grandmother. Judge Casey was not directly faulted by the press. Terri's court-appointed attorney, while critical of the quality of the testimony by the experts, supported the decision to return Terri on the basis of the evidence presented. Casey is reported as saying he had no other choice. He regrets the serious injury, but not the way he handled the case. The Kalamazoo Gazette noted the concern of several persons as to whether the agency might have an inadequate budget and insufficient personnel to do the job it was designed to achieve.

Casey suggests that no matter what controls are required, this type of situation will sometimes happen. "But, if you sit here all the time and think it's going to happen, you're never going to return a child home."

Later, the mother was to relinquish all rights to Terri. Proceedings were initiated against the putative father to terminate his rights. Terri is legally adoptable. But is she actually adoptable? A number of Kalamazoo County children and others across the country who have suffered severe handicaps have found adoption homes, often with the assistance of a wise subsidy law that assists adoptive parents with financing the special care these children require. Adoption hearings in the Kalamazoo court, that give more zest to Casey's court entry each Friday, from time to time include children such as Terri, some of the adoptive parents being assisted by subsidy funds.

The Terri case and observations arising from other abuse and neglect matters forced Judge Casey to recognize that other assisting persons were needed. True, the social services department provided parent aides for some families, to be a special visitor and advocate for them. The county had just one homemaker, whose role was to go into a family residence, assist with day-to-day home management, and thereby serve as a teacher and model. Parenting classes abounded, and were a routine part of a Casey order, but the groups involved parents with children of all ages, while certain presentations were largely age-specific.

He decided that what was needed was a Court Appointed Special Advocate program, citizen volunteers whose sole role is to protect the interests of a child and report findings to the court. Despite his affinity for the juvenile court lawyer's role, Casey knew the lawyer would not regularly visit the child or be sufficiently familiar with everyday developments. Casey notes, "Also, one day in court, a mother with a prostitution record was being grilled by the child's lawyer. She had done a generally good job of raising her kids except at certain intervals. But, tired of the cross-examination, she started asking the lawyer some questions: 'Have you ever talked to my children? Have you ever seen my children? Have you been to their foster home? Do you know what it's like in their foster home?' The lawyer had done none of this. With her rough language and all, it was a moving experience. That, plus my meetings with foster parents who told me they had never seen lawyers consult with the children or push for services that the caseworker wasn't providing, led me to the CASA program."

Judge Casey publicly announced this program, in late 1979, following a start-up grant award from the Kalamazoo Foundation of $10,000. In characteristic fashion, his press statement rejected criticism of attorneys. He noted that attorneys were doing an excellent job, but lacked the time to make the deeper investigation volunteers could provide. Without direct criticism of the social services department, he explained it would be one person looking at one child instead of twenty or thirty children being looked at by one person.

The volunteer was to form a close relationship with the child, serve as advocate for the child's needs, and inform the court about how the child is getting along in his own home or foster home. Casey had an additional interest with this concept, to open court proceedings to citizens. He wanted a larger public to know what happened in the court and to expand the number of informed citizens who might stimulate this community to better serve its children. But it has been difficult to recruit as many CASA volunteers as Casey wants. The commitment must be for at least a one-year period. It means involvements with serious family problems. In fact, only the most serious cases are assigned to the twenty volunteers.

However, these volunteers have been the link to the child and the child's link to the attorney and the courtroom. At review hearings, Casey gives special attention to their reports. When what they have discovered is communicated to the child's attorney and an emergency hearing is scheduled before the court, the welfare of a child has received better protection, affirming the merits of this program. Casey is committed to expanding this effort to assist children and the court. He has become the chairman of the CASA Committee of the National Council of Juvenile and Family Court Judges.

Jim Casey shifts to tell of another local program that is aiding his goal to bring greater accountability to the foster care system. Due largely to his efforts, Kalamazoo County became a demonstration site for a foster care review board. A half dozen or so citizen volunteers meet regularly to review the status of children in foster care and the responses of the children and their parents to the social service efforts that are to be provided. "The review board is discovering what I have been saying for a long time. The lack of accountability on the part of the social services department had frustrated us and now frustrates the review board. The agency's middle-management professionals are now hearing it from the lay citizens and this is helpful to me."

When Judge Casey enters his courtroom, his first action is to waive people to remain seated. There is enough formality, for him, in this spacious, contemporary, attractive room he helped design. Guards are not positioned in Kalamazoo courtrooms, though a sheriff's officer walks around the building during the day. Security concerns are not obvious in this juvenile court, but there is a button under Casey's bench to signal the sheriff's officer if an emergency arises.

Early in his judicial career, Casey invited staff comments on his conduct of hearings. As a professor he had found student evaluations of his teaching instructive. Feedback to a judge is more difficult to obtain, but one staff comment did change his hearing style. As in criminal courts, he would have juvenile defendants stand before his bench and strive to show interest in the youngsters, despite the awkwardness of this positioning, prior to entering his orders. Now, instead, all parties are seated at the large table Casey faces from a two-step-up bench.

What youngsters and others see as a now more confident Judge James S. Casey (as he enters the courtroom without closing the door on his flowing robe) is a kindly, full-faced man, "about five-foot-ten-inches tall, but shrinking". People tell him he doesn't stand up straight, but he has other concerns on his mind. Born in 1933, he appears his fifty years. His thinning hair is now gray, and parted left to right. His brown eyes look out through shell-rimmed glasses.

Though left-handed, he stretches out either or both hands in making explanations or asking questions. The United States flag is to his right, the Michigan flag to his left. A large metal seal of the State of Michigan looks down on the courtroom from behind Casey's chair. A staff member off to his left makes sure the electronic recording machine is capturing all in-court statements. Through wall windows he can look out to a cemetery across the road. A five-foot-tall potted tree stands near one window. There is also the lawyer's lectern, three rows of spectator benches in the back of the courtroom, and a large blackboard for attorney or party use. Unusual to juvenile courtrooms is a jury box. Michigan law provides juveniles with a jury trial right. Casey has held just one delinquency jury trial, but other juries have determined the facts with abuse and neglect cases in his courtroom. The jury box holds seven seats, one for a reserve, substitute juror. It is more often filled with the children and friends of adoptive parents who attend Casey's celebratory Friday adoption hearings. This is a cheery but stately courtroom.

In his adjacent chambers, where many hearings are pretried, Jim Casey is the discussion leader with attorneys and social service professionals. He smiles frequently, looks either to the record in front of him or into the eyes of the person he is addressing, jokes warmly, and maintains pleasant and collaborative working relationships. Meanwhile, his mind is filtering out the facts and hunting for the unresolved legal and social issues. He points an index finger in making an exception, listens attentively, sensitively asks for comments as to what he or others may be omitting, and indicates that disagreements should be frankly stated.

Framed color photographs of his six children are on one wall. His regularly used dictating machine and telephone are on a credenza behind his chair. His coffee cup recites, "Old lawyers never die, they just lose their appeal." In an alcove that is surrounded by three floor-to-ceiling cabinets of law books is a wooden bar, imprinted "Casey at the bat". County officials had this made and hung it over his bench at the time of the building's dedication. Deliberately, he omits framed degrees and certificates from his chambers. He believes these would make people less comfortable there.

On another credenza is a metal replica of Jonathan Livingston Seagull. For years this was his favorite book. Listening to the record of the book expands his enthusiasm to go further with his efforts . . . the seagull is pushed as far as he can go. Elsewhere in the chambers is a small model train, a gift from someone who knew about Casey's model railroad hobby. His chamber lacks windows. He laughs about providing an outdoor effect with Lake Michigan photos he has taken and a sailboat replica that reminds him of past vacations that involved sailing with his children.

One who enters his chambers or follows Judge Casey down the hall may well hear whistling. Whistling copes with some of the Casey tension. It is unconscious. His mother says her son whistles to control his nerves. "When he whistles, he has something on his mind."

What might be on his mind is an approaching neglected-child dispositional hearing. He may hold this in a jury deliberation room when the number of attorneys and social service personnel requires more space than his chambers provides. Here, as will occur shortly after in the courtroom, he hears the special language of this type of case. There is a report of early intervention, involvement of the child guidance clinic, case goals and participation in group therapy, minimum parenting skills and insecurity, trauma and head banging, referrals and resources, appropriate interactions and inappropriate anger, poor socialization skills and the need for emotional nurturing, the bonding process and permanency planning.

Casey has learned this language and the premises and operations of the human services agencies. He is too knowledgeable to be easily manipulated by the social work jargon. Rather, he manipulates agency accountability and the specifics concealed by the language. Further, there can be no complaint that his conferences or hearings are hurried. Social workers do complain that Judge Casey is overly reluctant to terminate the rights of neglectful parents. The Casey rebuttal is that he must rule on the evidence and that the law makes termination difficult.

Certainly, James Casey wants every child to have a stable, loving family. He recognizes that many parents fall below his own parenting standards, but knows these parents are still the natural family to a child who clings hard to a parental bloodline. Foster homes have their strengths and deficiencies. Children separated from their parents may languish between a series of temporary foster homes or even group residential programs. His own parents, whom he knew and loved, and his enduring experiences as a parent himself, form a refuge for him from the child trauma and parental shortcomings he absorbs daily at the court. Jim Casey believes it is important that juvenile court judges themselves be parents, and not just of one child. His six children have their differences. He knows stresses arise in loving homes. He can tolerate parenting styles different from his, but knows there is a line where children must be rescued.

James S. Casey was an only child. Born in Evanston, Illinois, June 8, 1933, his father was sixty-one years of age and his mother thirty-nine years of age at the time of his birth. The father's descent line was Irish, his mother's French-Irish. Casey was born two years following his parents' marriage. His father's first wife had died during childbirth some years earlier. Casey's father had grown up on a farm in Canada. He had enrolled in, but never completed, law school training in Canada and failed in his effort to transfer the credits he had earned to the University of Michigan Law School. But he steadily encouraged his son to pursue a career in law. His father was to be engaged in business in Grand Rapids, Michigan, and later in Kalamazoo, where he died, in 1957, at eighty-seven years of age. His mother, who had become a real estate broker in 1945, talks of Jim Casey's childhood, his father, and family life with obvious pride. As she reminisces, Jim Casey interrupts on several occasions to indicate he was not quite as good a boy as his mother recounts. His mother's sister intersperses additional memories.

"As a child, you could depend on him. He would be home when he was supposed to do his studies without being told." To this, Casey notes that he was less conforming during his high school experience.

"He had seven years of piano and organ. I would keep him interested in playing by darning socks nearby. He was very talented." Casey discounts any intuitive musical ability.

"He was an excellent student. He went to parochial school where a nun said she liked him because he had spunk, would discuss things, and tell her where he stood." Casey does not deny this.

"He had a wonderful dad. His father was a gentleman. When Jimmy was three or four years old, he was several blocks away from our house on his bicycle. His father finally found him and had to give him a mild spanking. Later, they would go fishing together. His father took him to Notre Dame football games and they listened to baseball games on the radio. Now and then they went to Detroit to see the Tigers play."

His aunt notes that James Casey always liked older people and would readily converse with them. "Our whole family loved him. During high school he would come by for lunch, have an omelet with us, and study."

His mother, Helen Casey, continues, "As a teenager, he was well thought of at school and he was interested in the girls. He was always busy with his school work and studying, along with his music. We kept him busy, so we had a pretty good boy, didn't we? We taught him that people were more important than the gifts they may bring him. Today, he thinks too much of others rather than of himself."

Jim Casey's favorite book as a child was about four little puppies named Wags, Tags, Rags and Obadiah. Helen Casey recalls reading this time and again to her son. "He liked the name of the fourth dog so much that it is surprising he didn't name one of his children Obadiah."

This was a gentle and caring household. Casey recalls his father getting up from the table after a meal, kissing his mother's hand, and saying this had been a very nice dinner. His father enjoyed telling jokes. Helen Casey indicates that her husband, like her son, could be angry about something or someone without others realizing this.

His parents were consistent with him. He recalls coming home once with flowers he had taken from a neighbor's garden. His mother rejected the gift because the neighbor's permission had not been requested. Casey adds, "My generation, in growing up, was more afraid about what would happen at home when we had done something wrong. Neighbors would tell your parents if they observed you misbehaving."

Casey recalls a police officer bringing him home one Halloween evening when he was caught soaping windows. "This scared me. I was very worried about what my parents might do or think." His memory also brings back the time he got kicked out of a high school study hall when he and others threw around pieces of corn as well as pennies. "We were just being bad." So he was transferred from the study hall to a typing class where, because of his piano playing experience, he became a rather good typist. This became an aid to his typing his papers at college and law school, and even the legal briefs he prepared as an attorney. He notes that his childhood pranks make him more tolerant of certain misbehaviors by youngsters who appear in his court.

At age five, Jim Casey had developed a severe problem with asthma. When he couldn't sleep at night, he would stay up for hours playing Monopoly with his mother. He was to outgrow this illness.

His parents were neither rich nor poor. They taught him responsibility. Instead of purchasing a bicycle for him, they made him earn the purchase price. They were generous with affection and encouragement. They provided him with his standard for family life, one he applies to his own home but needs to distinguish with court hearings.

Jim Casey's first five years of elementary education took place at a nearby private academy conducted by Catholic sisters. He wore the school uniform, believes he obtained a rather good education, learned French, and had no large problem with the tight discipline of this setting. For the next four years he attended the laboratory school at Western Michigan University, then went on to Saint Augustine High School in Kalamazoo, graduating in 1951. He went back and forth over the next five and a half years between Marquette University and Western Michigan University and Saint

Bonaventure University and Western Michigan University. It took this long to complete his undergraduate degree in early 1957. Part of the delay was due to Casey's uncertainty with his professional direction. He was, at different times, a pre-dental, pre-medical, and pre-law student.

He enrolled at the University of Notre Dame Law School in the fall of 1957, but left school before the end of the semester to return home and assist his mother. His father had died in the spring of 1957. Casey worked for a period at a local bank. His mother would give him his brown-bag lunch each day and say, "Do you want to carry a brown bag the rest of your life?" Helen Casey was doing reasonably well with her real estate brokerage, had relatives and friends who nurtured her, and insisted her son resume his law studies. This is what his father would have wanted.

Today, Judge James Casey enjoys confidence with his verbal skills. This was not always the case. During college, he was quiet in his classes, unsure of what he might say in front of others. He found a way to avoid the required college speech class. But something happened at law school when his moot court team was needled by another team. "This was my first competition. Our opponents said they would beat us because of their prior experience in speech and debate. I got mad, decided I would overcome my hesitancy, and I did. I worked hard at developing advocacy skills." An inspired Casey went on with his teammate to defeat a series of opposing teams and win the Notre Dame competition. The $350 prize was frosting on the cake for this senior law student who had found himself, or not quite. Casey's team lost out in the regional competition in Chicago. "But this all convinced me I was pretty good. My leadership was beginning to show. Soon, no one could get me off my feet." Jim Casey ranked an impressive number five in his senior law school class.

In Kalamazoo, during a law school summer vacation, he had begun courting the woman who was to become his wife. Joan Casey says, "We bowled each other over." She loved his enthusiasm, he was always fun to be with, was sensitive and eager to please, was intensely interested in her as well as in developing a career. Joan had graduated from Nazareth College, a Catholic women's institution in Kalamazoo. She never used her teaching certificate, but worked as a secretary at the Catholic social services agency. Both Joan and Jim Casey came from hard-working, financially conservative families. They were married the summer after his law school graduation.

Casey's job, as law clerk and legal assistant to the federal judge in

South Bend, paid $5,500 the first year, $7,500 the second. They banked the $60 a week Joan made as a legal secretary until, pregnant, she resigned. Their first child, Kathleen, was born in November 1962. Casey's clerkship provided opportunities to do extensive legal research and preliminary opinion drafting, observe good trial lawyers in operation, understand more about the workings of government. Some of the cases involved the prosecution of prominent public officials accused of corruption. Despite opportunities to join law firms in South Bend and in Champaign, Illinois, the Caseys returned to Kalamazoo, in 1963. They were close to their families, they liked their town, summer vacations on Lake Michigan attracted them. Still, Casey had qualms about opening a law practice back home. He says that at the time, "I was young looking." Friends and acquaintances would now have to see him as attorney James S. Casey.

The lawyer he joined, Harry Contos, Jr, talks about his early colleague. "His strength was with detail. His preparation was very thorough. He could analyze a legal issue as well as anyone. His intellect allowed him to dissect a law suit, come up with relevant issues, and determine what he needed to do with his case. He was as conscientious as any lawyer I have ever known. He agonized over problems, just as he does today as a judge. When he had resolved the problem, this stress would dissipate. There was no way this tiger could change his stripes."

Casey had some trouble shifting from the federal law clerk experience of working more extensively on a smaller number of cases to carrying instead a more general law practice, most cases being short-term in nature. What he particularly liked, however, were those cases that took him to the probate court, including appointments to represent juveniles. He knew that in time he would specialize in that arena, rather than generalize.

With the opening of his law practice, another opportunity opened for him. A lawyer acquaintance, who had been teaching a business law class at Western Michigan University, decided to stop teaching and recommended Casey as his replacement. For the next three and a half years, Jim Casey went back to his *alma mater* one night a week to teach contracts or agency or negotiable instruments at the University's College of Business. "The first night I taught I was more scared than at any time in my life." But he adjusted, was intrigued by teaching, and accepted appointment as a full-time assistant professor in 1967.

He enjoyed the stimulation of a university environment, had the opportunity to do research, liked the student interchanges, found teaching a challenge, and was aware of the university's plans to develop a law school. He could be in on the ground floor of the new law school. He was also able to maintain a part-time law practice, continue his developing specialty with probate law, and have enough money to take his growing family to the shores of Lake Michigan each summer. But the law school was never to be. The governor vetoed the bill that would have authorized Michigan's third state-funded law school. The legislature excised this appropriation when the concept was initiated a second time.

In time, Casey moved up to become an associate professor. He taught other courses: on the legal environment, business law, consumer law, sales, personal property, real property, legal controls of the business enterprise, and law and the administration of higher education. In 1971, he received the alumni award for teaching excellence, to which was attached a $1,000 prize. His interest in assisting with university committ e work, responsible participation, and leadership were also evident. He served on the admissions committee, the search committee for the dean of the College of Business, a faculty grievance committee, and was elected to the faculty senate, becoming its vice president and then president. Meanwhile, he was also carrying intricate probate court cases as an attorney. Also, he became a member of the board of directors of the Legal Aid Bureau and then its chairman. A news clipping announcing this appointment reports a typical Casey tactic. "The new chairman requested that the staff director draft proposed goals and objectives for the agency for the next two to five years."

Casey had been moved by his interactions with university students during the era of complaint against the war in Viet Nam. He identified with the students who were protesting at a time when the public could not understand opposition to the American involvement. This led Casey to a greater liberalism in his political viewpoint, and to a greater sensitivity to social issues, as well. It prompted his involvement at the Legal Aid Bureau.

There were other community efforts in which he was engaged. He joined the board of directors of Saint Agnes Foundling Home, chaired that board as it merged with Catholic Social Services, and then became president of the merged board known as Catholic Family Services. He also maintained bar association ties, quite predictably ending up as chairman of the continuing legal education committee as well as of the library committee.

In late 1975, Casey initiated his application for the about-to-be-vacated probate judgeship. A Republican, but neither a registered nor an active Republican, he obtained recommendations from local party officials as well as influential lawyers and citizens to the state's Republican governor. He emerged from the nominating commission interview with guarded optimism. The commission was comprised of eleven attorneys and one law professor. The law professor who ushered him into the interview had let him know that he was a fellow educator. An attorney member called him the next day to say Casey had done well. But the competition was strong and the three-month wait a lifetime until the governor called to signal Casey's appointment. Casey notes, "The five other candidates had better political credentials than I had. I viewed the appointment as a great honor."

He took Joan away for a brief vacation, but he took something else along on the trip, a cassette tape deck and an array of tape lectures on the law of evidence. His extensive lawyering in the probate court had given him security as he contemplated his judgeship. He felt less strong with his competency regarding technical evidence questions.

His family and friends attended the swearing in ceremony on March 10, 1976. His mother placed the black robe on him. The Gazette editorialized that the governor had made a "solid, interim choice." The new judge was forty-two years of age.

That he was unopposed in the following fall election for the final two-year term, and again unopposed in 1978 for a full six-year term provides testimony, according to community lawyers, of the respect Kalamazoo County holds for James S. Casey. One lawyer suggests that Casey probably doesn't have an enemy in town and is a judge who has escaped the usual lawyer criticisms of the judiciary.

Jim and Joan Casey are the parents of three boys and three girls, born from 1962 to 1979. A newspaper account of final son Matthew's birth reports the 5:30 a.m. dash to the hospital, the train that was stretched over the street crossing, and a frantic Casey's successful discussion with the switchman who parted the cars so the Caseys could proceed. The Gazette article carried a picture of Casey working at home on his model railroad hobby and a separate picture of Joan and baby Matthew. Asked by the reporter, "Did this experience lessen your enthusiasm for model railroading?" Casey retorted, "If anything, it increased it. Now I'll have three guys to help me."

The Casey home, ranch-style with a large yard, reflects the wear and tear of raising children. Kathleen and Molly, the two eldest, both study now at Saint Mary's College, an educational setting for women located across from the University of Notre Dame. Jim, Jr, and John were born in 1967 and 1969 respectively, Mary in 1972, and Matthew in mid-1979. The children's elementary and secondary education took place at nearby parochial schools. They lament that since their father became a judge, they have had to abandon their summers at the lake. Kathleen indicates that school associates began referring to her as the judge's daughter and suggested she must be different. "If my dad is a judge, then I must be a goody-two-shoes". Molly suggests that her associates were not really mean to her because of her father's status, but thought they were richer and therefore a little bit better than others.

Clearly, the children are proud of their father. And what have your parents taught you? Hard work, do your homework, get good grades, don't watch too much TV, no pot, drugs, or liquor, respect for teachers and for authority. What about discipline? Dad grounds us.

Son John, a promising young artist, tells more: "Dad grills hamburgers and chicken outside for us a lot in the summertime. And often he makes pancakes or waffles for our breakfast. He takes me to play ball, he buys me a hot dog, he takes me downtown to show me some of the new buildings. Last winter he helped us put up a large ice rink in the yard. We would ice skate and play hockey there, but it melted pretty quickly. We used to go sailing a lot at our cottage."

Joan Casey tells of her husband: "He's loving and very family-oriented, a good husband and father. He's very conscientious and hardworking, a perfectionist with his work. He seldom plays golf or tennis any more and we do not often go to the movies. His home is his retreat. We all enjoy his sense of humor. He's the head of the family just like my father was in our family. I prefer to be at home raising the kids and not to be active in the community. I appreciate that Jim doesn't drag me along to too many committee meetings. And his meetings are constant.

"But he's changed with his job. He's more serious. This is unfortunate because we don't see his sense of humor as much. Certainly he's not as relaxed. So many nights he brings his court file and work home." She adds that when they had first met years ago, Jim Casey had told her he could get by with three or four hours of sleep each night, but that he didn't tell her about the little catnaps he likes to take. Casey acknowledges he is a light sleeper. He will wake up in the middle of the night, turn on an all-night radio talk station from St Louis, and listen for hours. What he heard on this talk show during the autumn of 1981 made his usual difficulty in returning to sleep still more problematical. National attention had riveted on the Kalamazoo County probate court, not on account of Judge Casey, but because of a highly controversial case being heard by the judge of the recently created third seat of this court.

A neglect petition had been filed in that court division concerning an eleven-year-old girl. The girl was pregnant. The attorney appointed for the child asked that the judge order an abortion. The youngster was allegedly impregnated by a friend of her mother who had stayed with the family for periods of time. The girl's ten-year-old sister also was allegedly raped by the same man, but was not pregnant. The mother, divorced from the girls' father, held custody under the divorce. She opposed an abortion, though her view was never presented to the court. The girl was nineteen weeks pregnant at the time. The judge ruled, preliminarily, that he had no legal authority to order an abortion or to appoint a guardian to obtain one. Nine years earlier, the judge, then an attorney, had joined with his wife in submitting an anti-abortion letter to a Michigan newspaper. They had opposed abortion even with incest or rape. He had also signed a Mother's Day advertisement, in May 1981, opposing abortion, that appeared in the Kalamazoo Gazette.

Five days following the initial ruling, a full trial on the issue of child neglect began. The press, denied access to courtroom hearings by the judge, was highly visible in courtroom waiting areas, seeking information and disclosures from attorneys, social service workers, and court officials. It was not only the local media. Reporters from many other cities, even Canada, besieged the court. Helicopters carrying media representatives were landing at a nearby heliport and traversing over to the juvenile court building.

The prosecutor charged that the mother had allowed the alleged rapist to sleep in the same bedroom with the girls. The pregnant girl testified she tried to discuss the sexual encounters, but "mother stayed mad all the time", so she dropped the effort. The mother testified the man lived with the family for eight or nine years and she wasn't aware of the sex acts until finding out the eleven-year-old was pregnant. The judge ruled the girls had been neglected and made them wards of the court.

The lawyer for the girls asked that the court, as to the eleven-year-old, either order an abortion, appoint a guardian to make that decision, or give temporary custody to the father so the father could arrange an abortion. The judge stated he could not order an abortion unless it was to save the life of the minor. He ruled he had no authority to appoint a guardian. He didn't know enough about the father to determine whether he would grant temporary custody to the father. The judge continued the matter for fifteen days. Medical, psychological, and psychiatric evaluations were ordered. Meanwhile, the time clock was ticking away on medical abortion feasibility. Meanwhile, Casey's middle-of-the-night radio talk show listening yielded call after call on the pros and cons of the Kalamazoo abortion case.

The child's attorney, convinced that abortion was in her best interest, and concerned with the case delay, filed an appeal in the Kalamazoo County circuit court challenging the trial judge's failure to name the girl's father as her temporary guardian. While this was pending, the juvenile court judge took additional testimony at the continued hearing. Part of this concerned the social service worker's failure to obtain adequate information on the father for consideration by the judge. The judge entered no ruling at this hearing.

During this span of time, the twenty-nine-year-old "friend of the family" was charged with criminal sexual misconduct. He was later to be sentenced to seven to fifteen years in prison.

The attorney's appeal to the local circuit court was rejected, the circuit court judge deciding that the juvenile court judge had not abused his discretion in not appointing the father as the child's temporary guardian. Still, there was no final ruling from the juvenile court and the clock continued ticking. Her attorney then went to a federal court as the girl's pregnancy approached the twenty-four week legal abortion limit. The federal judge ruled that the juvenile court judge had violated the girl's constitutional rights in not entering a final ruling on the abortion question. His decree set a speedy deadline for a decision by the juvenile court judge. The latter judge appointed an attorney to represent the girl's unborn child. The child's lawyer objected, contending: "If you start weighing the constitutional rights of my client with the constitutional rights of the fetus, then you're fettering my client's constitutional rights." Several days later the judge's decision came down. He found that abortion was not in the best interests of the child. The decision noted that the risk of complications from abortion increases beyond the middle of the second trimester. The decision was to trigger other events.

Six nights later, nearly 200 citizens met in the public library to explore ways of ousting this judge from office. A request for investigation by the Michigan Judicial Tenure Commission was made. Seven months later, the commission determined there was insufficient evidence to justify taking action against the judge, although twenty-six grievances had been filed along with a number of petitions signed by citizens.

A case had also been filed before Judge Casey by the Kalamazoo Gazette asking that he, as chief judge, open the court file in this case to permit the newspaper to review transcripts and records. Two years earlier, Casey had issued a court policy, that courtrooms and court records shall be open to the media so long as names are not utilized. He then proceeded to authorize the newspaper to read the court files on this heavily publicized case. But several attorneys engaged in the hearing petitioned Casey to set aside this order. The statute provided that court records "shall be open only by order of the court to persons having a legitimate interest." Casey believed the newspaper had a legitimate interest in this case. But his final ruling set forth: "Since another judge is handling this case, he is better able to decide the questions presented by the requests to open the record and/or the courtroom. In fact, he has closed the courtroom. In fact, he has ordered the hospital not to disclose facts about the unborn child. It would be incongruous for me to open the record in light of those decisions." His initial policy directive had been published when he was the sole juvenile division judge.

In February 1982, a twelve-year-old mother gave birth to a five-pound-nine-ounce daughter by Caesarean section. In August 1982, this six-month-old little girl was made a temporary ward of the court by a visiting judge. The child was placed in a separate foster home from the foster home where her young mother resided. Two months later, the same visiting judge removed the young mother from guardianship of her child.

Casey's final opinion, that denied his authority to open the records of the other judge, reveals his deep interest in greater public understanding of the work of the court and of the toll this case had taken on the court. It states his belief that if the public is to misinterpret the workings of the court, this will happen in a "sensational case which is closed to the public." Conversely, "if the public is going to be aware of the process of the juvenile justice system and the work of the judges, referees, attorneys, and caseworkers, it will not be enlightened by a sterile article explaining the juvenile court process or the work of the department of social services." He added, "I cannot recall another case that has strained and drained the resources and personnel of this court as much as this case. It would appear from the publicity that the juvenile court handles no other cases. This case continues to have an impact on the work of this court, and as a result, an impact on all of the children and parents coming within the jurisdiction of this court. This is one case. It is an important case, but the hundreds of other cases in this court are also important to the people involved in those cases and the public. We must keep in perspective the total picture."

Casey indicates that he had become more reclusive during this period. He avoided public gatherings so as to escape needing to make or avert comments. Even on taking his children to a Notre Dame football game in South Bend, several Kalamazoo acquaintances had seen him and rushed up to ask about the abortion matter. A year after the abortion ruling, Casey had not fully recovered from the trauma this had brought to the court he loves.

Before, during, and after the celebrated case, Judge Casey was struggling with complicated but unpublicized controversies in his own courtroom, as well as his court administrative functions and the variety of teaching, committee work, and community participation that engages him. Certain of his written opinions tell us more about his workload.

One, a sixty-page ruling, had presented a different kind of custody question. This was a case "where childhood sweethearts reach a point of facing reality and a relationship of love turns to a degree of bitterness when they disagree on an important decision." The decision related to their out-of-wedlock child. The parents could not agree on the care of the child. The young mother petitioned the court to approve her relinquishing her rights to the child. She sought adoptive placement so the child could experience a father and a mother. But the young father wanted to raise the child. He believed that natural parents should raise their children. The parties had decided to become married on learning of the pregnancy, but the young woman later canceled this plan. The man sought counseling from a psychologist and his pastor, both of whom testified in support of his request. His parents offered to assist with the child's care and to provide financial assistance for their son who had just graduated from high school. Judge Casey ruled that the child's best interests would be served by granting custody to the father, but the custody grant must be deferred until the mother executes a formal release of her parental rights.

Another opinion recites the courtroom evidence and legal conclusions growing out of a series of hearings concerning the sexual abuse of two sisters and their two brothers. Probably, this grisly case was in Casey's mind when he suggested, that among the qualifications a juvenile court judge should possess, is a willingness "to listen to a lot of filthy, rotten, dirty stuff regularly, which is sexual abuse and neglect." The case also illustrates the uncertain validity of professional testimony that impacts the juvenile court hearing. The prediction of future behavior and the potential success of counseling intervention does, in reality, constitute a murky terrain, but is an integral part of the turf that is the juvenile court.

Judge Casey terminated forever the parental rights of the father to these four children. There was physical abuse by the father, for example, striking the children daily with a belt or a board. More important to the case was the sexual abuse. Court documents report that the parents forced all of their children to participate in sex acts with them and with each other. The parents also took pictures of some of the acts and engaged in their own acts in front of their children.

Out of fear, one girl allowed her father to have intercourse — often in the presence of the mother — and was forced into oral sex. When the daughter was injured from the incestuous acts, her father refused to allow her to seek medical attention.

Only the termination of the father's rights was before the court. The children wanted to live with their mother. A psychologist testified that the mother's fear of physical abuse of herself and the children was the motivation for her participation in the sexual abuse of the children. Therapy for the mother was recommended and her prognosis was held to be good. A second mental health professional testified that the mother could become an effective parent with the help of psychological counseling and assertiveness training. The mother testified she would cooperate fully and would now protect the children.

Based on this testimony, Judge Casey approved the return of the children from their foster homes to the mother at times seen as appropriate by the social services worker. He ordered the mother to continue individual mental health counseling, directed counseling for the children, that the counseling agency establish a sex education program for the children, and that a parent aide be assigned to the mother. He ordered the mother not to live with a male companion as long as the children were in her home and strongly recommended that she not establish new relationship with other men whose influence might be detrimental to the children.

Less than two months after the children were returned to their mother, a further complaint was filed. A man was living with the mother in the home. One daughter had to repeatedly fight off advances made by this man to force her into sexual intercourse. When she refused, he would slap and punish her. When she advised her mother, the mother denied that this could be true and refused to intervene. The adults frequently drank alcohol in the home, sometimes to excess. At Christmas time, the mother visited the father at the local jail where he awaited prosecution and had the girls wave to their father from the parking lot. The father, who had threatened suicide, was transferred to a hospital bed where the mother took the children to visit him. The mental health counselor testified that there had been two counseling sessions and nine other appointments that were canceled or ended up as "no shows". The court record recites the criminal history of the mother's live-in lover, which specified eleven criminal offenses aggregated over a twelve-year period.

This time Casey terminated the mother's rights to the children due to the blatant violations of his orders and the entirety of the evidence that the mother had caused or allowed the long-time neglect and abuse of the children. His ruling noted that the children's environment "was so indecent, so perverted, and so immoral that there is great likelihood that they will suffer permanent emotional damages." The children were placed in the permanent custody of the court so that long term planning could be initiated. The father, prosecuted in criminal court for sexual violations of the children, was convicted. His year in jail pending trial and sentence was equated as his sentence and he was released.

Judge Casey, of course, is deeply concerned with child abuse and neglect in all the forms this takes. How can abuse and neglect be reduced? He suggests the best way is prevention and that a practical type of family life education should begin with kindergarten and continue through high school. "A case worker recommends parent training with every single case of child abuse and neglect. And that's supposed to solve it. It often doesn't. But if it helps, we're solving it twenty-five years too late. It's pretty hard to change values, but we have to start someplace and that place is the schools, so that eventually we'll have new families better trained in parenting."

Casey wants to see more homemakers assisting neglecting parents in their homes and has high regard for parent-aide volunteers who visit the parents, befriend them, and talk over with them the raising of their children. He is concerned that social services workers have become more like case managers than case workers. They arrange the parent training, the counseling, the medical, psychological, and psychiatric evaluations or treatment, but provide too little direct service. He considers that most neglectful parents need "basic simple stuff, but we make available too much highfalutin'-type stuff. These parents need assistance with how to get along from day to day, to survive, how to keep a house, cook meals, supervise kids, arrange medical appointments."

Jim Casey believes that social agencies have become excessively reliant on psychological and psychiatric examinations and on the usual recommendation for follow-up mental health counseling. This should be used more selectively. More often, evaluations only confirm a lot of what is known. More relevant is the human touch, the one-to-one assistance that homemakers, parent aides, and social workers can provide.

Above all, Casey wants greater coordination of services to these children and families by the police, prosecutors, public social services agency, private childcare agencies, the court, and medical and mental health services. There needs to be improved case collaboration, clarification of service needs, prioritizations, and community provision of programs for particular groups rather than just working with each case individually.

After three years of effort, he has set up a broadly-based coordinating council. The council's focus will be on abuse and neglect, but is also to include adoption and delinquency. Assistance he obtained from the League of Women Voters finally brought the council into being. Agency heads comprise the council. The power people are necessary to this venture; assistants and middle managers are not welcome. Citizens intertwine with the council as task forces spin off to address particular areas for assessment and coordination. He is hopeful.

Judge Casey considers that citizen involvement is critical in the abuse and neglect arena. Citizen efforts helped establish another project, a child abuse and neglect council in Kalamazoo. The council annually sponsors a "You-Can-Help-Week". At that time, a speaker's bureau widely interprets needs and services. An expert is brought in to more formally address these issues. There are spot radio announcements along with question and answer programs and certain television programming. As expected, Casey has participated in media ventures.

All of this helps bring more cases to official attention. More children are now aware of the impropriety of sexual abuse and are reporting this. More aware teachers are reporting more abuse and neglect. Whether or not there is more child abuse and neglect, more is being reported. And he does give high marks to social services department screening efforts. Typically, the more serious cases are brought to the court's attention. No longer do "dirty home cases" dominate the court's calendar.

But he wants more volunteers working directly with these families and their children, in being special friends, to transport people for medical appointments, and to assist as a Court Appointed Special Advocate for children.

It is not that middle- and upper-income families do not neglect their children, though the forms this takes are somewhat different from the cases that Casey sees. These families utilize private medical and counseling resources and other alternatives, whereas the poor families seek out the public agency help or the public hospital examination that may well bring them into the juvenile court system.

All juvenile codes recite that a purpose of the juvenile court is to retain the family as a unit or to reunite the family members when there has been a separation. There are exceptions to this, of course. Some abused or neglected children never return home. Casey's orders, with a child placed in temporary foster care, specify the components of a plan aimed at the return of the child: The parents will counsel with a designated psychologist each Saturday morning at 11 a.m., the mother will obtain specified medical treatments at a specified hospital and will take her medication as prescribed, visitation with the children will be at the family residence one half to one day each week and the visitation will be supervised by a caseworker or agency volunteer, the parents shall attend parenting classes at the time and place scheduled by the caseworker, the parents shall maintain contact with the caseworker at least weekly, the parents shall attend all school conferences, the father shall file a written report each two weeks with the case worker detailing his efforts to find employment, a further review hearing will take place three months from date.

At each review hearing, Judge Casey is looking for the earliest return of the child. If return is not recommended, why not? If the parents are not complying with the order, why not? If the social services department is not obtaining the services ordered, why not? Deficiencies and failures occur in the execution of these plans. But even where there is full compliance and apparently stabilized progress, the judge who orders the child back home still takes chances. Parents may comply with every single court order, but there is no exact way to measure whether parenting classes have truly helped make parents better parents or whether counseling programs have indeed changed people's behaviors.

A judge tries to reduce the risks but cannot eliminate all risks to the child. And Casey notes that children sometimes suffer subsequent victimization in a different form. A father or stepfather abuses the child. The child is removed from the home. The mother will not separate from her abusing mate. She lives with him during the long wait for a criminal trial. She sits with him at the further hearings in juvenile court on the civil neglect matter. The child wants to live with her mother. But the court will not permit this so long as the father or stepfather remains with the mother. So the child must remain away from her mother. Further, the child has to testify in open court after she has earlier been questioned by police, social workers, a prosecutor, an attorney, a guardian, and others. "The child wonders if anyone believes her. She feels alone."

Casey experiences disgust and, indeed, anger at certain hearings. He has trained himself to recognize these feelings, deal with them, and do his utmost to look at the facts objectively. But Jim Casey is a feeling judge. Any number of these hearings get him down. He wants more for children than they are obtaining. He wants the happy home he experienced as a child. But his feelings turn to joy in his role as the adoption judge, particularly when the chosen child is one who had suffered abuse and neglect from a natural parent.

Observed in the Casey courtroom, waiting for the judge, is an adoptive family Casey knows well. Sitting in five chairs in the jury box are five youngsters, ranging into their teens, subjects of earlier Casey adoptions. Each has a physical handicap, or had earlier, significant emotional disturbance, or had been severely abused or neglected. They are smiling and laughing as the judge enters and is caught by the adoptive father's movie camera. Casey beams. A six-year-old girl in a yellow dress with a yellow ribbon in her hair and holding a red carnation climbs up to sit on the judge's lap. The adoptive mother uses a polaroid camera to preserve this moment for the family photo album.

The judge hears the report from the social worker recommending the approval of final adoption papers. He announces his pleasure at seeing "all of these good-looking children again." He signs the order, observed by the cameras. He steps down from the bench and announces that "You kids make me awfully happy." By now, everybody has come up front; pictures are taken, amid smiles and laughter, of the judge with all of the children. A court worker takes the next photo, the adopted child in the judge's chair with the judge and the adoptive parents encircling her. Casey is moved, obviously, and he is also at his best as he jests warmly with everyone. As a finale, Casey takes a picture of the entire adoptive family. He waves good-bye, saying, "Kids, you have made my day a happy one." The adoptive mothers tells him the family has made a scrapbook of all the adoptions.

This was a subsidized adoption, what Casey calls the best welfare program in the state. "You wouldn't believe the kind of people that are so devoted and give so much love to children with severe physical deformities and difficult emotional problems. They give them more love than anyone could give a child in an institution. It's a lot cheaper. And it has helped keep natural siblings together." The six-year-old girl in the yellow dress had joined her natural sister in this adoptive home. Another Casey adoption had involved seven siblings, all adopted by one family.

Another weekday that is different for Casey is Mondays, his administrative day. His administrative function is not limited to that day of the week, however. Most workdays begin between 7 and 8 a.m. with a conference with the juvenile court administrator. They usually confer after 5 p.m. as well and often during the day. Casey thoroughly enjoys being chief judge of this court and has been key to any number of projects that have improved the court's administration, though he remains restlessly dissatisfied with achievements to date. One of his early successes was recruiting and employing a highly competent court administrator. Together they are responsible for an annual budget that approximates $3,200,000. The court administers probation services, the detention center, foster homes for delinquent and status offense youngsters, a special residential program for these youths, and other community-based programs. Casey clearly understands where his responsibility ends and his administrator's begins. Judges set policy; administrators operationalize a policy. Judges may advise but not interfere with operations.

Casey believes he pretty well practices what he preaches when he says the chief judge needs daily communication with the administrator and must listen to that person's advice. Further, the judge should not create an environment where the administrator is to just blindly follow what the judge tells him to do. "The administrator shouldn't be so awed by the judge that he's not willing to tell you you're off base with a crazy idea."

Management achievements are impressive here. Some of these are showy, as with the word processing equipment and the computerized information system that helps the court keep track of its caseflow and enables instant retrieval of children's prior delinquency and court records. Vital, but less visible, are the prioritization guidelines for detaining youths that have cut back significantly on the detention of lesser juvenile offenders. This achievement coordinates with new court programs that serve youngsters in their homes, in lieu of detention, and serve other youngsters to avert the need to bring their cases into the formal court stream. Any number of other changes, from simplifying and modernizing forms to classifying youngsters for more intensive rather than less intensive probation services have been accomplished. Yet, the Casey conscience is relentless. Each slip-up in the system troubles him personally, each project that takes more time than anticipated forces him to question his administrative talents. But he knows he has effective management capabilities, as well as strong skills on the bench and in the community.

His admiring secretary successfully nominated Judge Casey as top boss of the year by the local chapter of the National Secretaries Association. The association cited Casey's achievements in community and public affairs. His secretary notes that her boss is a pleasure to work with, but a challenge. The challenge is the constant barrage of dictated memoranda, reports, directives, and expansive trial court decisions. She doesn't have to remind him to return phone calls or to complete certain tasks by a specified date. Jim Casey does this conscientiously, if not compulsively.

His regular telephone interchanges and meetings with judge friends in other districts are another joy of his job. His legal head is in demand from other judges who call to discuss pending cases. They interchange, also, to discuss upcoming educational conferences for which Casey is a frequent presenter and planning committee member. Since he takes responsibility seriously, requests for his teaching, speaking or committee participation are endless. When, in a teaching role, Casey is presented with an honorarium, his typical gesture is to transfer this to the court's trust fund used to assist with the special needs of children that cannot be obtained from budgeted monies.

Casey, in meetings, is an activist. Here, as with the administration of his court, he is very aware of costs to a county and a state that are facing economic hard times. Participating in a meeting of child abuse and neglect workers from different agencies, he suggests ways the social services department and court can utilize a specialized clinic at a nearby hospital. But then he checks out with his administrator whether the court has funds to pay for the referrals it makes. He suggests the use of an interagency, interdisciplinary group to perform case reviews prior to and at different stages of the court process. His comments reflect intensive knowledge of different agency programs. His tone is positive. His style is suggestive, not insistent, not dominating. The meeting is in the court building. Casey encourages community agencies to meet there.

He joins another meeting of court supervisory personnel as a sheriff's officer demonstrates and describes the value of videotape to law enforcement officials. Casey suggests to the group a formalized use of videotape for the pre-trial filming of the examination and cross-examination of child victims of sexual abuse and, otherwise, with physician witnesses. This could be less painful for the child, less inconveniencing for the physician, more efficient for the court. He notes the court purchased a videotape presentation concerned with the termination of parental rights for use with staff training and, characteristically, adds the court should use videotape more with staff development.

At a luncheon with the director of the children's unit of the Western Michigan State Psychiatric Hospital, Casey is briefed on a proposal for a new children's psychiatric facility. Other mental health groups consider that the projected eighty-bed facility is too large and too costly. Casey urges greater communication between different mental health organizations so that agreement can be obtained and a common front presented. He emphasizes one of his common themes, that of coordination between the different agencies so that clients are better served.

At an evening meeting of the county criminal justice commission, also held at the court, there is a presentation of the prosecutor's victim assistance program. Casey recommends that a staff member of the juvenile court be part of the committee to examine the potential for central videotaping of child sexual abuse victims to avoid multiple interviews by different functionaries.

At a meeting of probate judges in Lansing, the state capital, it is clear that Casey, as always, has done his homework. The judges are planning an educational conference that will focus on the court's juvenile jurisdiction. Casey, also on the planning committee for an earlier scheduled conference concerned with the entire range of probate court jurisdiction, describes that program so that coordination can better occur with the juvenile jurisdiction program. Casey, more than any participating judge, contributes ideas to seminar planning. He asks for staff comments on budget and faculty, synthesizes the discussion, then makes a number of suggestions to staff for further planning of the conference. Here again, Casey asserts leadership, enjoys the people he is working with, is looked to repeatedly for advice.

Casey's primary communication form is verbal, not written. He lectures from notes. He has not written articles for journals or law reviews, nor is a press release a customary vehicle for him. But several written Casey formats tell us more of this man's values, beliefs, and concerns.

He did write out a brief speech he presented on Law Day, in 1976, in Bronson Park, Kalamazoo. He used as his theme remarks made by Abraham Lincoln in this same park in 1856. Lincoln there referred to the great principle of equality found in the Constitution, the safeguard of our liberties. Casey noted that at the time of the Lincoln presentation, all persons were not equal, many were slaves. The Fourteenth Amendment was adopted later to bind the states to due process of law and equal protection of the laws. Casey continued that not until 1954 did the United States Supreme Court rule that there shall be no public school segregation on the basis of race. He commented the struggle was continuous to achieve for everyone the reality of the principles of the Constitution and the ideals of Abraham Lincoln. He warned that, if we stopped this pursuit, we are in trouble. Neither is society static nor are definitions of due process and equality. A commitment to the rule of law assists in attaining the goal of liberty for all.

Casey's advocacy of constitutional precepts is also evident in his 1980 presentation to the county board of commissioners that successfully urged board approval of a third judge for this court. He noted that the court "is totally committed to the judicial protection of human rights, whether it be a two-year-old abused child, a fifteen-year-old deliquent, or a mentally ill person." The third judge was necessary, he added, to help the court deal with its increased caseload and to help orchestrate effective early intervention with families so "we will be able to break the cycle that goes from abused/ neglected child to delinquent child to adult criminal to abusing and neglecting parents."

Casey's message contained in the court's 1979 annual report also records his concern with the cycle of neglect. "The juvenile court, which is at the vortex of the community's delinquency and abuse/ neglect problems, must be able to act swiftly and at the same time comply with due process of law." He adds that "We have learned from experience that neither 'getting tough' nor 'mollycoddling' provides exclusive answers to the many problems of youth who get involved in delinquent behavior."

His 1980 annual report message emphasized coordination. "The components of the juvenile justice system and the social system can no longer afford to function independently of each other. Unity of effort at all levels of the system is required to overcome escalating juvenile delinquency and child abuse problems." Another part of the Casey belief system is presented, "We must seek innovative ideas, though we must seek those ideas which will work when they are applied to the community's changing needs." He is an innovator. But positive results are more important than the innovation.

A year later, he published his concern about confidential court hearings in the annual report: "The secrecy now mandated by the statute has resulted in the curtailment of knowledge to the general public of a system which has a continuing definite impact on each and every one of our lives. It is more difficult to understand this system if one does not continually have an opportunity to read and hear about both good and bad aspects of the system, based upon factual accounts rather than rumor or hearsay." Jim Casey believes in the First Amendment as well as the Fourteenth Amendment.

And what do others say about this hardworking judge? The views contain considerable consistency. His judicial colleague, who handles the estates and disabilities section of the court, says that Carey is a workaholic, meticulous, a perfectionist. It is hard for Casey to delegate, he commiserates as to why he doesn't delegate more, and when he does delegate he fails to recognize that performance might not reach the level he could achieve himself. He sees Casey as knowledgeable, having a good analytic mind, and a good legal opinion writer. His only vices are his exaggerated virtues. He is very anxious to please and that is both good and bad.

His old law practice associate suggests that ever since he has known him, Casey has been like a bulldog when he undertakes the study and analysis of a matter. He cannot rest until this is finished. He agonizes over problems and cannot let go of these until he has reached his decision and acted on this. "He drips blood." Casey has an excellent judicial temperament, has great compassion, and "is a damn good judge."

A lawyer, frequently in Casey's court, says he is critical of judges, but has nothing but compliments for Casey. "He enjoys the best reputation among all judges of all courts in this county. He's just very, very good. He's well versed in the law, sensitive to all viewpoints, will stop specious arguments, will not allow lawyers to harass witnesses, is consistent, and is eminently predictable. He builds an impeccable record. I always get his orders in a couple of days, while from other courts I wait and wait. Social workers fault him as hesitant to terminate parental rights, but his legal decisions are sound as to when he can and cannot terminate rights."

The lead juvenile prosecutor is bothered when, on entering the courtroom, Casey signals everyone not to rise. The prosecutor's respect for Casey makes him want to stand for this judge when he enters. The prosecutor lauds Casey's knowledge of juvenile law, his dignity, and quiet control of his courtroom, his giving reasons for his decisions, and his encouragement of full-scale advocacy by lawyers. The prosecutor once accompanied Casey to the annual dinner that is given for the natural children of foster parents who care for foster children. Casey took the time to have his photograph taken with each child. Finally, "Judge Casey takes a fierce pride in this court and showed a lot of discipline in regard to the abortion case while feeling a great deal of hurt."

A private agency social worker considers him an excellent judge. She likes the respect he communicates to foster parents, finds him extremely thorough and conscientious, was upset about a decision where he did not find sufficient proof to terminate parental rights, but "he's super — I love him."

Casey's detention center director refers to the chief judge as "the leprechaun of juvenile justice". He sees Casey as careful, one who doesn't shoot from the hip, and emphasizes Casey's compassion for people and his high expectations of staff. When he identifies staff shortcomings, he is fair, firm, and very thorough. "He can be madder than hell at you for what you've done, and then it's over." The director also volunteers that Casey is very concerned with the court's image in the community, how hard Casey has worked personally to expand community respect for the court, and his shortcoming with delegating responsibilities to others.

Finally, his administrator states that Casey was the reason for his taking this position and that he is a blessing to work for. He doesn't preempt the administrator's role and does delegate 99 percent of the administration. He smiles in saying that: "The judge is much better now. He doesn't come in as often at 6:30 in the morning and work at the court till 10 p.m. or come in on Saturdays. But Casey has to learn to relax more. He has a lot of charged energy and so many things he wants to do, but the minute he gets free time, he volunteers for something else."

Jim Casey acknowledges that he's a worrier. He retreats more into his home and family on weekends. But he experiences challenge rather than boredom with his work. He is preoccupied, but he likes what he is preoccupied about. He sees hope with young people and wants to assist with their futures. He thoroughly enjoys being a pivotal person in his community and is constantly stimulated by the administrative dimensions of his chief judge role. And he does have victories.

He tells of an unusual adult adoption that recently occurred in his court. A foster child, immediately on turning eighteen years of age, petitioned to have her foster parents adopt her. Abused by her natural parents, termination proceedings had never been achieved. The girl, now an adult, in effect achieved termination and the legalization of an adoptive relationship. Forty persons watched him sign his James S. Casey. The next day he received this note. "Judge Casey: Thank you for being an understanding judge, especially for rushing the adoption through so fast, and before my graduation, and especially before the foster parent and family dinner that had meant so much to me. Thank you. Love."

CHAPTER 7

MEETING *EN BANC*

These five judges are strangers to each other. There have been no interchanges between them. If they were to sit down together to discuss their judging and their views, this is what we might imagine they would say.

Judge Casey to Judge Garff: You're the senior jurist of our group. So for the first round of this discussion, you should have the first say. What has your nearly quarter century as a juvenile court judge taught you about using this position of trust effectively?

Judge Garff: I'm not the bashful type and, as usual, there are lots of answers I could provide. But let me concentrate on one, the judge as the common denominator with the child. Let me use the example of the repetitive juvenile offender. Early on, probation officers, the first line of defense, have to involve the child as well as the parents, and have access to community resources that may be available. With recidivism, the question becomes whether probation should be continued and additional sanctions and resources added or whether out-of-home placement is in order. With a further reoffense, commitment to a state program may be indicated and one particular state program may appear more productive than another. Different agencies and agency workers are involved in this progression and the judge is in the best position to assess the strengths and weaknesses of these complementary approaches. In a hundred different ways I've learned the advantages and disadvantages of different programs and their fit with particular youngsters. In the eyes of the juvenile and of the community, the judge is the stabilizing factor. You get consistency by having the same judge deal with the same case over the period of time the court is involved. Chronic offenders learn how to manipulate the various agencies and workers to advantage, but hopefully the judge is above this type of manipulation and will add a considerable measure of consistency to the total program. I'm not sure Judge McLaughlin agrees with me, however.

Judge McLaughlin: I don't agree. True, there is merit to consistency and, like you, I see value in having the same judge hear the same case from beginning to end. But few judges possess the

212

graduate social work training you experienced and I'm emphatic about this being a nation of laws and not of men. I'm told that you have a better understanding of intervention programs than most professionals do. But this is unusual. We're on much firmer turf when a court begins with law and ends with law. My ten years on this bench have only confirmed what I believed my first day here. All matters coming before a judge require proof under law. Sure, I've learned about programs, but I'm not an MSW or a psychologist or an institutional director. Judges should be the experts on the law, the professionals should be the experts on behavior and intervention, and the judge should rule on the evidence presented to the court by these professionals. However, I would start with the precept that the first job of the judge is to make sure the Constitution and statutes are fully observed and that all youngsters and their parents are accorded their rights, not only by the court, but by all those who function to assist juveniles as well. I've said a thousand times that this is society's rule, not McLaughlin's rule. Juvenile courts protect children by protecting children's rights. Knowing what I've read about Judge Gelber, he seems to have a different agenda with how he views the judge's role.

Judge Gelber: Well, there is a crime called obstructing justice and I won't let lawyers do this in my court. A United States Supreme Court justice once said that the law is what the nine persons on the Supreme Court say it is. So it's my law in my court except when an appellate court has disabused me of my opinion. By and large I can control proceedings so that law and lawyers do not stand in the way of getting to the heart of an issue. At issue is whether the charge is true and, if so, what should be done about the offense. Where there are questions, I want strong advocacy from both sets of lawyers, but this is still a juvenile court and not the Supreme Court. However, coming back to the effective exercise of the judge role, I'd like to talk about the power this position holds for creating change and getting things done. A judge is more than a judge, he is a political figure. His vote is worth a thousand votes. If he makes any sense at all, people will listen and generally do what he wants. He can raise hell and the next minute the bureaucracy is in his chambers complaining about his demands but offering to go at least part way. Rehabilitation people function in their own system and their job survival is sometimes more important to them than serving kids. I treat them like I treat doctors and police, with great love and studied concern. Some lack any incentive except to avoid displeasing me. It's not that I'm fierce or usually disgruntled, but sometimes I'm far from being gruntled. My jabbing at the bureaucracy has brought positive results. So that I can get back to sipping my Postum, let's hear from Judge Powell.

Judge Powell: Well, gentlemen, I'm pleased that as the only lady in the group I was not the last to be called on. I'm pleased, as well, that you have not designated me the secretary to keep the minutes of this meeting. Surely I believe in the value of judicial consistency. And, if we didn't have the Constitution we have, this country would be in a lot worse shape. I also think I understand something about the power that vests in our position. Unlike Judge Gelber, I don't enjoy having running skirmishes going on all the time with the agencies I deal with each day. Just as I substituted honey for sugar at the detention center for our children, so I've found that honey goes a long way in getting what is needed from agency representatives. Having sworn myself in on my well-worn Bible, the truth is that the juvenile court judge is in a position to know more about the juvenile justice system than anyone. You can't sit there day after day and not become knowledged about children's problems and what helps children. And if a judge doesn't use that knowledge to improve the system, then he, and let me be the first to add this gentlemen, or she, has no business sitting in the juvenile court. There are so many things we keep needing to do to help that kid in front of us accept responsibility for what he or she has done and will do in the future, but that's only the beginning of our job. It takes meeting after meeting and phone call after phone call. We're in the best position to get what is needed to help youngsters help themselves. And I'm sure you'll agree with me, won't you Judge Casey?

Judge Casey: Certainly. You're referring to the system improvement and advocacy roles of the juvenile court judge. Each of you has made a very special if not extraordinary contribution to your community and beyond. Although I'm the junior member of this group, in terms of service, I'm rather proud of what my advocacy efforts have brought in the way of better services to the children and families of Kalamazoo County. I must confess, and thank you Judge McLaughlin for having first advised me of my constitutional rights, that there is much more I would like to have achieved. The juvenile court judge is in a unique position to call on a community to do more and to urge existing agencies to do better. I'm careful not to alienate these agencies, but the judge's focus must be on what is being done for the child and to let others know when their services appear deficient. As you know, I'm big on coordination. So even when a judge successfully stimulates a new program for a particular type of court child, we not only have to help this agency obtain continuing funding but insure that it collaborates with and draws on other helping services in the community. This has some similarity to my previous experience as a university professor. I not only had to convince the authorities that a particular new course was needed; I also had to make sure this was scheduled at a time when few, if any, required courses were offered so that more students could sign up for a new class.

Judge Gelber to Judge Casey: I believe my court hearings are the briefest in the five courts. I have found that professors, even professors turned judges, sometimes fail to notice that their audience is getting restless and that their time is up.

Judge Casey: I do carry a brief for the advocacy function, but since I mentioned something about my previous background, why don't we talk about our pre-judicial experience and whether that has been *prejudicial*, or at least how it has impacted the performance of our judge role. Teaching encouraged me to obtain a strong proficiency in a subject matter and, yes, I can pretty well recite our juvenile code verbatim and what each section number contains. I have read and reread prior appellate court decisions and draw on these quite specifically with my rulings. There is still the teacher in me. I thoroughly enjoy preparing for and teaching at training seminar after training seminar and, yes, I suppose that one of the reasons I like to write out important decisions is so I can teach the law. I want all children to have the best education that can be provided and I have high standards for the educational program at our detention center and the alternative school we sponsor. But I do try not to be pedantic with the youngsters I deal with. And I am sure that a juvenile has a leg up with me when he is doing well in school. If not, I want the probation officer to work with this boy to improve his attitude toward education and to work with the school to strengthen his educational program. While everyone is a teacher — parents, employers, older children, and judges too — I believe my priorities are in order. The law must come first and I want everyone, kids too, to understand this. Surely, I've encouraged a strong in-service training program for all court staff and want them to take advantage of outside seminars to the degree possible. I believe we all need training that broadens our thinking, provides new ideas, is practical, and can be applied. While it was important that I had served as a lawyer in this court before I took the bench, I believe Judge Powell's five years as a juvenile court referee was even better preparation for becoming a judge.

Judge Powell: I think so. I became used to wearing a robe as a referee so unlike you, Judge Casey, I didn't close the entry door on my robe as I tried to proceed into the courtroom. Referees have to fit their discretionary decisions with the policies and philosophy of the judge who appointed them. Still, my judge trusted me and gave me enough flexibility to pretty well be my own person. I conducted thousands of hearings as a referee and ruled on so many points of law that I had little new learning to achieve following my appointment except, perhaps, to learn how to handle the status of being a judge. I enjoy being Judge Powell and I believe I've succeeded in being a humane and not an arbitrary judge. But I would say that my experience as an attorney, lawyering for working-class folks, and the civil rights suits I was engaged in, very much influenced my judicial interests and emphases. Particularly, I want the poor to enjoy the fruits of this world and this comes from good parenting, getting an education, finding the right help when you need it, and taking advantage of opportunities. So I encourage this with children and their families. The Constitution, the supreme law that has been so helpful to my people over the last three or four decades, is present in my courtroom daily to protect all youngsters and their parents from inappropriate state intervention. I was never a teacher, but I'm accused of doing a lot of teaching in my court. While, earlier, I had defended many people in court, Judge Gelber had a lengthy background in prosecution.

Judge Gelber: I never was a real prosecutor. I didn't have an instinct for the jugular vein. But I loved the political environment of that office and my role in managing that office. There, I honed a management perspective that has been useful to me in juvenile court. And being in charge of grand jury investigations for years led me to some of the large-scale hearings I have conducted, as with the investigation of the detention center. The prosecution experience and the Miami area's long-term concern about crime and delinquency have made me protective of the public safety. It may be true that I'm prosecution-minded and perhaps I'm more honest than some judges when I openly acknowledge that, yes, I do presume that any police charge that has cleared the prosecutor's office is probably sound. But if a charge is contested, I call it straight. And I am tough on prosecutors when they foul up a case or, in my judgement, wrongly decide to switch a cherub to the criminal court. I ask them whether they really investigated this case and whether the charwoman or the cleanup man in the office made this decision? My graduate studies in criminal justice stimulated my interest in conducting court studies. I just completed a new one. We learned that most Pick-up Orders issued for a no-show juvenile defendant get little attention. When he's arrested six years later at age twenty-two on a traffic offense, we get to see him again. A smart delinquent doesn't need a good search and seizure lawyer. All he needs to do is not show up. We've just got to fill the cracks in our system. That's my crack for now. Judge Garff, with your social work background, do people in Salt Lake County see you as soft on crime?

Judge Garff: I suppose some do, but not the kids. I learned long ago that if you try to please everyone you please no one. One newspaper article described me as tough but fair and this, honestly, is a more apt characterization. I don't think I'm any less concerned than you are, Judge Gelber, with community safety. I don't get into many hassles with probation officers like you do. Utah judges administer the probation function, set probation officer employment standards, and get well qualified staff. Out our way, we'd say you raise too much dust about this, though down your way it could be said you raise a lot of sand. My social work background makes me think programmatically and to know quite a bit about youngsters' needs for controls. I'm constantly weighing the seriousness of an offense and a prior delinquency history against the different programs we have available and what a youngster seems to need. We've built a number of sound rehabilitation services, so when I move a juvenile to an institution it's because a youngster merits this measure or requires this control. I have no trouble sending someone to a state institution when it's indicated, but I look on this more as treatment, a legitimate way to get a juvenile's attention, force him to think through his actions, build greater regularity into his life, and quite possibly divert him from adult imprisonment. But, I'm a lawyer too. The law comes first and a judge must assure that proceedings are fair. What I can't understand about Judge McLaughlin is how a former prosecutor, and I think he did go for the jugular, seems more concerned about juveniles' rights than protecting public safety.

Judge McLaughlin: Fellow judges, and that includes Judge Powell: If you read the McLaughlin chapter as carefully as you read your own chapters, you will have noted that I answer questions differently from other judges. What evidence is on the McLaughlin record and how should it be weighed? Yes, I was a prosecutor; yes, my first task is to accord constitutional rights to all parties before me; true, I don't talk in terms of public safety to the degree the four of you do. As my friends, the Christian Brothers, teach, one must examine the assumptions behind a question or statement. The function of the prosecutor is to do justice and not solely to obtain a conviction. Prosecutors, too, are governed by legal ethics and a sense of fair play. They also have a duty to stand up to a howling mob. I have said before that the Constitution was written under the hand of God. It is the flywheel of a democratic and free society. Again, late last night as I was reading the History of Torture, what came through loud and clear was that a Constitution was absent from or went unenforced in those countries where torture took place. In this country, we do not approve of torture, but we authorize the state to sanction behavior that violates the official rules of society. You will recall that the thirteen colonies refused to accept our Constitution until it incorporated a Bill of Rights. This was because the colonists distrusted arbitrary governmental intervention. The colonists started with that principle, and this also is the wisest precedent for judges. The Bill of Rights does not limit its protections to adults. We are, of course, a nation comprised of fifty states. Fifty state legislatures have proclaimed their own juvenile codes. There are common threads but significant differences. For some historic reason, New York law, with one specialized exception, is silent as to any court responsibility for protecting community safety. Is my frame of reference to be other than the governing law? Am I to focus on protecting public safety when the people of New York have not directed me to do this? No, my oath is to the written not the unwritten law.

Judge Casey to Judge McLaughlin: Judge Powell and Judge Garff are appointed judges. Judge Gelber and I are elected judges but we have never had an opponent. You had opposition with your 1982 reelection. Wasn't the public vengeful? Didn't the public insist you do more to protect their welfare? Didn't the public tell you they wanted more order and less law?

Judge McLaughlin: Some did. But I don't like to pander to the crowd. My oath of office binds me to a higher authority. The Syracuse area public accepted my contention that my job was to administer the law. If the public doesn't like the law, it should go to the legislature and not to a judge to change the law. I will follow whatever law society gives me. If in conscience I cannot follow the law, I will resign from the bench. Judges are not annointed to their positions, but are appointed, or elected. Since you're really referring to more serious and repetitive delinquency offenses and offenders, I'd like to hear what your laws permit you to do with these cases. Will anyone join me in a cup of coffee?

Judge Garff: Let me come back in on this one. As a Mormon, I don't drink coffee. Traditionally we don't smoke either and I'm pleased to see that none of you smoke though this is probably not due to your religious convictions. Yes, Utah seems to be the only state where juveniles are brought into court for smoking cigarettes. However, Judge McLaughlin, that is the Utah law and my duty is to enforce the law. But this aside helps illustrate the present subject. Illegal cigarette smoking is not a serious offense. It may be a repetitive offense. Society is not injured when a juvenile smokes. His body is not injured by this in the short run though this may happen in the long run. Might this be a reason why my colleagues have been wise enough to abandon this habit if they had earlier used tobacco? What we're really talking about is the hard customers and the chronic offenders who injure people, threaten significant harm to others, or are responsible for property thefts. Generally, offenses against persons are more significant than offenses against property, but certain property offenses are of real concern to me. I'm not talking about a minor shoplift from a department or grocery store but I do include burglaries of occupied dwellings. Stealing a television set from a home is serious. Entering someone's home, becoming frightened and leaving without even taking any property is also a serious offense. Judge McLaughlin will remind us that the Fourth Amendment protects the right of the people to be secure in their homes against unreasonable searches and seizures, and while this provision refers to governmental intrusion, state laws make it a crime and thereby a delinquent act for juveniles to burglarize. Further, in a moment of panic, a juvenile burglar might impulsively use a weapon if he is surprised in the home. He could also be on the receiving end of a homeowner's shotgun.

As I said when I opened our *en banc* meeting, a community needs different levels of intervention capability. By law, the most drastic actions a judge can take in Utah and most states is to lock up a juvenile in a state training school or transfer him to a criminal court for handling as an adult. The field of social work has long advocated alternatives to institutionalization for delinquents, the mentally ill and retarded, and certain adult criminals. So what you need, and what we've obtained pretty well through hard work, is a wide range of program alternatives that enrich our options between standard probation and the state institution. Counseling juvenile probationers and their families is helpful, though rehabilitation often takes more than counseling. I often fine youngsters for their misdeeds, order them to perform community service work with public and private agencies, pay back their victims, and in other ways be held responsible for what they've done. But stronger sanctions are needed for some youths. That's why I will let some juveniles spend time in the detention center pending hearing. I make sure an armed robber spends time in a state evaluation center or institution because he needs to understand I do not look lightly on his offense. And certain juveniles are definitely untreatable, or at least untreatable by what we now can do or have available. As Judge Gelber says, we can't save them all. However, all of our youngsters have an opportunity to save themselves.

Judge Powell: Let me jump in here to make it sooner rather than later that the issue of delinquencies committed by minority youngsters is discussed. A moment ago I borrowed Judge Gelber's national statistics report and it does confirm what I believed and what I assumed most others thought, that black youngsters commit a disproportionate percentage of crimes against persons. They are overrepresented with certain property crimes as well. Black children are severely overrepresented, also, in the poverty class where crime normally is more common. I hope it's no consolation to the white community that blacks offend more often against blacks. Certainly, it's no consolation to me that with self-report delinquency studies, when youngsters are asked to confidentially acknowledge different offenses which they have committed and for which they have not been apprehended, that both white and black children report extensive violations for which they are never caught. We need to work harder at equalizing opportunities in this country and to become more aware of our prejudices. But we also need to deal with the realities of the cases before us. Children of all races are responsible to the law; people of all races have a right not to be victimized.

Yet, poor families don't have the opportunities that middle class black and white youngsters have when they are in trouble. Their parents cannot afford the private psychiatrists or the private educational settings that otherwise could result in police or probation intake officials deciding to let a family handle this instead of the court. Being poor, and especially being black and poor, doesn't mean you will necessarily become a delinquent. Any number of good kids come out of bad neighbourhoods. But many start with two strikes against them and are headed for the big leagues, and I mean the state prison systems rather than the Atlanta Braves or the New York Yankees. The schools have to do more, employers must do more, juvenile courts must do more. That's why I'm so insistent that juveniles know what the rules are and are held accountable, while they are young, when they break the rules. Virtually all of the juveniles I transfer to a criminal court have experienced a state juvenile institution at least once. The juvenile court has shortstopped any number of criminal careers but the public foolishly expects us to abort all potential criminal careers, doesn't it, Judge Casey?

Judge Casey: I'm sensitive to the term abort. May I substitute the word thwart? With great patience I've told my community that it needs to enrich education and other opportunities for all children and that the court needs its help in order to do better. But the court can't and shouldn't try to do everything. Sure, I'm still shaping up our probation program and, yes, I'll probably never be satisfied with this. And I've gotten countless volunteers to help with our different programs, foundation monies to help streamline our operations, and additional budget funds to expand what we can do both with early delinquency patterns and more significant reoffenders. Lightning has struck a few times in my bedroom when I can't sleep and am thinking about the court. Some good program ideas have emerged from middle-of-the-night inspirations, which makes it even harder for me to return to sleep. We've been filling in with more community-based alternatives, but the dollars are tight in Michigan so we can't do as much as we'd like. I transfer some youngsters to criminal court though my most difficult decision is with a serious first offender who has had no or little prior court-ordered program involvement. Still, I have transferred first offender cases involving murder, armed robbery, or rape where there was scant evidence the juvenile could be rehabilitated within the juvenile system. But I can say with confidence that I will not transfer a repetitive property offender to the criminal court unless he has first been through the range of local and state facility programs. In Michigan and Georgia, juvenile courts handle offenses until one's seventeenth birthday. New York as we have learned, cuts this age limit off a year earlier. I suppose, Judge McLaughlin, that you see fewer serious and repetitive youngsters than I do because of this.

Judge McLaughlin: Yes, that's bound to be true. Another reason I see fewer serious juvenile offenders is because the legislature, in 1978, authorized initial criminal court filings for certain thirteen- to fifteen-year-old juveniles. I would rather that our jurisdiction extended to one's eighteenth birthday, as with Judge Garff and Judge Gelber, and I would rather that our code, unlike all of yours, permitted me to transfer certain clearly criminalistic youngsters, which is not now possible in New York and a few other states. But I've also written an article suggesting we think seriously of ending the noble juvenile court experiment and begin all delinquencies in a criminal court, though separate juvenile institutions would be retained. What we're really discussing is punishment and my law says nothing about punishment. This is hypocritical. What do you think a kid truly thinks as he goes to sleep in his institutional bed? That he was sent there for treatment, like the law says, or for punishment because he did something wrong, which is not what the law says. Like my opinion in the *Felder* case pointed out, when law, as with the New York designated felony act, requires with commitment that the juvenile be institutionalized for a mandatory minimum period of time, that is a punishment that is criminal in nature. Institutionalization may result in a cure in six days, six weeks, six months, one year, or never. But if rehabilitated within the mandatory minimum time period, a juvenile still has to serve the full term. So treatment becomes indistinguishable from punishment and the Constitution compels the right to a jury trial if punishment looms, a right denied in juvenile courts in New York and most other states. Maybe it is time to end the hypocrisies, abolish the juvenile court, use the word punishment, and then give juveniles their full constitutional rights in a criminal court. Does anyone agree with me?

Chorus of judges: No, no.

Judge McLaughlin: Not even you, Judge Gelber? You appear hard-line.

Judge Gelber: No. I am not enamored of the criminal courts. True, more than many juvenile court judges, I think a larger share of juvenile marauders belong in the criminal courts. There they have the right to bail and the jury trial, but they will also face an undermanned probation operation or a seething prison. At the end of that line there is little to help that offender. Let's face it, he's out of circulation for a while, maybe a long while, so society does not have to worry about him making their streets unsafe. But I also know about half of the juveniles who start in the criminal court go nowhere, really. They get probation, get fined, or their cases are not prosecuted because a prosecutor does not think this offender is a serious enough case for adult courts. Perhaps you've been so busy writing legal opinions, Judge McLaughlin, that you didn't notice in my chapter a proposal to keep more juveniles in the juvenile system. I want authority to sentence hard-core juveniles, fourteen years and older, to an up-to-five year sentence in a juvenile institution.

Judge McLaughlin: I don't have any constitutional problem with that if the kid can get out when he is ehabilitated without having to serve a minimum time period sentence, but my proviso would undermine what you're recommending. Five years must be seen as a long time in a child's life and I have to worry about how judges would go about deciding which youngsters would merit the five years. In fact I did read your chapter. You must have been quite a softball pitcher when you were young. But now that you're older you sound like you'd prefer to play hard ball with kids. And while otherwise you seem like a charming gentleman, you would probably want all of the discretion in the world to decide which kids go where. I'd have trouble granting even you that much power. Yes, I know you'll answer that judges should have flexibility and discretion, but that leads to arbitrary decisions and idiosyncratic decision making.

Judge Gelber: I think I know what that word means, but in other writings I do for the newspapers I do my best to use words that have no more than ten letters, like punishment and jail.

Judge McLaughlin: It means that fifty different judges in Florida would make fifty different decisions about who should go off for up to five years. No, by legislation or by court rule, we need precise guidelines, or the public will look on the court as capricious, an institution to punish the poor.

Judge Gelber: I've got to get in a few more words, short words that is. I don't subscribe to the theory that a state facility is a school for crime. They don't go up there and learn how to break into a house. They learn by breaking into a house and talking to the guys on the corner. They already know bad people. Generally they are not plucked out of a gentle home life and sent to this horrible place. They've lived in a horrible place before they were sent here. Anyway, most of these kids are lousy at what they do. They're lousy burglars. True, at state schools they talk with others about better techniques to break into houses, but they learn more watching TV in terms of techniques. TV doesn't force you to commit the crime, but it sure gives you style. Television shows more sophisticated criminal techniques than they learn from the lousy burglars they're living with at the state school.

Judge Powell: May I shift this, gentlemen, to our views on less severe offenders, what we call status offenders, the runaways and incorrigibles and truants. I think it has been a grave error for the states to restrict what we can do with these youngsters. I battled this in the legislature but the carrot of federal dollars was overwhelming and I lost. So today I have very limited powers with these youngsters. Status offenders are as much a threat if not more of a threat to society as a child who is delinquent. Future society is jeopardized when these youngsters grow up without respect for authority. Now we are prohibited from doing much about their rebelliousness. I see many such children come back into my court as adults, the parents of abandoned, abused, and neglected children. True, I have found a way that I am confident is legal to find such children in contempt of my orders to attend school or adhere to their parents' rules and then to place them in our detention center for a period of time so they understand my orders are to be followed.

Judge Casey: These cases are frustrating, but just because juvenile courts for decades could lock up these youngsters doesn't mean it was good policy. I know, Judge Powell, that you've developed crisis counselors and shelter homes and other programs like we have that have been suitable substitutes for many children. When I first came on the bench, I didn't see any difference between status offenders and delinquent offenders. Now I do. It is better that we not send them to state institutions with delinquents. Despite what Judge Gelber suggests, they can be contaminated by the more chronic offenders there.

Judge Gelber: I thought status offenders were a non-issue. We have status offenders in Miami but the helping efforts are largely done outside of court. This doesn't satisfy the schools, though I think they should do more with children. It certainly doesn't satisfy parents who want us to take over their responsibilities. It doesn't even satisfy some of our social work agencies who still want us to lock up youngsters in their care who don't follow their rules. When I do hear these cases, the kids don't know that I lack the power to carry through if they disobey further. I don't resort to using contempt because I don't think this was the intent of the legislation that stripped me of the incarcerating power. I suppose the kids go back to school for a while. These cases don't come back before me very often. Perhaps it's because people understand the court can't do much with these matters.

Judge McLaughlin: There are a lot of judges who agree we should not lock up status offenders in JD institutions. Few judges agree that at the front end of the system we should not accept these youngsters. I am one of them, but not for the reasons you might think. It is not that I'm a raving liberal, in fact I'm a Republican. I have two reasons for this view, over and above the fact that as a kid I had bright red hair, was Irish, and used to get in a little trouble now and then. Fundamentally, this issue has to do with the role of the court. Judge Powell was hinting at this. Courts are to provide due process and apply muscle. Normally, if someone fails to follow our order, we are granted authority to take steps to enforce that order. Now, we've been denied that muscle, so why provide the courts as a recourse? A further starting point is that these youngsters have not broken the criminal law. Instead, they stay away from home for one of many reasons, keep a dirty room when they stay home, prefer being out with their friends to coming home and being seen as "goody goodies", or find the streets or highways more adventuresome than school. I don't do the systematic statistical research Judge Gelber performs, but I think my estimates are pretty good. These kids fit into two subgroupings, about equally divided. One consists of those who are desperately looking for help and will accept any help offered. So why label them a court kid to give them help? The other half wants everyone to get out of their lives. They reject treatment. You put them somewhere and they'll run. They've got problems but won't accept treatment. Why give them another burden to carry? So present policy deceives children, demeans the court, and labels two groups of children, neither of whom deserves it. In the early days, young bucks took off for the western frontier and that was the last we heard from them, for better or for worse. Maybe their grandchildren are now in Judge Garff's court for a status offense.

Judge Garff: Probably. I think we see some Irish kids whose roots go back to New York. Actually, I started out with Judge Powell's approach. I was "doggoned" if I was going to stand by and let the legislature throw these kids to the winds. Actually, I don't think they would have. They and I consider it a vital state function to provide necessary services as well as necessary behavioral controls. We've moved the court into a last-resort posture and, by law, grant the primary service responsibility to the Division of Family Services. The Division, or with truancy cases the school system, must document the earnest and persistent efforts it has undertaken which have failed to correct the situation, together with what formal court intervention is expected to achieve, which cannot be obtained through voluntary alternatives, before we can consider the case. We've added a number of alternatives in lieu of court and instead of secure detention and, believe it or not, I have become comfortable with no longer sending these youngsters off to a state institution. This overall approach makes sense for Utah and I'm happy with it. But I'm not happy with going on with our discussion without taking a stretch. In our courtrooms, when we need a break or need to go to a bathroom, we're in control and can call for a recess, though I notice that Judge Powell can hang in there for three hours without taking a break. "Recess".

Judge Garff (resuming): I'd like us to discuss the question of detaining youngsters before trial, the juvenile analog to adults who are jailed pending trial. A present issue in many less populous areas of our nation is to get these youngsters out of the adult jails where they are often housed, or out of the juvenile units of adult jails where it is difficult if not impossible to maintain full sight and sound separation from adults. Besides, these are not usually nice places for kids, even tough kids. Our five communities all maintain separate juvenile detention facilities, so our issues deal with who we lock up there and why, the alternatives we provide to secure detention, and the expected benefits of this experience. Let me ask, what is the capacity of our detention centers?

Judge McLaughlin: Thirty two.

Judge Casey: Forty.

Judge Powell: Seventy-two.

Judge Gelber: One hundred twenty with an average population of one hundred seventy-five.

Judge Garff: Fifty-six. But, Judge Gelber, how come you're well over capacity?

Judge Gelber: That's a very long story. Our law favors detention rather than freedom. I believe that immobilization, if you will permit me an occasional lengthy word, is valuable; our community would see the juvenile court as a cream-puff operation if far fewer youngsters were held and then we'd get still tougher legislation for dealing with juveniles.

Judge McLaughlin: That irks me. It would be hard to visualize how

Florida laws could become still more punitive. You set the cap. Why wait for the federal courts to tell you you're overcrowded?

Judge Gelber: We've speeded up case processing. We hold detention hearings the day after a kid is confined. Detained youngsters get a far quicker trial date than those released to the community. At any time we have sixty kids, who could be detained, on home detention under close supervision by state agency staff. Our county's population is over 1,700,000; juvenile court age goes to the eighteenth birthday; and youngsters targeted by the prosecutor for direct criminal filings start off in our detention center. Miami has severe pockets of poverty, has had to integrate the Marielitos and other recent immigrant groups, and is a completely different community from yours.

Judge McLaughlin: True, our communities and our laws are different. New York's law makes it extremely difficult to detain a youth. If you will allow me to pontificate a moment, juvenile courts do one heck of a lot of preventive detention that criminal courts do not approve for adults. And remember, a juvenile detention center is still a jail. State after state says juveniles may be detained if their release would endanger the community or themselves, a very vague standard. It allows us to punish youngsters by taking away their freedom before trial, when they are presumed innocent, based on the thinnest of proof standards, far lower than that required to incarcerate juveniles following trial. How do you justify locking up many more kids pre-trial on this *de minimus* standard than you lock up after you have found them delinquent beyond a reasonable doubt?

Judge Garff: Let me jump in here. Look, I see nothing wrong with the detention criteria. Most youngsters are not locked up. The juvenile system is different. It is now a legal system, but juveniles have never been granted the same panoply of rights conferred on adult offenders. Most juveniles are released within a couple of days after they have been restabilized, have had a mild taste of freedom deprivation, and can better follow the rules and take responsibility. Besides, our detention center is quite a nice place, nicer than I'd actually prefer for some repeat offenders, and a lot of these kids would jeopardize the community if they were not held. I might sound too virtuous, but I know of no other juvenile system that has looked at its detention practices more than we have, looked so hard at the kind of kids it was holding, and developed as many alternative programs so youngsters would not have to be locked up.

Judge Powell: Nationally we overdetain. In our court, we used to overdetain. Our center was built for 144 juveniles. We couldn't staff this facility effectively and any number of youngsters were being transferred to jail because we couldn't handle them. So we passed a court rule setting a detention cap at 72 and we've never exceeded this population limit. We have eight detention priorities. Lower priority youngsters are released if we reach the cap. Helping us are detention screening staff that are onsite around the clock. They try to restabilize a family so we can send a youngster home or to find non-secure alternatives so they don't need to be locked up. At the next day's detention hearing, not only must there be a strong social reason to keep a youngster detained, but also evidence showing probable cause to believe this youth committed the particular offense. We detain the serious or repetitive offender whose detention is necessary for the security of the community. And in Georgia, a child has the right to bail on the request of his parents.

Judge Casey: Michigan law provides a bail right, too, though we know only a dozen or so states allow this. Bail has worked well in our community. If parents put up $100 bail, they'll get $90 back when the child appears at the hearing. Parents will help the court detain the minor at home and out of trouble since they don't want to lose their money. We are required to hold detention hearings on Saturdays, which keeps the population down and, like Atlanta, we established priority groupings as to those that may be detained. We've brought this pre-trial detention population down significantly, I'm quite sure with no serious risk to the community, by encouraging others to set up shelter care for status offenders and by our home detention program that is our pride and joy. Serious assaultive crimes are pretty well assured lockup time, property offenses less so on the first time round, more so with repetition. We're averaging eleven under capacity and we got to that point because we really worked at it and better decided who should be held.

Judge Gelber: There is another type of juvenile court case we haven't discussed, child abuse and neglect matters, that Judge Casey has specialized with for a number of years. Will you lead off on this?

Judge Casey: Well, I've had a number of victories but some defeats. These are about the most difficult cases one can hear in juvenile court; one of the most complex and emotionally draining areas of social work practice; the only type of case I think lawyers, when they represent parents, want to lose; matters that we ask so much from foster parents; cases where we see no "sooper-dooper", gold-star juvenile court families. My memory takes me back to an early case which became a long-drawn-out matter because of the repetitive births this mother experienced. She happened to have been, earlier, a neglected child and a ward of this court. During the process of hearing the case of her first baby, she agreed to relinquish her rights to this child who was then placed. With her second baby, neglect was again apparent. Her rights to this child were terminated involuntarily because when she has a child, she goes into a depression, sits in her room, and leaves the child in a crib for a day and a half while she sits there. Then she had a third child and we found a foster home willing to take in both mother and child to provide training for the mother. But the foster parents gave up on her because the mother was just letting them do all the work. So we tried her back in her own home with the child and within two weeks the mother was back into the same depression, people knocking on the door and not being let in, the child in the crib for a day and a half. I'm hearing the evidence on that now. Termination of parental rights has been petitioned. But now she's pregnant with a fourth child. Obviously, so little constructive effort has been accomplished except to get these children rather quickly away from their mother and into foster care, and then into adoptive homes. This mother was ill-equipped for motherhood. As a child she had been, in effect, adopted by the social services department but never really adopted by anyone. Throughout her whole young life, her only friends were agency people. As an adult, the only people she looked to for guidance or help or friendship were agency people, so here we go again. That case is more depressing than shocking.

Another difficult scenario comes with mentally ill or retarded parents who are good people but just don't have the ability to parent. The problem is with our statute that only allows me to terminate parental rights if parents are able to parent and fail to fulfill this responsibility. These people are not able to parent effectively in the first place. So how do you design a treatment program to help them take care of the child when the experts say they can't learn to even take care of themselves? In any event, our law requires that whatever efforts are made must cover a span of two years before termination can be effectuated. So we have a lot of kids waiting in limbo for two years, for their parents who will never be able to put it together, until we can go into permanency planning. We've got to address that dilemma.

Judge Gelber: You appear rather pessimistic.

Judge Casey: I am more pessimistic because I have seen a decline in services over the last three or four years. I've seen social workers burn out, replaced by new, underpaid, and overworked social workers who need months to get truly familiar with the case. And it seems we have had so many new prosecutors, who are responsible for bringing these cases for the department of social services, coming into and out of this court that I'm afraid to take a recess during a hearing for fear I'll be facing a new prosecutor when the case picks up again. Further, legal developments are turning more toward a parent orientation with termination, judges are sometimes more hesitant to terminate, and it's also more difficult to terminate.

But we've done some good things, too. We now have specialized foster homes for more disturbed youngsters; the review hearings I conduct have achieved far greater accountability and better case planning; I get a report each six months on any child I have freed for adoption, advising me whether adoption is in readiness and if not, why not; we've made inroads on earlier case findings with child abuse; and we're doing a better job with training and supervision of foster parents. Still, the court's role is useful but limited. We are not a prevention agency, though I make talks on the need for prevention and have expressed some ideas on this. I would like to hear what another judge has to say about preventing or reducing the incidence of these types of cases.

Judge Garff: I don't think we can other than by improving the economy. Unemployment and underemployment further family tensions that increase maltreatment of children. A more complicated society seems to increase abuse and neglect, and I don't see those development alleviating. I believe that even in the best of homes, kids can really drive their parents to the brink, and if you don't have the kinds of controls that parents should have, and which a lot of parents don't have, everything goes black and parents can't control themselves. Also, I think we've all noticed more sexual abuse. My own theory is that this is related to more permissive societal attitudes toward sexual standards. I think a lot of men develop an attitude that since sex is so acceptable in society, it's just one more step to little children, and it's okay there, too. I think this is more true with men who move in with a woman who has children. I once publicly urged more assertiveness training for young girls and for women so that they would be able to say to a guy, "get your hands off me", or "you can't do that to my kid and if you're going to do it, get out". But I was taken to task for not saying we should teach young men to be more respectful for young women. The point was a good one, but I think the basic idea is one of the lines of defense.

I believe a reason we cannot see the light at the end of the tunnel, also, is because so many teenage girls are having babies and keeping them. It takes a really skillful single parent to rear children in a healthy way, and I'm talking about young teenage girls who can't handle their own problems let alone the problems of a child. They have a gap of many years in their growing-up life experiences that they can't integrate and share with that child. And we're going to reap a whirlwind as these babies grow up without the right kind of parenting. Overall, professionals have worked very hard and often quite well in trying to remedy abuse and neglect situations. Different disciplines have worked well together. But I think teachers, if they were willing to make a stronger effort, could detect and report more abuse and neglect. I share Judge Casey's belief that the schools are way behind with their curricula and need to initiate programs and classes to teach young people how to parent. Further, many people don't want to interfere with somebody else's family life or the way they discipline their child. But sometimes this results in important referrals that are not made and in continuing neglect.

If citizen groups became involved in agency work and became familiar with the total problem, they could be helpful by pounding on the legislative door to insist this problem gets attention. Now you get the PTAs and a few social workers or judges up there trying to plead the case but we need more grassroot support to get larger agency budgets. Private agencies can be valuable here as well and this means citizen involvement. We use citizen volunteers with the court's guardian program but it is important they receive good training, not fall by the wayside, and that they are able to be used once trained. There are several other comments I would like to make. One is that prosecutors appear to be filing a significantly greater number of criminal cases against a parent or the adult abuser. This was rare ten and fifteen years ago. Prosecutions fall into two classes. One is an unvarnished strategy to obtain a criminal punishment. The alternative situation is where the criminal case is filed as a lever to promote a parent's cooperation with the juvenile court case in admitting responsibility and accepting the assistance of social work and medical personnel.

But what really surprised me was what our experts are now telling us, that child abuse, including sexual abuse and even incest, are some of the most hopeful areas in the entire neglect arena. A number of these children can be returned to their parents safely. The experts contend these are specific rather than generalized problems. If they can unearth the early causes for this abuse, they can grapple with it. There was a crisis, a reaction to the crisis, and then the explosion. They say they can deal with that, but I'm skeptical.

Judge Powell: I would require, in the eleventh and twelfth grades of high school, courses in parenting, family relationships, the role of the child in the family, the role and responsibilities of parents to children. True, a number of potential parents drop out before eleventh grade, so maybe Judge Casey was right when he said in his chapter this should begin in some form in kindergarten and continue all the way through high school. Many young people have the simple idea that they will marry, become parents, live a long and happy life thereafter in a white house with flowers and lawn. I've heard so often from parents who feel that since they have birthed this child they have the right to do with this child as they want to. But they need to learn to enjoy that child without causing the child any physical, mental, or emotional pain and suffering, that parenting is no easy task, and that there will be crises of all forms. They need to think through how to deal with crises, prevent crises, where to get help before a crisis explodes, how to reduce the impact of a crisis, as well as how to build structure into a home, teach useful values, and help their children achieve more than a minimum kind of existence. I also think television could be more useful. While youngsters are getting this foundation in school before they become parents, present parents need to know about the same kinds of things I would teach kids in high school. Many people will not read but do watch the tube. Public television can take people through the different phases of childhood, what to expect, what to relate to, though unfortunately any number of parents who should view this will instead switch to other channels.

Child abuse and neglect cut across all economic classes, but there are several dimensions that have a special poverty implication. Community mental health services are helpful but more of their services should be free. The small charge or the sliding fee scale acts to discourage use of this service. Parents say they are already in a financial bind, and sometimes will not go for help unless coerced by the court or an agency. They think of their financial distress more than the help they may obtain. The other is the reluctance on the part of private physicians to report suspected abuse or neglect. Public hospitals, where the poor go, report these problems for investigation. The private physicians are more cautious. They are afraid of losing patients. The word would go out that "Dr Jones reported me so don't go to him". They are also worried about a possible misdiagnosis and being sued for making a false report. Still, private physicians are bound by the same reporting requirements. I'll tell you what some private doctors are doing. They tell these parents to take their child to a hospital, suggesting they cannot provide the particular diagnostic or treatment services the hospital can furnish. If the family goes to the hospital, the problem is then spotted and reported, protective services can make its investigation, a court might become involved.

As to citizens, I would urge Right to Life groups to become deeply involved with abuse and neglect. Then they could better understand why a person who feels she cannot be a good parent wants an abortion. They could provide homes for certain children, develop other foster homes, serve as free babysitters for parents who need time away, or be a support group for parents who cannot emotionally cope with certain situations. I certainly feel church groups should take the lead in protecting children. They can conduct educational programs on parenting skills and problems, and help develop foster homes and other community resources. Also, children need to understand their right not to be abused and what steps to take when they are abused. My eyes were opened last year when I spoke to a group of sixth- and seventh-grade classes. The children asked me: If I am abused and don't want to tell my teacher, where can I get help? What would happen to my parents if I reported this? Would my parents be locked up? I felt the children preferred to accept abuse in order to avoid their parents being incarcerated.

Judge McLaughlin: I really don't know if abuse and neglect have increased. The statistics recite an increase but we have encouraged people to report these problems more than ever before. Really, I only see what comes into court, what caseworkers think I should see. It's like with delinquency and crime. The courts only see people who the police have arrested and not all the people who commit the crimes. I don't see very many emotional neglect cases but the ones I see are relatively serious. Am I to conclude this type of case has decreased or is it better to suggest these cases are more typically handled outside of court and that social agencies now essentially bring to my attention the physical and sexual abuse cases? I don't think we need additional services in my community, though I would stand to be corrected by people who know more about this. What is needed is to be able to make much more quickly the ultimate decisions with regard to children. Presently, it is taking ten to twelve weeks to go through all the hearings and have a final disposition, and I know this is speedier than in many courts. If, pending all this, a neglected child has been retained at home, it would be an odd case where this family did not need help from society during this period. But if the child has been placed with a foster parent, professionals will come in and say you shouldn't return the child to his natural mother because he has bonded to the foster mother, even when the mother isn't all that bad.

I really empathize with the underpaid case workers in the child protective service who are given responsibilities for fifty or sixty children instead of a more ideal twenty children. They become discouraged and a lot of the discouragement is due to their workload. It's rare to see a caseworker keeping her job more than three or four years. They do need more training and understanding of the court's responsibility. I have to articulate the reasons why I make a determination and the caseworkers need to be trained to articulate their findings and reasons. You ask them why they picked up one child and didn't pick up another and they say they don't know or something, or they tell about a feeling they had. But if you probe why they did or did not do something you find they have very good reasons for their decisions. As to the parents, the most serious cases of child abuse I see involve people who belong to fundamentalist Christian churches. I'm not talking about being hit with a strap, but about four broken ribs and three broken legs and four broken arms. I'm talking about serious, serious physical abuse. Whether those churches attract the people who do it or whether a person walks into the church and then somehow the church justifies it, I don't know. I would say this involves 15 to 20 percent of the serious physical abuse cases I see.

One of you commented on the citizen role in helping obtain satisfactory budgets for the social services departments. Legislators like to spend money in areas where their constituencies are critical and will be glad they fought for them. If the schools raise hell and fight and the teachers fall down and gnash their teeth and slam their heads on the ground and threaten to strike, they're going to get more money. But the commissioner of social services is more intimidated. He is hired by county government and has to go to the county government for a budget. He's got to want citizen help, which has to be an organized effort because the tighter the budget, the more organization is needed. But, I'm especially interested in citizens as court watchers. The court belongs to the people. Is it running the way they want it to run? There's only one way to find out. Come on in and watch. Sitting in the courtroom day after day, they learn how the court and all the players are conducting themselves and what is happening with children. If they complain to the judge, they have credibility. If this fails and they take an issue to the media, they can say, "I sat there for three months and, let me tell you, this is what's going on". Finally, and Judge Gelber has said the same type of thing about when you can take risks with delinquency cases, the public is far less critical of the problems of foster care and repetitive foster care replacements and even forms of abuse that occur in foster homes than they are tolerant of a judge's returning these youngsters to their own homes.

Judge Gelber: I will note that our discussion with this subject area has been more somber, as I think it should be. With this type of case, failure is not something unusual. I've had situations where I've rejected the idea of the state taking the child and the child has experienced subsequent neglect, but not severe abuse. I play the ball as it lies. These are emotional cases and you have to try to look at them without getting involved, which is just about impossible. You have to consider all kinds of things and different opinions, together with the law, so you are bound to make mistakes, but I don't get shell shocked by this. If I'm wrong, I'm wrong. I suppose a judge's background becomes a part of the decision-making process, but you have to think in terms of the environment the parents and the child are in, and that often involves different cultures and different standards. Then you don't decide that this house is a pigsty, as described by the social worker, and automatically take the kid away. Or that the mother is drunk twice a week or she and her boyfriend slug each other regularly or that she leaves the kid with the grandmother. A lot of people leave children with grandmothers, a lot of people drink and a lot of people are pretty damned filthy. The test is, how is that child flourishing or surviving in that environment? And you can be amazed that a lot of those things, at least on the surface, don't appear to be causing any tremendous problems. You have to become oriented to different cultures and their upbringing approaches and you have to watch out not to overimpose your own standards.

As to reducing the incidence of abuse and neglect in the first place, we don't have any control over the external problems that prey on parents causing them to go over the edge where they have to beat up on their kids. It could be the job, it could be the marital relationship, their upbringing. It would be helpful if home conditions were better, and the father had a job and didn't come home mad, and that there were no alcohol problems. But child abuse is the net result of all the problems that plague families and that plague people and plague the world. I would hope that parents can be made aware that there is help available for their problem and that while there is a stigma attached to seeking help, this is not something parents can hide from the whole world. We can make people more aware that if they have a propensity in this direction, someone can help them, and that the preference of society is not to take their child away or lock them up, but to be helpful. They should know it is more acceptable to seek help than to keep this problem in the closet.

Judge McLaughlin: I think it's in order to switch to a happier theme. Let's talk about the joys and satisfactions of being a juvenile court judge and let me get the first word in on this. Juvenile and family courts, like other courts, are building a cathedral that preserves society by according people their rights. I get rewards adding more stones to this building and by having other officials help me with the masonry. This makes me think of the man who was walking across the fields of France in the twelfth century. He had never seen a building more than one or two stories high. Suddenly he sees a cathedral being built into the sky. He has to ask what this is. Though maybe we'll never finish this cathedral, recall that it took centuries to build some of the European cathedrals and we're still a young nation.

But I have a good foreman, the Constitution. Training the lawyers on all sides to be good lawyers, to present and to challenge the evidence, helps this construction effort. I've pretty well gotten my court to run on time. We've done better than our time-processing standards require, which is satisfying. I've enjoyed jiggling the bait and being the yeast for new programs that have benefited the community and the clients of my court. And because I believe in the family, I take pleasure in having prevented the reach of the law from yanking boys and girls away from their families and into juvenile jails unless courtroom evidence required this. You know how strongly I feel about the eternal values of justice and due process of law and following society's rules, so you can understand my gratification with the opportunity I have each day in executing my oath to assure fairness to all concerned. I celebrate the judgeship opportunity when

I get a bureaucracy to abide by the law and, of course, when it does a better job serving children. It's more than ego when I have an opinion published, it's the resolution of a legal dispute and a teaching of the law. Writing and teaching students and practitioners lets me participate in constructing a cathedral of learning which in turn strengthens this cathedral of justice. This has been hard work but a joy. However, my recent hernia operation has forced me to reassess the pace of my construction.

Judge Gelber: Being of the Jewish faith, I would prefer a reference to the temple of justice. My labor in the vineyards has borne fruit and I believe I've saved my community from the bitter fruit of certain destructive activities by juveniles. The pleasure I've obtained from harassing the bureaucracies of the school, rehabilitation, and even justice system have brought better services to children. Juvenile delinquency rehabilitation is not dead, it's just in a state of remission. That's a difficult admission from a longtime liberal who grew up believing that good intentions and a well-funded alphabet agency could solve almost any social problem. But my needling has helped and my advocacy for greater private sector involvement with delinquents has brought some gains as well as personal satisfaction. Some of the private organizations have converted losers into winners to everyone's benefit.

Lately, as you know, I've been looking at the cracks in our system. While my style is to knock some agency heads together, rather than using the mason's trowel, I'm getting some greater coordination and accountability. For example, youngsters I had sent to the state school were told that successful completion of classes there would result in a grade promotion when they returned to Miami schools. But when they did return, they received no credit. So I got our local educators to go up to the state school and work this out. I enjoy controlling court proceedings so I don't have lengthy trials or need to work overtime, and of course I like seeing my views and articles in print along with newspaper photos of me wearing a nice bow tie and my half glasses. It has been useful to chair the criminal justice council, help make sure monies are allocated for useful purposes, and energize the community to take action with its complaints about delinquency and crime. Conducting studies, massaging statistics, and writing articles about juvenile justice issues reduces my weekend boredom and keeps me away from the greyhound racetrack where Judge Si Gelber has not been running too well recently.

Judge Casey: As you'd expect, my biggest joys come from the adoption hearings, particularly those where a child with a previously disjointed life is placed with a loving family and has a greater opportunity to participate in the opportunities this society provides. The task of administering this court, however, is not an easy one. But I like the challenge and really am pleased when I've been able to change things and make them better. My town of Kalamazoo used to be known because of the popular song about it that was a big hit in the '40s. You can still hear it now and then on the radio. I'm happy that the juvenile court in Kalamazoo is now known as well, and that has something to do with my record as a judge. Specializing as I have, or as we have, has given us expertise. I like having mastered our given area of the law and how social agencies need to fit in with the law. In other words, I enjoy being a Mr Juvenile Court who is using this position to further what our community is doing for children and therefore what it is doing for itself. Helping new programs get underway has been gratifying. And imagine, I can do all of this without relinquishing my old pleasures in teaching. It's just great to lecture to people in this field. In this job, you also learn a lot from psychiatric and psychologist witnesses who testify about the unconscious and the hidden reasons behind our attitudes and beliefs. So, and let me couch this carefully, I must enjoy having things to worry about. I'm always worrying about the court and the kids, so there's no end to that "pleasure".

Judge Powell: It certainly gives me satisfaction when a delinquent youngster I dealt with comes back a year or two later, knocks on my chamber door, and tells me he has straightened out his life. Or when, on the streets of downtown Atlanta, someone asks if I'm Judge Powell and then proceeds to tell me how well she is doing now. What I had personally done was to strongly urge that youngsters make the most of themselves and their education and to not blame anyone but themselves for breaking the rules or squandering their futures. Otherwise, my influence was less direct. I've helped build a good probation department and those ladies and gentlemen really deserve more credit. I've been somewhat of a community force for better schools, improved health and mental health services, vocational training, and job opportunities for young people. The people who work in those settings also deserve more credit. I am rewarded when a new probation officer develops into an extremely effective worker with young people or when a community agency I have supported in one of a number of ways successfully helps a child.

I've had satisfaction in strengthening the legal procedures of our court and in making sure constitutional rights are protected. But I also stress one's responsibilities to the law so this is all very civilizing. I've met so many wonderful people through my work that I otherwise would not have known: citizen members of community agency boards, school and governmental officials, agency directors and staff members, and fine judges such as you all. And then, I've been part of a movement to retain a movement, to help one of the greatest inventions in history to remain a vital and viable instrument. So I am blessed many times over.

Judge Garff: My work has made me a better person. Observing misfortunes daily and the adversities so many of our families experience has made me more humble, which colleagues say is no easy task. Being so close to family problems helped me be a better husband and father. Trying to suture families each day helped me learn how to prevent or reduce family problems at home. Knowing more, from my court work, about adolescent stresses helped me understand and be a more effective parent as my children went through that stage of development. Fine tuning my court judgments has made me wiser with my out-of-court judgments. I like to see kids shape up and feel I had some role in strengthening their capacity to resist temptations. It's been rewarding to have been in on the ground floor as we began modernizing our juvenile court system, to have been somewhat of a key to the legislation, structure, organization, and implementation of this effort, and to have been around long enough to help it mature.

I really like kids and I get pleasure out of solving problems in the system that stand in the way of helping kids more. We've innovated all over the place and will never have a status quo as far as I'm concerned. So there are always new problems and interrelationship problems and budget problems that I usually like to work on and must work on so we can reduce our juvenile problem. Sometimes I give others grief, but this is purposeful. None of us will ever become rich as juvenile court judges, but we have achieved an inner wealth that is incalculable. And now what should we say about the future of the juvenile court and the role of the judge? I'd expect to hear different thoughts on this, since what has become clear to me is that we are different people, have different backgrounds, run our courts differently, and from each of our soapboxes urge certain differing remedies to the problems we confront.

Judge Casey: The critical problem of abused and neglected children requires intensive court involvement. The juvenile court is in the best position to oversee that social service, medical, and mental health services do a good job with these difficult cases. Because of the court, parents obtain a better insight as to their legal responsibilities and their legal rights. But all juvenile courts and juvenile court judges do not commit sufficient time and energy to this vital workload. With delinquency and status offense cases, I believe we are on the correct track in focusing more attention on the former and moving to a backup role on the latter. I'm not happy with the national trend to remove more serious and repetitive offenders from the juvenile court to criminal court handling. I would prefer that legislators grant juvenile court judges the authority to sentence the most difficult of these juveniles to lengthier stays in juvenile institutions, though this would require careful guidelines to protect against abusing this power with more rank and file delinquent youngsters. Few will disagree that the conversion of juvenile courts into settings ruled quite clearly by regularized legal procedures has been a positive development.

We must continue to make the case for a broader array of services to meet the differing needs of youngsters more effectively. We have been blamed for failures that are beyond the court's control but must stand accountable for deficiencies we can do something about. All this requires greater citizen understanding. It is a forever task and judges must take the lead in interpreting our needs. We should involve citizens more broadly throughout the range of our activities. We need more judges willing to accept the responsibilities and visualize the opportunities of this office. These should be judges who know themselves quite well and can control their biases by adhering to law and a very careful exercise of their discretion. It is necessary that this nation allocate more than rhetoric to its long held assertion that children are our most precious resource.

Judge Gelber: I am not one who can see down the road very far and I have always been better at dealing with the here-and-now. There is a lack of public confidence in juvenile courts, not entirely unwarranted, and the consequence has been our partial emasculation by the legislatures of our states. The old concept of trying to motivate a kid by counseling therapy is being replaced by trying to instill good work habits. I have no big problem with this. We'll always need counselors to talk things over with youngsters but talk, including my talk, sinks in only so far. A few minutes in the courtroom, a half an hour in the counselor's office cannot compete with the around-the-clock influence of a delinquent's peer group.

More of this juvenile's time must be taken over by community service work, pre-vocational and vocational experiences, and more effective schooling.

Properly, we've moved from trying to understand delinquent acts and then trying to help youngsters to, instead, holding juveniles accountable for their acts while trying to assist them but holding them still more significantly accountable for a future offense. I see some merit in the beginning trend to accept punishment as a legitimate function of the juvenile court and to gear the extent of the punishment to offense severity or offense history. But I would oppose overly structured requirements that compel judges to function like a computer. True, more equitable justice can be achieved if you weight each offense, tie this into a matrix of punishments, and just add this up and there you are. Maybe we'll go further in that direction to gain more uniformity, so youngsters can be told ahead of time that such or such an offense will bring you six months or eighteen months of probation or thirty days or nine months in a juvenile slammer. But I want more discretion than that, and society objects to an automatic rule of law without an individualizing capability.

I'm also convinced that while we are dealing with the here and now, we need to make a very strong commitment to a long-term approach to reducing the future delinquencies of impoverished children. This will take a crash educational effort, beginning at age three, exhaustive efforts in fact, so that poor children can be brought to some parity with better off youngsters in achieving the education so critical for their futures. I would, with Judge Casey, seek to reclaim some of the youngsters we have lost to criminal court by allowing us a lengthier sentence option, but this should be limited to older juveniles. I do not believe that a juvenile court needs to be separately organized from the other courts. It is part of the general court in Miami and I am convinced it's a better court than when it used to be separate some years ago. I'm proud to be associated with such highly qualified specialist judges as the four of you. But I have seen specialized juvenile court judges who thought they were God Almighty and were unbelievable. It is true that in my court, assignment to the juvenile division is not a high priority of judges, but there is a useful role for citizens to become informed about a juvenile division of the general court and then to go to the chief judge to say, make this division of higher or highest priority.

Improved management of the courts, not a particularly exciting call to arms, probably holds more payoff than anything we can put our hands on now. Monitor the system and make it accountable. Close the cracks in our system so we don't let juveniles fall into a hole in the ground and then disappear once they get into the system. What's the good in developing programs to handle serious offenders or to treat the learning-disabled, if sloppy administration cannot carry out the mission? And I'm not pitching a curve ball when I suggest that the more private sector involvement we can get into direct work with delinquents, non-profit agencies or even for-profit agencies, the better off we will be.

Judge Powell: At the moment I'm gloomy about future juvenile court prospects. Setting aside for a moment the issue of abused and neglected children, three major trends are evident today and I can agree with only one of them, the continuing extension of due-process requirements with juvenile court proceedings. The inhumane direction for adult handling of juveniles is clearly wrong. We know how ugly our prisons are and how limited are the rehabilitation programs there. I can't see that many come back from prison having been improved by that experience. Admittedly, there are some youngsters the juvenile system cannot manage, who require criminal court handling, though these are far fewer in number than legislative policy makers or the general public believes. But, despite new, harsher handling policies, legislators have not stopped the forward march of expanding legal protections for juveniles, and I'm convinced that strong due-process safeguards are here to stay. In a way it's true that we are now more like a junior criminal court, but I see nothing wrong with that as long as they let us keep working with junior criminals and let us retain some flexibility in dealing with them.

As you know, the third development, restraining what we can do with status offenders, has been a mistake as far as I'm concerned. These youngsters require court authority and controls. True, with fewer such cases, I can devote more time to abused and neglected children which is extremely important. Some judges worry that if we keep losing more delinquent youths to criminal courts, narrow the entry door for the status offender, deal only with the more serious abuse and neglect matters, and continue to pass off juvenile traffic offenders to the traffic courts, there will not be enough responsibility remaining to justify the juvenile court. I am convinced there will be. I don't go along with the national trend to end separate juvenile courts and attach their jurisdiction to the general trial courts. Those judges, except for Judge Gelber and some others, just don't have the commitment during their six months or one year or so assignment to the juvenile division or family division to provide the leadership this position requires. Strengthening the juvenile court is no sport for the shortwinded. I hope those who read what we say here will join and help us climb back up that mountain.

Judge McLaughlin: And join in helping us construct that cathedral of justice. I start with my statement that fairness is the best teacher. Juvenile as well as adult offenders are not offended when courts play by society's rules. This does not guarantee they will in turn play by society's rules, but it removes an additional reason or excuse that might in their minds justify a reoffense. Despite my regard for Judge Powell as a long-distance runner in this field, and although I've been a specialist judge, I'm less sure about the special merit of long-term tenure. A judge who is a good lawyer and sees the Constitution as a living document can be a valuable judge in this court even for just a year. The first duty is to insure the fair administration of justice to those who come into the courtroom. It's quite nice to have a judge do more than that and to do some of the things we've done in our off-the-bench hours.

But we have to be careful of a holier-than-thou attitude that prompts us to think that only the judge can do all of these things. Even very decent juvenile court judges may not know what they're talking about, advocate worthless programs, or suggest simplistic panaceas. Do save our children from judges who are very rigid with their moral standards, have a sophomoric law and order perspective, or are so certain that one plus one must equal two. Watch out against judges who are empire- rather than cathedral-builders, who think their opinion on any subject dwarfs those of everyone else, who want deference from all creatures large and small. Judges can run away with this spirit of improving the system and fail to more thoroughly examine the constitutionality of the laws and procedures they administer daily. I am still attracted to the Irish concept of a "Brehon" judge, a Gaelic term referring to both a man and a woman. A judge there is to have the best qualifications of a man and a woman. The judge shall have studied law for years and years. We must begin with the law.

Judge Garff: Yes, let us start with law but not stop there. Let us know more about how children grow up in today's complex society, how to communicate with children and parents, and to be watchful of our manipulation by all those who appear in our courts. We must know how to integrate the contributions of the professionals we work with, but know that, first and foremost, we are judges. To be effective juvenile court judges, we need a working knowledge of human behavior, the types of services and facilities needed to assist with human misbehaviors, and to avoid usurping the prerogatives of those who work on a day-by-day basis with youngsters and families. We occupy a position of power and influence. The art is to use this power to further the administration of justice and to achieve better services for people coming into our courts. We need to protect the community while acting in the best interests of children and upholding the dignity of law and the public's faith in the judicial system. Involved judges can influence public policy and then administer their courts to achieve these objectives. Juvenile courts have adapted to change without losing the advantages of the original concepts.

I am confident that there will never be a fully mechanized justice scheme with children, for this would be a manifest injustice. Rehabilitation efforts are being reshaped, we have properly incorporated due process safeguards, the public has some legitimate concerns we are responding to, we have ways to deprive youngsters of their freedom in order to teach them we are serious about their offenses and insist on their accountability, and we continue to experiment to seek new and different ways to unravel the riddles of youthful behavior and misbehavior. I tell the youngsters in my court that I will be honest and I am a person of my word. If I say I will do something, I do this, otherwise I will create distrust, disrespect, and confusion. So let me be completely honest here today as well. The juvenile court, itself, is on trial. There is evidence of our failures, some unwarranted, others true, and of our achievements, some overblown, others understated. The public, rather than the judiciary, will ultimately weigh the evidence and determine the future of the juvenile court concept. I still believe that this court has been one of the nobler inventions in American history. It cannot be patented so that each court within a state or in the fifty states functions precisely the same way. I have seen that five judges are not patented either, nor are our different communities or the youngsters we confront. But another great invention was the watch and mine says that our time is up. We have said our words. Society judges us more by our actions. My court hearing calendar tells me it's time to get back on the bench. I have ten delinquency cases to wrestle with this afternoon, how about you Judge Powell?

Judge Powell: Twelve delinquencies but I'm prepared to go until seven o'clock.

Judge Gelber: Seventeen delinquencies and I'll be done by 3.45.

Judge Casey: Eight abuse and neglect reviews and I'm speaking tonight to the League of Women Voters.

Judge McLaughlin: Two child support cases, five delinquencies, an abused child, three abused wives, some lawyers' arguments, and then to pick up writing a legal opinion on a most interesting case that is titled, "Five Juvenile Court Judges in the Interests of Children, Families, and the Community." Between us, and *ex cathedra*, the case was proven beyond a reasonable doubt.

ABOUT THE JUDGES

JUDGE REGNAL W. GARFF, Jr, is administrative judge of the Second District Juvenile Court, Salt Lake City, Utah. He has been a judge of this separately organized juvenile court since 1959.

JUDGE ROMAE TURNER POWELL is a judge of the Fulton County Juvenile Court, Atlanta, Georgia. She has been a judge of this separately organized juvenile court since 1973.

JUDGE SEYMOUR GELBER is administrative judge of the Juvenile Division of the Circuit Court, Eleventh Judicial Circuit, Miami, Florida. He has been a judge of this general trial court since 1974, and has served exclusively in its juvenile division.

JUDGE EDWARD J. MCLAUGHLIN is administrative judge of the Family Court of the State of New York for the County of Onondaga, Syracuse. He has been a judge of this separately organized family court since 1973.

JUDGE JAMES S. CASEY is chief judge of the Probate Court for the County of Kalamazoo, Kalamazoo, Michigan. He has been a judge of this separately organized probate court since 1976, and has devoted his efforts largely to juvenile matters.

H. TED RUBIN

ABOUT THE AUTHOR

H. TED RUBIN is one of the nation's leading authorities on juvenile justice. As judge of the Denver Juvenile Court, 1965–71, he pioneered due process reforms and community-based rehabilitation programs during that period. He architected the major provisions of the model Colorado Children's Code enacted in early 1967. Previously, as a Colorado state legislator, Rubin developed forestry camp programs for delinquent youths and mental health legislation and services.

Senior Associate, Juvenile and Criminal Justice, for the Institute for Court Management of the National Center for State Courts, Denver, he has directed the Institute's juvenile justice education and research program since 1971. He teaches juvenile justice administration at the University of Colorado, Denver, has taught extensively at the University of Colorado, Boulder, has served as Visiting Professor, School of Criminal Justice, State University of New York at Albany, and was primary American instructor for the American University Institute on Juvenile Justice in Great Britain and the United States, London, England.

Rubin has been a consultant to the President's Commission on Law Enforcement and Administration of Justice, the Joint Commission on Correctional Manpower and Training, the Institute of Judicial Administration-American Bar Association Juvenile Justice Standards Project, the National Advisory Committee on Criminal Justice Standards and Goals, and numerous additional projects.

He holds graduate degrees in both law and social work, earlier worked in children's agencies, and has published over forty articles, mostly focused on juvenile justice, court, and rehabilitation issues. He is also the author of *The Courts: Fulcrum of the Justice System*, 2nd ed.(Random House, 1984), *Juvenile Justice: Policy, Practice, and Law*, 2nd ed.(Random House,1985), and is editor of *Juveniles in Justice: A Book of Readings* (Goodyear, 1980).